"*Ahead of the Game* is a truly refreshing startup story that vividly chronicles the rise of a scrappy company in a thriving industry. It's also a moving, beautifully written portrait of a founder whose story—and whose reach—extends far beyond Silicon Valley."

—Christine Lagorio-Chafkin,
author of *We Are the Nerds*

"The wonder of Kevin Ryan's work here is the way he effortlessly reinvents a classic tale—the triumph over the odds—for the golden era of video games. In fact, *Ahead of the Game* chronicles three triumphs for the price of one: the rise of an unlikely entrepreneur, the birth of a high school gaming team, and the explosion of esports itself. Make that four triumphs."

—Devin Gordon,
author of *So Many Ways to Lose*

"Delane Parnell's rise to startup stardom is as riveting as it is unlikely. Kevin Ryan's account of how PlayVS started, got funding, and captured the imagination of millions is as thrilling and addictive as any video game out there."

—James Ledbetter,
chief content officer at Clarim
Media and former editor-in-chief of *Inc.*

"A great read about a great founder—and so much more. More so than almost any other book out there, Kevin Ryan's enthralling *Ahead of the Game* gets at the precise stuff about how an entrepreneur succeeds and all that such a journey requires. But it also tells a much bigger tale. One in which a culture around gaming takes root and spreads to everywhere from Alaska to Alabama. One in which outsiders become heroes. And one where Delane Parnell makes his way from one of Detroit's toughest neighborhoods to the innermost circles of tech and Hollywood, willing himself into becoming one of the world's most fascinating and inspiring tech founders—all before he reaches his late twenties."

—Jon Fine,
author of *Your Band Sucks*

"Told with the pace and energy of a *Fortnite* tournament, *Ahead of the Game* is *Friday Night Lights* meets *How I Built This*. Whether he's taking you inside a Silicon Valley boardroom or a small-town high school classroom, Kevin Ryan's curiosity and enthusiasm make him an ideal tour guide. A must-read for anyone interested in entrepreneurship or the booming esports business."

—Jeff Bercovici,
Los Angeles Times deputy
business editor and author of *Play On:
The New Science of Elite Performance at Any Age*

AHEAD OF THE GAME

THE UNLIKELY RISE OF A DETROIT KID WHO
FOREVER CHANGED THE ESPORTS INDUSTRY

KEVIN J. RYAN

FOREWORD BY SEAN "DIDDY" COMBS

HARPERCOLLINS
LEADERSHIP

AN IMPRINT OF HARPERCOLLINS

Published by HarperCollins Leadership, an imprint of HarperCollins Focus LLC.

Any internet addresses, phone numbers, or company or product information printed in this book are offered as a resource and are not intended in any way to be or to imply an endorsement by HarperCollins Leadership, nor does HarperCollins Leadership vouch for the existence, content, or services of these sites, phone numbers, companies, or products beyond the life of this book.

Cover photograph by Sean Yalda

ISBN 978-1-4002-2451-7 (eBook)
ISBN 978-1-4002-2450-0 (HC)

Library of Congress Cataloging-in-Publication Data
Library of Congress Cataloging-in-Publication application has been submitted.

Printed in the United States of America
22 23 24 25 26 LSC 10 9 8 7 6 5 4 3 2 1

For Nana; I know she's proud.

CONTENTS

Foreword by Sean "Diddy" Combs xi

Author's Note xv

Prologue xvii

1. Phenomenon 1

2. The Forgotten Ones 15

3. "This Is Not a Pity Story" 31

4. The Kid from Detroit 65

5. Fate on the Dance Floor 77

6. High School Legends 91

7. Big Deal 107

8. Liftoff 141

9. The Making of a Hustler 175

10. Next Level 189

11. Guiding Light 227

12. Achievement Unlocked 239

Acknowledgments 287

Sources 291

About the Author 297

FOREWORD

BY SEAN "DIDDY" COMBS

Less than five years ago, Delane Parnell set out to change the landscape of esports for young people. In that time, his PlayVS platform has made video games an organized high school varsity sport—alongside basketball, football, baseball, volleyball, etc. Even saying that out loud seems unbelievable! *Ahead of the Game* takes you behind the scenes of his upbringing and documents how he raised more than $100 million in venture capital and, in doing so, kicked in the door of the tech world unlike any other African American before him—placing him in the less than 1 percent of Black people in leadership in the tech industry.

Because I have always known that Black Americans are a culturally rich people, too often trapped by society's limited expectations rather than our own, I am never surprised by the heights we reach in any arena. The surprise is in our ability to navigate the obstacle course, to maneuver around the traps and landmines, and, despite them all, to fulfill our God-given destiny. This and more is what Delane has accomplished.

I am known around the world as a hip-hop mogul, dealmaker, record executive, producer, cultural influencer, and rapper. But what you may not know is that my path as an entrepreneur began with a paper route. I still remember the sense of exhilaration I'd feel whenever I sold out of those papers—almost as much as my disappointment when I was told that it didn't matter how great a salesman I'd become; each kid could only have one route.

What to do? I convinced five friends to start routes—and then, I bought them out. Years later, when I left Howard University early to go to work as an intern at Uptown Records for my mentor, Andre Harrell, I did so because hip-hop (still in its infancy but on its way to becoming a multibillion-dollar-a-year industry) was the next frontier, and I knew I couldn't wait. A few years later, when I left Uptown and started Bad Boy Records, it was with that same sense of urgency. Already, it was clear to me that my superpower, above and beyond my other creative impulses, was entrepreneurship itself.

It's that same hustler's spirit I picked up from Delane immediately when I first met him in 2018. I take a lot of meetings, so I'm used to new people coming by my home or office ready to sell me on something—an idea, a brand deal, a new artist, and everything in-between. Delane showed up at my house as himself and was more interested in getting to know me than figuring out how or if we could do business together. I'm a firm believer in the philosophy that businesses are built on good relationships. Delane understood this principle early on.

It was also clear to me that he was a smart, hungry, innovative thinker. The more I got to know him and learned about the key partnerships he forged to put his company in a position to make history, the more he reminded me of the days back when I was producing records for artists like Mary J. Blige and Notorious B.I.G. I was constantly in talent-scout mode, looking for people with new beats and rhymes to make music.

Putting creatives in one room for a collective mission is difficult. Delane does this every day with a team of 120-plus chasing the PlayVS mission. That said, I think he's one of the greatest talent scouts and dealmakers of his generation.

Delane grew up in the hood, on the west side of Detroit, immersed in hip-hop and basketball culture. Like me, he left college early, before graduating, because the entrepreneurial impulse kept calling his name: from a lawn-mowing business he started with his brother as a kid to partnering on several retail businesses, such as cell-phone stores and rental-car dealerships—all before graduating high school. Other ventures would follow. Of course, I see myself in him.

At the same time, Delane's on his own journey. Truth be told, I feel lucky to have a front-row seat, to watch this Black Man Magic, this hustler's spirit, unfold right in front of my eyes. He understands that there is rarely anything more magical than putting this art of entrepreneurship to work to build something bigger than yourself.

Delane and his PlayVS team built both a market category and simultaneously a universal tent that welcomes students from all walks of life. The universe that PlayVS built is helping these young people to grow academically, socially, and in their leadership abilities. Most had never participated in extracurricular activities or earned varsity letters before. Today, there are more than nine thousand schools and twelve hundred colleges with esports teams competing and repping their schools through PlayVS, with many more to come.

Delane once told me that it was watching me and Jay-Z making bold moves when he was a teen that helped him to imagine that this level of greatness was possible. I'm humbled to know I was an inspiration for his willingness to never stop dreaming. Unlike the hip-hop industry, where Black youth are the primary driving creative force of the culture, the tech world has long been the domain of Ivy League–educated white guys. Delane decided he could thrive in that world and put his entrepreneurial impulses to work to make it so. I revel in the fact that he is on a mission to create Black wealth from this space. It's been a long time coming. Now, the next Black kid who wants to chase a dream will know what's possible by watching Delane. This is the frontier of a new generation.

This book is the beginning of that story.

AUTHOR'S NOTE

ESPORTS IS ONE of the fastest-growing activities in America, but you're forgiven if you don't really get it. I didn't either back in spring 2018, when a pitch about a new gaming startup arrived in my inbox at *Inc.* magazine. The company, a small Santa Monica outfit known as PlayVS, was preparing to launch the first season of official high school esports. Students across America were about to begin earning varsity letters—for playing *video games*? I hadn't owned a video game console in more than a decade, but this made me raise an eyebrow. I took the interview.

It was one of the best decisions I ever made. During my first conversation with Delane Parnell, I couldn't believe what I was hearing. As a tech journalist, you spend a lot of time covering people who, to use an analogy borrowed from a colleague, were born on third base. Delane was the exception. Still just twenty-five, he'd already overcome more adversity than many people will face in a lifetime. Yet here he was, blazing a path through one of the hottest industries in America, accomplishing feats no one had before.

That interview resulted in a piece for Inc.com. Within several hours of its publishing, a literary manager named Chris George reached out to tell me he saw potential for the story as a book. Delane and I casually discussed the idea. He was flattered but hesitant; despite what his company has already accomplished, he thought it was too soon for his life to be worthy of a book. Plus, he had a business to run.

I understood. Still, I kept reporting on Delane and his startup. High schoolers booted up their computers for the first season of officially sanctioned esports, and anecdotes from the frontlines began trickling in. Esports, I came to learn, was about much more than just a controller and a screen. Meanwhile, PlayVS continued to fight its way to huge funding dollars, unprecedented deals, and national expansion. It quickly became clear that there were more layers to this story. Delane eventually agreed that a book was in order.

I'm thrilled that he did.

The result, *Ahead of the Game*, is the product of three years of reporting and writing, a process that included interviews with more than seventy people: Delane, his friends and family, colleagues and PlayVS employees past and present, venture capitalists, entrepreneurs, gaming executives, educators, coaches, students, and many others. In some cases, especially those involving Delane's life in Detroit, I haven't included people's names even if they were known to me. I've also opted not to use full names for the high schoolers in this book, given their ages at the time I was reporting. Typos and shorthand are mostly kept in place within reprinted texts, emails, tweets, etc., and their content might be slightly changed, though only when necessary for clarity. And while the vast majority of this work is based on my own firsthand reporting, I've compiled a list at the back of the book for instances in which other sources were used.

It's funny to think back to the way I thought about esports just a few years ago, when I would have wholly agreed with all the parents and teachers out there telling their kids to put down the damn controller and pick up a book. Now, I think it's not quite so simple. But in this case, dear reader, I'm grateful you chose to do just that.

PROLOGUE

FOUR TEENAGE BOYS sit on the small cement porch, clinging to the last days of summer. Two are brothers; the older boy rests in a rocking chair their grandfather built. The shade from two oak trees on the front lawn offers some respite from the day's stickiness. Rhymes and bass from a new rap album flow from the portable stereo sitting by their feet.

Another boy they know from the neighborhood walks by. He shouts a few words to them and comes to a stop on the sidewalk in front of the house. The boys on the porch start to chat with him. The conversation is friendly.

The boy in the rocking chair notices it first. In front of the neighbor's house, a passing car has slowed to a crawl and the front window is down. This isn't a good combination. The boy sits up a little straighter.

There isn't time to react—it's already begun.

BANG. BANG. BANG-BANG-BANG.

Shots ring out, metallic and deafening. The front of the house pops as bullets pierce its siding. The boys hurtle over the railing, tumble down the steps, sprint along the side of the house toward the back. Others fling the front door open and run inside, keeping low to the ground just like they've learned.

They all reach the backyard, wide-eyed and panting. They listen. The shooting has stopped. The sound of a car speeding into the distance drifts over the neighboring houses.

The boys check themselves and each other. Somehow, nobody has been hit. They wait a few moments. When they're sure the coast is clear, they cautiously make their way back to the front of the house. The neighborhood boy is gone. The teens examine the damage. Bullet holes mark the street side of one of the oak trees. Several more are scattered across the house's vinyl siding, just a few feet from where they were sitting. The boys have gotten lucky. They decide to spend the rest of the day in the backyard, where it's safer.

Later, some of the boys will visit the local hardware store. They'll buy some plywood, bring it home, and nail it over the bullet holes. It's not the world's best repair job. It's not even a good one. The holes are still there. But at least they can't be seen.

1

PHENOMENON

IF YOU WANTED to find Rick Yang in the late 1990s and early 2000s, the first place to look was the swimming pool. The brainy, athletic teen spent hours after school honing his freestyle in the lanes at J. J. Pearce High in the Dallas suburb of Richardson. The work paid off. His freshman year, Yang won the school's Outstanding Swimmer of the Year award. He repeated the feat the following year, and the year after that. By his senior year, the honor was a foregone conclusion, so he also added two First Team All-American honors and became Texas's state champion in the 100-meter freestyle for good measure. Yang's athletic and academic prowess earned him a spot on Stanford University's swim team, one of the top programs in the country.

Yang also had a bit of a secret life. Unbeknownst to most of his classmates—and his teammates—he would come home after practice, breeze through his homework, boot up his computer, and play the game *World of Warcraft*. This activity was not, by any means, considered "cool." Known for its elves, dragons, and other fantasy imagery, the game once had an entire *South Park* episode dedicated to mocking the nerdy culture around it. Yang developed a second social circle in addition to his swim circle, one that played games together in each other's bedrooms or basements. On weekends they'd get together and play *WoW*, as it was known among gamers, or *Ultima Online*, another game characterized by healthy doses of magic and dorkiness.

One swim season, Yang's coach approached him in need of help. The team's roster was smaller than usual, and he needed more bodies to round it out. Yang dipped into the only other pool he knew: his gaming buddies. He convinced a few to sign up. Most had never played an organized sport in their lives. The first day of practice didn't exactly go, well, swimmingly.

"Some of the guys couldn't even finish a lap," recalled Yang.

After he graduated, Yang continued his dominance of the classroom and the pool lanes at Stanford, helping the men's swim team finish second at the national championships in three of his four years. After a quick stint as a financial analyst in the mid-aughts, he landed a job at the venture capital firm New Enterprise Associates (NEA), based in Menlo Park, California, the heart of Silicon Valley. During Yang's tenure, NEA invested in companies like Uber, Snap, BuzzFeed, Groupon, Coursera, 23andMe, Cloudflare, and Robinhood. Its funds under management would balloon to more than $20 billion, making it one of the largest VC firms in the world.

In 2012, Yang helped lead an investment in the payment platform Braintree. PayPal shelled out $800 million to acquire the company the following year, and Yang soon found himself promoted to partner. Through all the success, and long after he put away his swim cap for good, one constant remained: video games. As an adult and father, he reveled in the nights he could get his two kids to bed early and sneak away to play for a few minutes or watch other people compete against each other on the streaming platform Twitch.

Jon Sakoda, another investor at NEA, rose through the ranks on a trajectory parallel with Yang's. After he cofounded a messaging platform called IMlogic and sold it to Symantec, he joined the venture firm as an early-stage investor and was promoted to general partner in 2014. When he was studying a startup, Sakoda had a set of prerequisites—three boxes he needed to see checked before deciding to invest. The criteria weren't groundbreaking, but they laid the foundation for a startup to have at least a decent chance of success. They were:

1. A massive potential market
2. A competitive advantage within said market
3. A great founder

Sakoda wasn't much of a gamer himself, but he could identify a phenomenon-in-the-making when he saw one. Playing video games was no longer about turning on a Nintendo or PlayStation and competing against the computer. More and more games were being created with team play in mind, giving those teams the option to play against one another online. These competitive, team-based matches were known as esports. In their early days as NEA partners, Sakoda and Yang spotted a cultural transition playing out across America. For gamers, the dual life was becoming a thing of the past. High school basketball and soccer stars were picking up controllers and playing video games after school, and they weren't hiding it.

"For the younger demographics," said Yang, "video games were becoming a part of mainstream culture."

Gaming, in other words, wasn't just for the nerds anymore. For a couple of venture capitalists, this meant there was a lot of money to be made. The data told a similar story. In 2012, worldwide esports revenues—including media rights, advertising, sponsorships, merchandise, tickets, and game publisher fees—totaled $130 million, according to the industry tracker Newzoo. Two years later, that number climbed to a shade under $200 million. During that same span, Twitch's streaming platform saw its average number of concurrent users climb from 100,000 to 400,000. In August 2014, Amazon sent a jolt through the gaming world—and beyond—by announcing it was buying Twitch for $970 million. In just two years, the company had gone from an upstart unknown outside of the fiercest gaming circles to having a valuation of nearly a billion dollars. The sale was eye-opening for investors and tech firms. If a company like Amazon was taking esports seriously, why shouldn't they? Venture capitalists, those at NEA very much included, started scouring the market for the next big thing.

"Twitch's exit led people to believe that there were some more big esports companies to come," said Sakoda. "We thought it was even bigger than what most people were saying. We had a thesis that esports was going to be explosive."

This thesis, of course, was correct. Between 2014 and 2017, global esports revenues would grow by more than 250 percent, reaching $655 million. While the industry expanded, Yang and Sakoda searched for the company that could be the next unicorn. They listened to pitches from a handful of game-makers, known in the industry as publishers. The upshot of betting on the right publisher could be huge: Riot Games, for example, grew its game *League of Legends* from zero to 100 million monthly users in six years; and Epic Games, the company behind *Fortnite*, gained 200 million registered users in sixteen months and would go on to be valued at $17 billion.

But for every *League of Legends* or *Fortnite*, there were many, many flops. Predicting what titles would take off was seemingly impossible. Yang and Sakoda wanted to find a company that was less vulnerable to the capricious nature of consumer tastes. A company that could instead capitalize on the industry's macro trends. A company that could tap into the market in a new and profound way.

In the spring of 2018, they found it.

•   •   •

PETER PHAM WAS a difficult man to ignore. Sometimes it was because of the giant cowboy hat he wore to parties and conferences. More often it was because of the dancing. Pham, short and taut with a big white smile and about zero percent body fat, used any excuse to bust out his moves. Sometimes the excuse was the Burning Man festival, where he was known to work himself into a shirtless sweat for hours on end in the hot Nevada desert. Other times it was a beat he liked coming over the PA system of a convention center ballroom. "First on the dance floor," read the opening sentence of his Twitter bio, below an image of him mid-move in a gold sequin shirt. The man had rhythm—and he knew it.

But Pham was well known in VC and startup circles for more than just his ability to find a beat. Back in the mid-aughts, he was the fifth employee and president of business development at the image hosting company Photobucket. When the firm sold to Fox Interactive Media for $300 million in 2007, he ended up a millionaire. But his full earn-out required him staying on at Fox Interactive for two years. He left after nine months.

"I'm not a corporate person," he said later. "I have ADHD. I just couldn't do it."

A few years later, Pham joined up with several other entrepreneurs to found the location-based photosharing company Color Labs. The Palo Alto startup scored $41 million from investors including Sequoia and Bain Capital while in stealth mode, then emerged to the public in 2011 to much media coverage and fanfare. The hype was short lived. The Color app confused users and failed to gain any significant traction. Pham, seeing where things were heading, bailed. Not long after, the startup's CEO reportedly stepped away, and the company collapsed nearly as quickly and spectacularly as it had arrived, eventually selling to Apple for pennies on the dollar.

Pham was living in the Bay Area a short time later when he met up with Mike Jones at a conference in Hawaii. The two had known each other since the early Photobucket days, when Jones was cofounder and CEO of the web chat platform Userplane. Back then, they had privately discussed the possibility of launching a startup incubator should they ever get paydays that would make it possible. Pham's windfall came at Photobucket; Jones would go on to get his when Userplane sold to AOL for a reported $40 million. Now, on an island in the middle of the Pacific together, Pham and Jones were both unemployed. It was the moment they'd been waiting for. "He turned to me," Pham recalled, "and said 'Hey, remember that incubator idea? Do you want to do it?' I said 'Yes, let's go,' and decided to move back to Los Angeles, where he lived. It was a one-minute conversation."

The two teamed up with Greg Gilman and Tom Dare, two other endeavoring types who had spent most of their lives in the California tech world. They raised $10 million in additional funds from investors that included Tomorrow Ventures, a firm run by former Google CEO Eric Schmidt, and founded Science later that year. The concept was that Science would provide young startups with space in its Santa Monica office, constant access to its experienced staff, and potentially funding to help them grow into profitable companies. One of its first projects was a charismatic entrepreneur with an idea for a shaving-kit-by-mail subscription service. Science provided Michael Dubin with his first investment and helped him hone his business plan. The company, Dollar Shave Club, grew to 3 million subscribers and $200 million in revenue within five years. In 2016, it sold to Unilever for $1 billion. Science had its first big exit, and Pham had multiplied his net worth yet again.

In the weeks leading up to April 6, 2018, Pham sent dozens of emails to investors across Silicon Valley about a new entrepreneur he was particularly excited about. Science had given the young founder a few hundred thousand in seed money and set up a desk for him in its office. Now it was time for him to try to raise a full-on venture round.

A few minutes before 2 p.m., Pham confidently strolled into NEA's Menlo Park headquarters. Walking alongside him was the entrepreneur in question. Delane Parnell was twenty-five years old. He had no college degree. He wore not a suit nor a vest over a button-down, but a hoodie. His startup had just two full-time employees. But Pham had vouched for him, going so far as to compare his entrepreneurial chops to Dubin's. As such, several firms, NEA included, had agreed to meet with him.

Yang and Sakoda escorted Pham and Delane to a large-windowed conference room. The two pairs seated themselves on opposite sides of the table. Sakoda thought about his three requirements. There was no denying that Delane's startup, PlayVS, existed in a massive market: the company was building software for esports. At that time, a small number of high schools across the country had created esports clubs. Students could show up after school and play against one another or, occasionally, against another school. Most of the clubs were grassroots in nature. What Delane was creating at PlayVS was a platform that could give high school esports some much-needed infrastructure. The company would help the schools that didn't yet have clubs—the vast majority of America's 24,000 high schools—form and launch them. Then it would arrange the teams into leagues, schedule matches, host those matches online, compile the relevant statistics and records, organize and stream the postseason, and, ultimately, help crown state champions.

This was where Sakoda's second requirement—a competitive advantage—came into play. Unbeknownst to the public at the time, PlayVS had recently signed a deal with the National Federation of State High School Associations, or NFHS. The NFHS is to high school sports what the NCAA is to college: a body that writes the rules for athletics, determines student-athlete eligibility, and offers guidance on issues like coaching and athlete safety. For years, the NFHS had been considering making esports an officially sanctioned high school sport. Its agreement with PlayVS meant that when that happened at some time in the near future, the startup's software was going to be the platform on which all high school esports would operate. The deal contained something critical for PlayVS: an exclusivity clause. This meant that no other esports company could cut a similar deal with the NFHS for the next five years. PlayVS, despite being a three-person startup no one had heard of, had built a tall and sturdy wall of defense against competitors—exactly the kind of edge Sakoda looked for.

The way the company had managed to do that had a lot to do with Sakoda's third factor: the entrepreneur. Sakoda knew as much from his conversations with Pham. Now he was getting to see it firsthand. Almost as soon as the kid started talking, Sakoda found he couldn't look away from his smile. It changed Delane's whole face, puffing up his cheeks and narrowing his eyes into squints. Sakoda liked this smile. A few minutes into the meeting, Delane was off and running, standing near the monitor on the wall and walking the investors through the various features of the software.

"This is where a coach can log in to manage their roster." A click of a slide. "This is where they can see their team's stats and upcoming matchups." A click of a slide. Delane talked about the fact that high school esports would be a no-cut sport, allowing kids of all skill levels to participate and thereby creating a wider user base. He spoke about teams being coed, with competitions taking place in person under the guidance of an adult—as opposed to online and anonymous—which he theorized would neutralize much of the toxicity that plagued the world of gaming. He discussed the platform's potential, as an after-school program, to keep kids off the streets.

Yang and Sakoda listened intently. "You just don't hear those types of things in a pitch about a gaming company," Yang said later.

Pham, normally a bundle of energy in these meetings, knew to take a back seat today. He grabbed some snacks from the spread and brought them back to his seat at the table, munching quietly while the VCs asked questions.

"How do we know PlayVS will actually get schools and students to sign up?"

"We will," Delane reassured them. "We're talking about video games. And what schools wouldn't want to give their students the chance to be involved in something after school?"

An even bigger unknown: not a single game publisher had agreed to let PlayVS license its games. Many were notoriously stingy about such deals.

"What's the likelihood that PlayVS can sign deals with publishers?"

Delane grinned. "Having a contract with the NFHS means we have access to sixteen million high school students," he said. "Why *wouldn't* the publishers do it?"

Continually, the investors asked him questions, and continually, he had answers—sometimes in the form of a rhetorical question right back at them.

"He had such a certainty, such a positivity," Sakoda recalled. "He would just smile and say, 'Yeah, we'll get the big publishers to do these deals.' No matter what he was talking about, even if it seemed risky or seemed like it would be difficult, you just believed he was going to be able to do it."

Here was the NEA office nestled in the rolling greenery of Menlo Park, across the street from a country club in the heart of Silicon Valley. You could walk out the door and reach the offices of some of the other most renowned VC firms in the world—Kleiner Perkins, Sequoia, Andreessen Horowitz—in under a minute; the headquarters of Google, Facebook, or Apple in less than twenty. And here was Delane Parnell, the twenty-five-year-old Black entrepreneur from the impoverished neighborhood just off Seven Mile Road in Detroit, standing in the center of it all, pitching his heart out for two seasoned investors.

"It was magical to watch," Sakoda recalled. "We caught the bug."

Which was why, twenty minutes into the meeting, Sakoda turned to Yang in his chair. "We have to invest in this company," he blurted out.

That was just what Pham needed to hear. He stepped back into the conversation, and he and the two investors started discussing potential terms. PlayVS needed a firm to lead this Series A funding round—the firm that would sign the largest check, help set the round's terms, vet the other potential investors, and take a seat on the startup's board of directors.

This time, Sakoda turned to Yang before turning back to Pham: "NEA is interested in being that firm."

When the conversation ended, the four men shook hands, and Delane and Pham were on their way to their next pitch meeting, the eleventh of thirteen they'd attend in the span of thirty hours. Even if none of the other firms were interested, they had earned a verbal commitment from a lead investor. There was still a long way to go, but this was a critical first step in acquiring the millions of dollars PlayVS would need to hire a staff and get this thing off the ground.

For Yang and Sakoda, Delane represented a potential answer to their four-year search for the right esports entrepreneur. Everything they'd heard that day had convinced them so. It wasn't just about the positivity and the confidence and the ability to sell an idea, although those factors surely helped. There was more to Delane. Much, much more. They had learned so in that pitch meeting, before Delane spoke about PlayVS's software or the NFHS or potential publisher deals. They learned it when Delane took them back. Back to the apartment in the crack-infested projects. Back to the gangs. Back to his mother, the shootings, the shed in his backyard.

"Context," Delane would say later, "is super important."

Yang would agree. "If it wasn't for Delane talking about the mission-driven nature of this company and his own background," he said, "and why that all led him to be the perfect founder for this type of company, the rest of the pitch wouldn't have been as powerful as it was. That's an important part of understanding who Delane is and how it drives him."

The reality of investing in early-stage companies is that it's impossible to know how a product will land once it hits the market. But watching Delane in front of the room that day, Yang and Sakoda knew one thing with certainty: If PlayVS ever failed, it wouldn't be because of its founder. Delane Parnell wasn't going to give anything less than everything he had to offer. He had already come too far.

2

THE FORGOTTEN ONES

THE TOWN OF Orange sits in the western part of Massachusetts, eighty miles from Boston and an hour by car from the nearest interstate. On the drive from the highway to the town limits, you'll pass a tractor dealership, two dozen American flags, several horses, and zero traffic lights. Main Street is quiet—among the handful of functioning storefronts are a barber shop, an outdoors store, a pub, and a pizzeria. Nearby, a small bridge spans a river lined with boxy brick buildings, textile mills from the town's glory days, most more than a century old and long abandoned. Just down the road is the town's biggest employer, the Walmart where some residents shop for their clothes and their groceries.

On an overcast winter afternoon at the bottom of a small hill nearby, the 2:05 p.m. bell rang to signal the end of the day's final period at Ralph C. Mahar Regional School. A dark-bearded Kyle Magoffin stood in the middle of the school's main corridor dressed in his usual physical education teacher garb of a half-zip pullover and gym shorts. Students rushed by, blurs of dark clothes, camo and flannel, the occasional streak of green or purple hair, most looking like they wouldn't be out of place at a peak grunge-era Soundgarden concert. Nearby were the only two unlocked bathrooms in the school; the rest had been closed in an effort to curb the fights that were being filmed inside them and uploaded to an anonymously operated Instagram account. A boy and girl walked past Magoffin, the girl with jeans ripped to shreds across the front.

"Did you make those rips yourself, or did you have to pay extra for them?" Magoffin asked.

The girl rolled her eyes playfully. "Every. Time," she muttered to the boy, loud enough for Magoffin to hear.

Magoffin kept his head on a swivel, seeking out more students to trade barbs with. A moment later, a boy cut through the crowd toward him, a senior named Isaiah with swooping black hair and an easy smile. With his wiry build, usually hidden beneath a dark hoodie and khaki cargo pants, Isaiah looked like he might play point guard for the basketball team. He didn't, of course, unless that court was pixelated. Magoffin stuck his hand out for a high-five.

"Start getting set up," Magoffin told him. "I'll be right there."

Isaiah did as his coach asked, and a few moments later he was wheeling a pair of tall padded chairs into the engineering classroom. During the school day, the large room was the domain of Ms. Cote, a teacher with a firm two-handed handshake and a serious but warm demeanor. A small group of students, part of the school's after-school engineering club, sat at some desks in the corner, waiting for her. She was near the classroom's entrance, waiting for Coach Magoffin. In he came, dragging another pair of gaming chairs.

Cote stopped him in his tracks. "I apologize for the smell," she said quietly. "An exceptionally immature eight-grader released fart spray in here earlier."

"Ah, fantastic," said Magoffin with mock enthusiasm, positioning the chairs in front of a row of computer monitors.

One by one, boys entered the room. One by one, they covered their noses and gagged dramatically.

"Smells like butt in here," muttered one, his eyes watering.

Magoffin left the classroom and came back in wheeling a four-foot-tall industrial fan that might have predated the school itself, positioned it in front of the doorway, plugged it in, and turned it on with a *whoosh*. "Now we're talking!" he yelled.

Sitting at a desk with the rest of the engineering club at the far end of the room, an eighth-grade boy with full cheeks and blond hair listened to Ms. Cote talk. His name was Ben, but the other students on the team called him Benji, or Beanie, or just Bean. And if the kids called him that, that meant Magoffin did, too. A year and a half earlier, Magoffin hadn't known anything about esports. His experience with video games was that of the average nineties kid. He'd played Nintendo 64 classics like *GoldenEye 007* and *Mario Kart*, and he occasionally dusted off the game cartridges to play with his buddies in college. But Magoffin was fully embracing his role as Mahar Regional High School's esports coach. He couldn't talk strategy like the students could, and he didn't play much on his own, but he was learning. Before that season, in an effort to round out his roster with the five players necessary for the game *League of Legends*, he'd dipped down into the middle school class to recruit Benji. The coach sought out students who didn't have the biggest friend groups but seemed like they'd take to esports. Benji fit the mold. Even though his family didn't even own a computer, the kid was in the *engineering club*, so an interest in video games didn't seem like a stretch.

In walked Meeker. He took a seat next to Isaiah at the row of computers, an eighth-grade apprentice learning from a seasoned senior. Just over a month into the season, his first ever as a varsity esports player, Meeks was rapidly improving. Tall and quiet, he had a young face that rarely changed expression. But he knew how to play. Sitting side by side in gaming chairs, he and Isaiah booted up *League of Legends* on their computers and started to practice. Soon Benji strolled across the classroom to join his teammates. He scanned the room.

"Where's Justin?" he squeaked.

"He's coming," Magoffin assured him. "He'll be here."

Today had been a weird day. That morning, the coach received some bad news about one of his players. He'd been having headaches recently, and a trip to the doctor had revealed excess fluid around his brain. The prognosis wasn't dire, and the condition was expected to resolve itself within a few months, but that meant he was going to be homeschooled for the rest of the school year. Magoffin was worried about what that would mean for his team. More specifically, he was worried about what it would mean for Justin. The previous year, as a member of the school's inaugural *League of Legends* team, Justin had found a new identity for himself. It was a whirlwind—playing video games after school, qualifying for the state playoffs, being the subject of writeups in the local paper. Then, the next year, one of the team's players had decided at the last minute to play football instead. That left a squad of only four—one short of a full lineup. Magoffin decided not to field a team. Justin didn't handle it well. He started skipping school again. His grades dropped. For a few months, competitive video games had succeeded in painting over the bad parts of Justin's life. With that gone, the cracks were exposed again.

This time around, Magoffin wanted to see if there was another option. During his lunch break, he visited the PlayVS website, typed in his credentials, and pulled up the official *League of Legends* competition rules and regulations. There it was: teams may compete with fewer than five players. It wasn't against the rules; it would just be a huge disadvantage.

Now it was getting closer to 3:30 p.m.—match time. A few more students seated themselves at computers and began practicing the hybrid soccer-racecar game *Rocket League*. But the *League of Legends* team's leader was still missing.

"Has anyone talked to Justin lately?" Magoffin asked the room.

"He's probably with some girl," replied Isaiah, turning in his chair to show a sly smile. Magoffin pulled out his phone and started composing a text to his player. "Call him a simp," urged Isaiah, using a derogatory internet term for a guy who puts a girl up on a pedestal.

"What's that?" the coach asked.

"Just say it."

Several more clicks. Text sent. A few minutes later, in walked Justin, surprisingly upbeat. He wore a black T-shirt and gray gym shorts, his getup punctuated by a pair of green, yellow, and blue Vans. Brown curls sat close to his head. Isaiah chided him about the girl that had made him late to practice. Justin laughed sheepishly and brushed it off.

"I was thinking," he said, diving straight into strategy mode, "what if we start with Garen and then bring in Lucian later?"

Immediately, the kids began hashing out the details of which characters—or champions, in *League of Legends* parlance—they would each choose for their match. The rules of PlayVS competitions also allowed both teams to "ban" three champions from the match, meaning no player could use them. While the students debated, Magoffin reached into his backpack, pulled out a laptop and laid it on the table in front of him. On his screen appeared a spreadsheet: the roster of the esports team at Oliver Ames High in the Boston suburb of Easton. Next to each student's name sat a list of the champions they used most frequently and what the team's winning percentage was when they chose them. As the Mahar football special teams coach, Magoffin had been tasked with scouting the opponent before each game. Now the ritual had carried over to *League of Legends*.

"Their best player has an 80 percent win rate as Neeko," the coach announced. "He has a 100 percent win rate as Aatrox."

The implication didn't need to be said out loud. *We should ban Aatrox.*

"I want to use Aatrox, though," Justin said. The rest of the kids fell silent. "That way I can front-line everything. How about we put me on Aatrox the first game and see how it goes. Then, if and when they ban Aatrox, I switch to Yi."

Isaiah pushed back. "No. I want Aatrox banned."

It was his view against Justin's. Best friend against best friend. Magoffin leaned back in his chair, letting the boys hash it out themselves. Isaiah objectively was a better player, but any opinion coming from Justin, the team captain and founder, bore more weight. Justin stared down his pal, a slight smirk on his face.

"Okay," Isaiah said, finally relenting. "But I don't know about this."

Magoffin glanced at Benji, who sat observing the conversation with wide eyes. "And what are we gonna do with Beanie?" he asked.

Justin and Isaiah put forth their strategy for the least talented player on the team. Benji would hide back in the wings while the other players did the bulk of the actual combat. "Don't go out in the open where you'll be vulnerable," Justin told Benji. It was a defensive strategy. Don't attack. Don't draw attention to yourself. Just try to survive as long as possible.

Magoffin nodded his head in approval as he stood up from his chair. "Hey, Beanie. You know what cattle prods are?" Beanie nodded. "I have a pair. If I see you traveling too far I'm going to come up behind you"—he pinched Beanie gently on the back of his neck—"and *zoot* you." Beanie jumped, then giggled. Point taken.

Magoffin sat back down at his laptop and exchanged a few messages with the opposing coach. Earlier in the day, before he'd found it in the rules, Magoffin had asked the Ames coach if he knew whether it was legal to play with four players. The coach had replied that it was, and that his team had done so in the past. Now he was curious: Which of Mahar's players was missing the match? "I'm not answering that," Magoffin said with a wry smile. "We're already at enough of a disadvantage. Let's not give him any more information than he needs." Then, to the room: "Everyone good to go?"

The four boys brought the game's main menu up on their monitors. Across their screens flashed wizards, warriors, dragons, monsters, and beasts both ferocious and cuddly. From their four cushioned seats, the kids chose their champions and submitted their ban list. Off to the side, Magoffin stood grasping a blue plastic and metal chair. "You guys ready to do this?" he asked loudly, picking it up and pounding it on the ground with each word.

"I guess," said Isaiah.

"Where's the confidence, guys?" Magoffin yelled. "Where's the blind confidence? Let's go!"

Justin, Isaiah, Benji, and Meeks pulled on their headsets. The clock struck the bottom of the hour. Magoffin walked behind the row of thrones, pausing as he passed each kid to pat him lightly on the chest. "Good luck, boys."

Serious now, the students stared into their monitors, where colorful pixels danced on their screens. The action had moved from the real world to the animated one.

It was game time.

EIGHTEEN MONTHS EARLIER, on the first morning of the school year, Kyle Magoffin found himself face-to-face with a distressed Justin. The two were already familiar with each other. Each middle schooler at Mahar had to get a scoliosis test, which meant ducking behind a screen, taking off your shirt, and bending over to touch your toes. It was Magoffin's duty as one of the phys ed teachers to administer the exam to the boys in the class. Justin stepped behind the screen where the teacher was waiting and pulled off his hoodie. As he did, a pair of women's underwear fell out and onto the hardwood floor. Magoffin had been a teacher for half a decade, but this was a new one. Justin didn't notice, already working on removing his T-shirt.

"Justin," Magoffin said quietly. "Do you have a sister?"

"No," replied Justin, confused. "Why?"

Magoffin motioned his head toward the skivvies crumpled on the ground. Justin looked. His eyes grew.

"Oh my God," he uttered, trying to stay quiet so the students nearby wouldn't hear.

They were his mom's—they must have gotten caught up his sleeve when she did their laundry. But the explanation didn't matter. They were his mother's underwear. Middle school social lives had been terminated over less. Magoffin tried to stifle his laughter, at the same time understanding that anything less than a complete coverup would create a legacy that would follow this thirteen-year-old around the halls for the next half-decade. What to do? Other kids were waiting to step behind the screen. Justin was rendered useless, staring at the underwear and muttering awkwardly.

"Just throw them in the trash," Magoffin told him.

A good plan.

But Justin wasn't about to touch his mom's underwear with his bare hands. He ran over to the paper towel dispenser and grabbed a handful, scampered back, scooped up the undies, jogged to the nearby trash can, and dropped them in—all while the other kids looked on from afar, probably wondering if this was a new addition to the spinal curvature test. A red-faced Justin shook his head through the rest of the screening, and Magoffin did his very best not to burst into laughter in the poor kid's face. For the next few years, any time the two of them passed each other in the hall, they gave each other a knowing look. If Justin acted out in gym class, Magoffin would dangle the threat over his head. "Hey, Justin," he'd say with mock menace, "just remember that I know your secret." It was blackmail sufficient to keep any teen on his absolute best behavior.

Now, four years later, Justin sat in the classroom with Magoffin. Mahar had created a new before-school program in which the students would start the day in a small group with a teacher. The idea was to provide each kid with an advocate in the building, someone they could trust and talk to about any problems. Magoffin knew about Justin's spotty attendance—he'd missed school dozens of times the year before—and low GPA, which the student joked "resembled the low end of a pH scale." To Magoffin, it was clear the brains were there. The effort was not.

It was hard to blame the kid. When Justin's parents divorced years earlier, his dad moved out of state and was now more or less out of the picture. Justin and his older brother lived with their mom in a dilapidated trailer on a dead-end street. After a back injury, their mother had been out of work for years, surviving on disability checks. It was known around town that they didn't always go toward essentials. Out in front of the trailer, red gas cans used for heat sat on a wooden porch that had rotted or broken away in many places. Inside, three cats and a dog had free rein, and feces sometimes sat on the floor for days. Some nights, Justin would wake up shaking from the cold and find that the beat-up front door had blown open during the night. After the divorce, Justin's mom had dated a man for several years. He'd become something of a father figure to Justin. One night, the boyfriend overdosed and died in the trailer. It was scarring, to say the least. Justin's older brother became his rock. Then he enrolled in community college, dropped out, and moved in with a girl he'd met while working at Dunkin' Donuts. It was now just Justin and his mom in the old trailer. She worked at the Walmart in town when she felt up to it. When she didn't, it was back to the disability checks.

When Justin was fourteen, his brother got an especially hefty tax return and used part of it to buy Justin a gaming computer. The machine became Justin's lifeline, giving him something to do in the many hours between when he got home each day around 2:30 and when he went to sleep. He played war games like *Call of Duty*, *Counter-Strike*, and *Rainbow Six*. Sometimes he and Isaiah would log on at the same time and compete against each other online or team up to take on some randomly assigned opponents. Gaming became Justin's primary source of joy. Still, it had its limitations. Some mornings, the sadness would become too much, and he would ignore his alarm clock and lie in bed and cry. Those were the days he didn't bother coming into school.

Magoffin didn't know much of this when he got his advisory assignment. He was happy to see Justin's name—good ole momma's panties Justin.

On the first day of school, Magoffin thought he was asking the kid a simple question, "What's on your mind?" Little did he realize he was about to take the cork out of the barrel.

The day before, August 26, 2018, there had been a *Madden* tournament in Jacksonville. During a match, a charismatic twenty-two-year-old named Elijah Clayton spoke to an audience via video livestream while he played. For a brief moment, a red dot appeared on his chest. Then gunshots pierced the broadcast and the feed cut out. When the chaos settled, reports revealed that Clayton and another competitor had been killed.

A twenty-four-year-old gamer had shot them after losing in the tournament, then turned the gun on himself.

Justin was upset. He was upset about the senseless killings, and he was upset that the incident had already reignited discussions about the connection between video games and violence. To Justin, this was an isolated incident that probably stemmed from a mental health issue—nobody in a healthy state of mind shoots someone over video games. (Days later, reports would reveal that the shooter had received treatment for psychiatric issues and had been prescribed antidepressants and antipsychotic drugs.)

"For a lot of people," Justin told Magoffin, "this will cement their view of gamers. We're misunderstood. People tend to stigmatize gamers. They think we're overly aggressive or violent. They don't appreciate us for the people we really are."

When Justin finally finished, Magoffin quietly asked, "Well, why don't you do something about it?"

Justin left school that day with something to think about. Just before dinner, he wrote a brief email.

Coach Mags, were you serious about that?

Indeed he was. Magoffin told Justin to see if he could find some other students who would want to be part of an esports club. A few days later, Justin and twenty other kids showed up for their first meeting.

"I came into it thinking it was just gonna be a club where we sit back and watch matches or just talk about why we love esports," Justin said later, "and I was fine with that."

Magoffin didn't have much of a strategy either. He asked the kids what they wanted the club to look like. The best suggestions involved watching matches on YouTube. He tried another approach. Before they could determine *what* they wanted to be collectively, he thought, they needed to talk about *who* they were individually. He posed them that exact question and, one by one, the answers came in.

"I think of myself as an outcast," said one.

"Loner," said another.

"Forgotten."

"I feel like I don't have a place."

Magoffin's heart dropped. "As a teacher," he said later, "it breaks your heart to hear that you have students who don't think they have a place in your school. Here are a bunch of kids who have a passion about something, and they're getting told that it's stupid by someone at home, by a teacher, by whoever. So that sort of piqued my interest."

As soon as he got home, Magoffin started scouring the internet for ideas on what to do with a group of high school kids who loved video games. His Google search brought him to PlayVS. The website was pretty bare bones, but the basic information was there. Officially sanctioned by the NFHS. Sixty-four dollars per player per season. Season begins in October. Magoffin copied the link and emailed it to Justin with a note:

Check this out. What do you think?

In a cramped trailer on the other side of town, Justin's eyes lit up. Competitive video games . . . at school? PlayVS had not yet announced which games it would be offering, but Justin guessed *League of Legends* would be one of them, given that its publisher, Riot Games, was known for liberally licensing its software. Justin didn't play *League* himself, but he could learn.

He wrote Magoffin back:

This looks legit.

Justin wasted no time recruiting teammates. Isaiah, already a big *League* player, was an obvious choice. He asked a few kids from class who he knew played at home. Word spread quickly. Within a few days, the squad stood at eighteen kids—enough to form three teams with some subs.

The next step, a significantly harder one than finding a bunch of kids willing to play video games, would be to pitch the idea to the administration. For starters, the $64 fee per student meant $1,152 for a team of eighteen—nothing that would break the bank, but still a previously unaccounted-for expense at a school in a lower-middle-class area. Then there was the need to get the principals and superintendent on board with the idea of having a club built around video games, the very thing that parents across America can't pry their kids away from when it's time to set the table or do their homework. It wouldn't be an easy sell.

Magoffin had an idea.

"You want this more than anyone," he told Justin. "The administration might be most persuaded if a student like you who is, let's say, not exactly known for his school involvement were the one making the pitch."

For the next few days, Justin used his free time to do research. Soon, he and a friend found themselves standing in between a PowerPoint presentation and a group that included the school's superintendent and co-principals. The words poured quickly from Justin's mouth.

"Gaming requires teamwork." "Tens of millions of kids play across the US." "Eighteen students at Mahar are already interested and many more will surely follow."

It was the most passionate any of the half-dozen people in the audience had seen Justin about anything. Scott Hemlin, one of the co-principals, sat attentively in his chair trying to digest it all. With a graying goatee and a high and tight buzz cut—a holdover from his Marine Corps days—he didn't look like someone who cared much for video games, and he wasn't. Hemlin was more of a football and ice hockey guy. But as he listened to Justin explain this new concept, he heard some things he liked.

"Sometimes," Hemlin said later, "kids pitch things and I don't understand it one bit after they leave the room. When I saw this presentation, what I heard was that this wasn't going to be some small club with two or three kids playing. It was going to be a whole bunch of kids, and it was going to be competitive."

When the pitch concluded, the committee voted: Mahar would form an esports team, and it would be guaranteed funding for its first two seasons.

Kyle Magoffin was officially a varsity-level esports coach—one of the first in the country. Now he just had to figure out what *League of Legends* was.

3

"THIS IS NOT

A PITY STORY"

A YOUNG COMPANY called Groupon was all the rage in the startup world of late 2010. The upstart's innovative business model let customers earn discounts if a certain number of people signed up to use a particular deal, thereby encouraging users to share promotions with their social networks. Participating businesses could include online retailers as well as restaurants, museums, salons, apparel shops, and just about any other kind of physical storefront. Just two years after launching, the company had 35 million users and was operating in 250 cities worldwide.

Though Groupon was headquartered in Chicago, two of its cofounders, Brad Keywell and Eric Lefkofsky, had grown up in the Detroit suburbs, which made the company particularly intriguing to Delane. But its Michigan connections weren't the only thing that drew him in. Delane found the model fascinating. In the age of ecommerce and Amazon, an internet company was driving people into brick-and-mortar shops instead of out of them. At the time, Delane was working at a physical storefront himself. His mom had recently connected him with an enterprising man she knew from the neighborhood named Mark who owned a collision shop. Mark had started a car rental business and loaned to people whose vehicles were under repair. He decided to take on Delane, who was only a high school senior but had already proven himself to be a capable businessman.

As the end of the school year rolled around, Delane's friends wanted to rent luxury cars for prom, but most agencies required renters to be twenty-five and possess a credit card. Delane convinced Mark to lower the establishment's minimum age to eighteen, accept cash, and stock its inventory with higher-class models. Local students soon flowed in. Business took off, and the company kept the model in place, finding a niche among customers with bad or no credit. Within a few short years, the company expanded to sixteen locations across Michigan and the southeastern United States.

Almost all of Delane's jobs to that point had revolved around brick-and-mortar businesses. The internet was still a somewhat new phenomenon to him—his family had only gotten access to the web a few years prior. The fact that a company like Groupon could not only exist, but also have a positive impact on the real world, amazed him. Studying the company's business model more closely, though, Delane perceived a few flaws: it required businesses to heavily discount their products and services, and it rarely created loyal customers. He envisioned a web application that was part coupon machine, part customer relationship management platform. Through the app, businesses would create profiles on which they could offer discounts. Customers would be able to follow their favorite shops, get support directly through the app, and receive deals for being frequent patrons, while businesses would be able to communicate with and track the behavior of their clientele. Delane called his idea Plenty Discounts and set out to build it. Over the next six months, he created an overly elaborate product mockup using PowerPoint Shapes that numbered more than a hundred slides. He drafted financial models to find the margins that would generate profits for both the company and its partners. He approached local businesses with the concept and got a handful to agree to sign up before its launch. But Delane knew he would need money to get the thing off the ground—and venture capital was scarce in Detroit at the time.

The solution to Delane's funding problem came to him in the form of a local news story. Just a few paragraphs long, it announced the creation of Detroit Venture Partners, a new VC firm being launched by a group that included Quicken Loans founder and Cleveland Cavaliers owner Dan Gilbert, a Detroit native, and Josh Linkner, the founder of ePrize, a Michigan-based online rewards and promotions company that Gilbert had financially backed. Linkner, Delane thought, was just the person who could help bring his idea to life. He knew he had to get in a room with him. Soon after, Delane learned that the TEDx Conference was coming to Detroit and, sure enough, Linkner was going to be speaking there. But Delane was on the fence about going. He had recently lost a loved one and was struggling to find meaning or motivation. He was plugging away at his car rental job. Making any traction with someone like Linkner seemed like a long shot anyway.

Delane's girlfriend, Ashley, wasn't having any of it. She surprised him with a ticket to the conference, plus a business casual outfit—button-down shirt, cardigan, pair of khakis—as well as a leather binder and a set of business cards.

"You've got this business idea," she told him, "and you need to do something with it. You're going."

He did just that. In an ornate music hall in midtown, Delane mingled with the crowd and watched inspiring people speak on stage. After Linkner gave his talk, Delane spotted his opening. He approached Linkner, introduced himself, and told him he was excited to hear about the new venture firm.

"I have some ideas," Delane told him. "I'd love to set up a meeting."

Linkner appreciated the forwardness. He had his assistant make arrangements.

The next week, Delane found himself on the tenth floor of the Compuware Building, the new home of Quicken Loans. It was the first time he'd been in a building that tall. He looked out the window over downtown, seeing his city from an entirely new perspective. When Linkner walked into the room, Delane sat down at his laptop and took him through the deck. He showed Linkner how a business would set up its profile, what a customer would see, and how to use the platform's many features. Linkner was patient. This wasn't at all how a pitch was supposed to go, but Delane didn't know that yet. About forty slides in, Linkner intervened. He suggested Delane meet with Bizdom, a startup accelerator that Gilbert had recently founded. Delane left the meeting unsatisfied, feeling like Linkner was skeptical he could get it done. Still, he did as Linkner suggested and took the idea to Bizdom. It didn't go anywhere. Delane started to get an inkling that he wasn't being taken seriously. Over the next few weeks, an unpleasant truth set in: his business concept had been rebuffed.

"I took it hard," Delane recalled. "As a kid from Detroit, to hear that from somebody who has been successful in Detroit, and who you admire, you immediately think, 'He must know.' Maybe he just wasn't mindful of how him saying that would affect me. Maybe he was inured to that. Also, I was feeling down already, so maybe that level of rejection just hit me harder. But I kind of fell into this depression around it. It was hard to get out of."

Of course, Linkner couldn't have known all this. Delane was young, inexperienced, and seeking advice, and he had gotten himself face time with one of the more established entrepreneurs in Detroit. But to Delane, it felt like a failure. His desire to work on the idea faded. He set it aside and turned his attention back to the car rental business, where he did whatever Mark needed, whether it was renting out the cars or washing them.

The itch to break into tech never quite went away. After he met Jake Cohen, another DVP partner, at an event, Delane followed up with an email.

Thanks again for taking the time to speak at the conference. I forgot to ask you in person, but is DVP hiring in any support roles? I'm quitting my job to fully immerse myself in the space. I want to be in a position where I can learn and grow.

Cohen replied and told him DVP wasn't hiring at the moment. Not long after, the firm had an opening for the role of Cohen's assistant. Delane, still without much traditional job experience on his resume, applied for the position. He didn't get it.

One day a few months later, Delane saw a tweet from Jonathon Triest, a partner at Detroit-based Ludlow Ventures. The VC firm was a sponsor for the startup-centric Launch Festival in San Francisco, and Triest had some tickets—valued at $400 apiece—he could give away. Delane tweeted at him several times with no response. So he tracked down Triest's email address and typed something up.

Hi Jon. I hate to seem like a pest about winning the Launch festival ticket. And, I just wanted to explain to you why the opportunity would mean so much to me.

Growing up in my neighborhood, all everyone wanted was to be an athlete or a musician. All I wanted to be was the best entrepreneur the world has ever seen. Before I even knew the basics of founding a web-based company, running an internet business has always intrigued me. The only problem is growing up I had no resources/mentors in this industry I desperately wanted to be a part of. To make a long story short, I have conquered every

challenge I've been faced with in my life thus far. I'm positive with
my knowledge and multitude of skills I can succeed in the startup
space, I just need the opportunity to prove myself to the world.

This is not a pity story, I just wanted to let you know that the
opportunity to attend the Launch festival would be an amazing
experience for me as I attempt to begin my professional career in the
tech world.

A few hours later, Triest sent Delane a free ticket along with
a brief note:

go kill it dude!

Delane was just as excited as he was terrified. He'd never been
on a plane nor left Detroit on his own. He found a hotel room
near San Francisco International and booked the cheapest round-
trip flight he could find. Touching down in San Francisco was
like arriving in a new world. Sleek offices that housed thriving
tech companies. A fledgling app called Uber that let you hail a
black car from your phone. Hills everywhere.

The Launch Festival's home was the Concourse Exhibition
Center, a dingy multipurpose hall that also hosted craft beer festivals and baseball card shows. To Delane, it was nothing short
of incredible. He watched the angel investor Jason Calacanis, the
festival's founder, interview entrepreneurs and venture capitalists
on stage. Hundreds of people roamed the floor, where founders
showed off their startups to passing guests with tabletop displays.
Delane visited every one of them. He spoke with every person he
came across. When he finished each conversation, he scribbled
a few notes about their chat on the back of the person's business
card. That night, he followed up by email with every one of his
new contacts.

From the demo pit floor, Delane watched a speaker named Thomas Korte, an investor who had recently launched a startup accelerator with his wife called AngelPad. When he left the stage, Delane approached him. Korte gave him a few minutes, then politely told him he needed to peruse the floor for potential candidates for the fund's premier class. "But," he told Delane, "you can walk and talk with me."

"I've already seen every company," responded Delane, "so let me take you to some that were really interesting."

Impressed, Korte took him up on his offer. While they walked around the floor checking out companies, he told Delane he should come work with the fund in San Francisco. There was just one catch. It wasn't a paid position.

"I need to be making money," Delane responded honestly. "So I'll have to decline the offer." (Little did he know AngelPad would go on to become one of the most highly regarded accelerators in the US.)

Still, the experience reignited his desire to try to crack into the tech startup world. It also made him want to bring a version of the Launch Festival to Detroit, a city still very much in recovery mode following the 2007–2008 financial crash. Events like Launch simply didn't take place in southeastern Michigan.

Entrepreneurship was so uncommon in Detroit that some twentysomethings didn't even know what it was. Around the same time Delane came back from his first trip to the Bay Area, an industrious recent Michigan State University grad named Amanda Lewan had taken a job as the second employee at a newly formed advertising agency.

"I had no idea what a startup was," Lewan recounted. "That's how blue-collar Detroit was. It felt like everyone here worked in the auto industry or, like my parents—a janitor and a secretary—had the same job their whole lives. I didn't know the concept of entre-preneurship as a career path."

At the ad firm, Lewan was tasked with making early hires and managing marketing campaigns for local businesses. She caught the startup bug. At the time, though, the city had almost no support system in place for startups. If you were looking for a coworking space, Bizdom was your lone legitimate option. But getting in required applying and having your business idea accepted, which Lewan attempted and struck out. One night, Lewan's boyfriend, Marc Hudson, came home gushing about a young local guy he had just met at a pitch event at the Garden Bowl, a century-old bowling alley in the city's center. Sure enough, that guy was Delane. Lewan and Hudson befriended him, and they soon met a group of three other wannabe entrepreneurs, some of whom similarly had been turned down by Bizdom. "We were the rejects," said Lewan, "so we all became close."

Lewan, Delane, and the three young men agreed that Detroit's startup scene was severely lacking—and they wanted to do something about it. The father of one of the guys ran a construction company and owned a building downtown near Ford Field, home of the NFL's Detroit Lions. The two-thousand-square-foot space sat on the second floor above a bail bond business and below a music studio. It had old wood floors, exposed brick, and the perfect amount of charm to serve as a hub for entrepreneurs. Lewan and the three guys decided to turn it into a place where founders and developers could network and get work done. They bought $5,000 worth of Ikea furniture and converted it into a coworking space they called Bamboo. For $99 a month, members got all-day access to a workstation, conference room, copy machine, and printer. The coworking space concept would soon take off thanks in large part to WeWork, but at the time it was novel; Bamboo was the first of its kind in downtown Detroit.

Delane decided not to come on as a co-owner, instead viewing the space as a home for the events he'd been hoping to bring to his city. He started securing guests like TechStars cofounder Brad Feld and Mozilla cocreator Mitch Kapor to come talk at Bamboo. The speakers flew in from all over the country, in some cases setting foot in Detroit for the first time. Delane called his new event series Fifty Founders—with the rather ambitious idea being that he would throw that many events—and he and the Bamboo folks charged twenty to thirty bucks per ticket, essentially the cost of the pizza and beer they would serve. "Nothing like that existed in Detroit yet," recalled Lewan. "There weren't these fun events where you could just bump into people and network and hear founders talk about building a company." The first talks drew just a few dozen people, but word soon spread. The group secured sponsorships, which allowed them to offer free admission, and the events eventually crammed two hundred people into the space and flirted with fire code violations.

As the series grew, so did Delane's passion for Detroit's startup scene. He realized what he wanted most was to support entrepreneurs and get paid for it, whether that meant working for an accelerator or finding an entry-level job in venture capital. Gilbert's Detroit Venture Partners began sponsoring the events, which Delane started using as a chance to get his foot in the door in the tech world. Even as Bamboo's membership steadily climbed, he didn't have any regrets about not joining the ownership group. He had other plans.

IN A STARBUCKS in the upper-middle-class Detroit suburb of Birmingham, Hajj Flemings sat across the table from the kid he'd been hearing all about. Flemings, bespectacled and the owner of an impeccable fashion sense, was nearly twenty years Delane's senior. An engineer by training who'd joined the auto industry and then fled it during the financial crash to pursue entrepreneurship, he'd earned a reputation in the Detroit startup scene as someone willing to help out founders. He launched a branding conference called Brand Camp University while still working in the automotive industry, and now he was gradually growing the series. He knew people, and they knew him.

Flemings had heard a lot about Delane in the leadup to the meeting. The reviews were mixed: he's smart and full of ideas, but he's stubborn and difficult to work with—"A bull in a china shop," as someone once described him. Still, Flemings was intrigued. *I like the work he's doing*, he thought. *I've got to talk to him and see for myself.* Now, seated in the coffee shop, Delane spoke about his desire to build something in the startup world and his hope to see Detroit transform into a tech hub. As Delane talked, Flemings fairly quickly identified Delane as someone who could help him. For all his connections, what Flemings didn't have was someone with whom he could go to war. Or, more specifically, to pitch meetings.

"It can be really difficult to find somebody who has the same kind of passion as you and who can go secure the bag," Flemings said later. "In my gut, I knew that there was something special about him. It was the energy. When you talked to him, you just knew this was not your average twenty-one-year-old." As a one-hour conversation became a two-hour one, Flemings decided, *This young man is going to be my new business partner.*

Soon Flemings was bringing Delane with him to pitch potential investors and partners who could help him expand his series. He quickly learned that Delane was a secret weapon of sorts. Not only did he possess an unparalleled ability to connect with people, he also prepared for a meeting like it was the bar exam. If Delane wanted your business, he would come into the room with research decks on not only your company, but a dozen of your closest competitors. He was just as confident in a room with a single angel investor as he was talking to the brass of a billion-dollar state economic commission. He also knew how to work his network. When Flemings needed someone's contact info, Delane would find a way to track it down, often within minutes.

The relationship was mutually beneficial. For Delane, Flemings served as the adult in the room, someone who could open doors that often remained shut to someone barely old enough to drink. Maybe someone involved in Detroit's tech scene in 2013 hadn't heard of Delane Parnell, but they had heard of Hajj Flemings. Attaching his name to things gave Delane credibility and helped him earn time with important people. Together, the duo would earn some grant money for an event here, a several-thousand-dollar investment there.

Sometimes, though, Flemings ran into the brashness he'd been warned about. After some back and forth with the folks at a local accelerator cofounded by one of the Big Three automotive companies, Flemings and Delane secured a meeting with the firm's leadership. They settled into the downtown office and began their pitch. Things began smoothly, but when Delane started to sense they weren't headed toward a favorable outcome, he changed gears with little warning.

"Look," he told the CEO. "What you guys are doing, it sucks. You're having no impact," he said, proceeding to run through a laundry list of what he perceived as problems with the way the accelerator operated.

Flemings held his cool, but inside he was boiling. It wasn't the first time Delane had failed to sugarcoat something when it would've been in their best interest to do so. "I come out of the meeting," Flemings recalled, "and I'm like, 'Delane, you know that you're my guy. What you said in there, you were spot on. But if you keep going in these rooms and doing this, we're not going to be able to get money from anybody, because nobody is going to like us.' And he said, 'Man, but it's true.' I was like, 'It is true, but that doesn't mean you have to say it!'"

Flemings and Delane had their share of disagreements as they built out their respective projects. They would quarrel about branding or domain names or the speakers they should book for an event. Sometimes the arguments would escalate nearly to the point of coming to blows. "He doesn't back down from anything," Flemings said. "He's going to go toe-to-toe. He's like Kobe— they'll prod you, but they don't respect you if you just fall in line." The pair would have a spat, walk away thinking the partnership was over, then reconnect and find that things were even better than before. They grew to be friends in spite of the age difference. Both event series benefited. Brand Camp University rose in stature. Fifty Founders signed speakers like Reddit cofounder Alexis Ohanian, and it soon outgrew the Bamboo space. Delane renamed the series Starter Talks and moved it to the atrium of a building attached to Ford Field. He booked Kickstarter cofounder Charles Adler, sold tickets on Eventbrite for $25 apiece, and, in September 2014, held an event in front of a crowd of 1,500.

Delane, meanwhile, still had one eye on the venture capital space. He continually checked in with firms about opportunities, most of them based on the coasts. For one event he landed Tom LaSorda, the former Chrysler CEO who had recently launched a venture firm in Detroit, IncWell, with a handful of other automotive industry expats. Delane and LaSorda got to know each other, and when IncWell had an opening for an associate position, the two met at a Coney Island restaurant in Birmingham. "IncWell has struggled in its first year," LaSorda explained to Delane. "We want to increase the number of companies pouring in through the top of the funnel." It was something Delane's connections to Silicon Valley and the tech world were well suited to assist.

After the meeting, LaSorda reached out to Flemings for a character reference. "Delane won't be shy about his opinions, for better or worse," Flemings told him, "but he will work his ass off."

As a final step, LaSorda decided to bring Delane into the Inc-Well office for a meet-and-greet with Simon Boag and some of the other company leadership. From his desk, Reda Jaber, a newly hired partner, watched the first half of the meeting through the conference room's glass walls.

"Delane starts giving Tom and Simon a presentation on how IncWell can improve, what his strategy would be, what we're doing wrong, what companies we should look at, and why we should look at them," remembered Jaber. "He's standing up and the two of them are sitting. They weren't even expecting this—they had just been expecting a conversation. It got to a point where Tom waved a few of us to come over, and we just sat there. I was in awe. He's in his early twenties, standing there in a boardroom with the former CEO of Chrysler, and the confidence that he had—it was just like, how can we not bring him on?"

LaSorda offered him a job. Delane wound down the event series and started working with the group of millionaires and billionaires. IncWell invested in early stage companies, usually in amounts up to $250,000. Almost all of the firm's investments to that point had been in Michigan-based companies.

"At that time, the best startups, the most exciting startups, came out of the coasts," said Jaber. "We're sitting there in Michigan. How do we attract startups to even pay attention to us? Delane had this amazing network of the top people in the entrepreneurial space—the biggest investors, the biggest entrepreneurs, the best startups. He had their numbers in his phone somehow. Almost instantly, we were getting face time with some of the top startups in the country."

Though Jaber was technically one of Delane's bosses, he watched him work with wonder. Delane's style differed greatly from his own. Jaber was quieter, more introverted, uninterested in stirring things up. With Delane next to him, silence was something that simply didn't exist. The kid was constantly on the phone or talking about a company that excited him. Fairly quickly, Delane had an idea for a total revamping of IncWell's intake process. Companies reaching out to the firm had to enter an online portal and fill out information, including a pitch deck and a business plan, then sign off on the firm's legal terms and conditions. Delane believed the system was cumbersome and discouraged founders from applying. He wanted a more informal procedure—a note from a founder that could lead to a casual conversation. After he told the partners as much, they took his advice and pared down the process.

With the barrier to entry now lowered and Delane working his contacts, a bevy of new startups ended up on IncWell's radar. Among the first that Delane presented to the firm was Calendly, a calendar automation app that helped people block off time on one another's schedules. IncWell invested $200,000 in its seed round; six years later, the app had 10 million monthly users, $70 million in annual revenue, and a valuation of more than $3 billion. But for each success, it felt like there were many more missed opportunities. Delane pitched the partners on Managed by Q, an office management company that had just been formed in New York. They passed. Five years later, it would sell to WeWork for $220 million. He couldn't convince the firm to invest in the biotech company Ginkgo Bioworks, which would later go public in a $17.5 billion SPAC deal.

The noninvestment that irked Delane the most, though, was one right in the firm's wheelhouse. Cruise, a San Francisco-based startup that made software and hardware for self-driving cars, was fresh out of the Y Combinator accelerator and valued at about $20 million. Delane used his connections to earn Inc-Well a call. It quickly became apparent that the startup's leadership didn't quite see the value of a firm that made investments of just a few hundred thousand dollars. After a few minutes of chatting, though, Cruise came up with a proposition: in exchange for equity, IncWell, with all its automotive experience, could make an investment and take on an advisory role.

The IncWell partners huddled up after the call. The opportunity was interesting, but advising wasn't what IncWell did, and they had some serious doubts about the startup's ability to commercialize. They decided to pass. Less than two years later, Cruise would be acquired by GM for $581 million. Five years after that, it raised money at a valuation of $30 billion—fifteen hundred times what it was worth when IncWell turned it down.

"In the VC world," Jaber said later, "sometimes people ask, 'What investment do you regret most?' The answer a lot of times is not which investment you made that failed. It's the one you could have made but didn't. A deal like that could have been a career maker."

Delane started growing frustrated. It didn't help that he was supposed to remain in the office throughout the day, which limited his preferred face-to-face interactions only to companies willing to visit IncWell's building. The job's corporate nature weighed on him. Every morning began with an 8:00 a.m. standup meeting, and any latecomers had to put a dollar in a tip jar that would later be used to buy the company lunch. "Delane filled that thing up," Jaber said. "He was always like one minute late. It was a funny thing, but it was kind of a microcosm of how a process like that clashed with his style."

That spring, LaSorda had to take a personal leave from the company. With his longest-running connection to IncWell gone,

Delane had even more of a strained relationship with the firm's leadership. Fed up one day, he told one of the partners that the company needed to rethink its approach if it wanted to make an impact. It didn't take.

By the time the fund stopped making new investments, Delane was already long gone.

IN 2010, GOOGLE announced that it would be choosing one location for a pilot test of its new high-speed broadband service, Google Fiber, and invited cities and towns across the US to apply. More than a thousand did. Many resorted to attention-grabbing tactics to separate themselves from the competition. Peoria, Illinois, flew a banner over the company's Silicon Valley headquarters. Greenville, South Carolina, recruited a thousand residents to spell out *Google* using glow sticks in the brand's colors. The mayor of Duluth, Minnesota, jumped into Lake Superior in February under the guise of needing a faster search for the definition of *hypothermia*. Some temporarily changed their names, with varying degrees of creativity: Topeka christened itself as Google, Kansas; Rancho Cucamonga became Rancho Googlemonga. In the end, the company selected Kansas City, and Google Fiber came online there soon after. The effects were swift. The city passed a $15-million technological revamp initiative called the Smart City Project. An entrepreneurial hub named the Kansas City Startup Village sprang up. Local companies and business organizations created an incubator called Digital Sandbox KC. Startups added more than 80,000 jobs in a four-year span. Long a blue-collar town, Kansas City began a gradual but undeniable transformation into a twenty-first-century city.

Marc Hudson sat at home in Detroit one night in late 2012 reading about some of these developments. Hudson had recently started working for Quicken Loans after Dan Gilbert moved the company's headquarters from the suburbs to downtown in an effort to revitalize the area. Hudson didn't think Detroit should wait until it won some contest to get high-speed broadband. He drafted up a pitch for Quicken Loans to create a fiber optics arm and submitted it into the Cheese Factory, a portal through which employees could send ideas for improving the company.

The idea gained traction, continually escalating through the various layers of the firm's hierarchy, until one day Hudson and two of his colleagues found themselves pitching it directly to Gilbert. When their presentation concluded, Gilbert looked out at the three faces staring hopefully back at him. "I don't know what you do today," he admitted, "but you don't do that anymore. This is your job now." Gilbert agreed to form a new company called Rocket Fiber with the objective of bringing fiber-optic broadband to Detroit. He backed it with $31 million and named Hudson its CEO.

Delane, meanwhile, was starting to feel like it was time to move on from IncWell. When he spotted a job listing on the newly formed Rocket Fiber's website for a role leading the development of a new retail store, he called up Hudson to tell him he would be applying. Hudson hesitated. Delane had some retail experience, he knew, but it hardly seemed like an ideal fit. Plus, he told Delane, Rocket Fiber had already interviewed candidates with extensive backgrounds in developing new stores. Still, Delane persisted, so Hudson convinced the rest of the Rocket Fiber staff to meet with his friend. They reluctantly agreed to interview the eleventh-hour applicant whose only retail experience was peddling cell phones. It looked like a classic case of nepotism.

Delane showed up for his interview at the Rocket Fiber office carrying a handful of stapled packets. He'd drafted up a pitch deck outlining what the store's interior would look like and the types of products it would offer. The shop he proposed would be something of a next-generation Best Buy, a business that sold cutting-edge hardware and connected devices that could leverage Rocket Fiber's broadband: drones, entertainment systems, internet-of-things-connected household devices.

"We had publicly said very little about what we wanted to build," Hudson said, "and he basically came in and pitched a concept that was a mirror image of what we had envisioned without having prior knowledge of it. The team, without me even saying anything, looked at each other and said, 'This is the person we need to hire.'" Hudson told Delane he'd been chosen for the job. Over the next few days, Delane sent text after text promising he wouldn't let Hudson down.

Internally, Rocket Fiber had been thinking about the retail store as more of a marketing ploy than a reliable source of profit. The business would be located downtown in an area with a lot of foot traffic. For assistance with the store's design, Delane suggested the company speak with the renowned firms Eight Inc.—designer of the first Apple Stores—and IDEO. He secured meetings with both companies in San Francisco. Hudson, despite his new status as a tech company CEO, had never been to the Bay Area. His guide for his first pilgrimage would be Delane.

When they arrived for their stay at a beautiful boutique hotel in downtown, Hudson asked how he was able to keep the trip within the startup's skimpy travel budget. "He told me," recalled Hudson, "that when he was younger and he'd come out to San Francisco, he didn't have enough money to stay at one of these nice hotels, so he looked up a senior VP on LinkedIn and messaged him. And the guy was like, 'Yeah, you can stay here any time. Here's my discount code.' So that was the first indication that I was traveling with the right person."

The pair had productive meetings with the two firms regarding how to approach designing Rocket Fiber's store. Afterward,

Delane decided he and Hudson should pay a visit to Kapor Capital, the VC firm founded by the tech entrepreneur and billionaire Mitch Kapor. In the elevator on the way up, Delane started a friendly chat with a man and encouraged Hudson to tell him what they were building at Rocket Fiber. He did. When the man stepped off the elevator, Delane turned to Hudson.

"You just pitched your company to Mitch Kapor," Delane told him.

Hudson couldn't believe it. Here was Delane, six years younger and a newer arrival to the tech scene, guiding him all over town like he was the mayor of San Francisco. Nothing ever came of the introduction, but Hudson looked at Delane in a different light after that. "The trip highlighted one of Delane's superpowers," he said. "It was very clear that he had an ability to connect with very powerful, influential people in a way that most people can't."

The pair flew back to Detroit and Delane continued plugging away at the retail project. His desk in the office was next to that of D'Andre Ealy, another young local with a taste for entrepreneurship. Delane and Ealy had gotten to know each other a bit in the Bamboo days, when Ealy would come in to work on his startup, a college campus–centric meal and grocery delivery service called Runn. He had started developing it while at Central Michigan University, then dropped out to pursue it full-time. The platform would accept orders on behalf of restaurants and grocery stores, then have local students deliver them in exchange for a fee, which at the time was a fairly innovative concept. The cofounders had earned some clout in Detroit's nascent startup scene because they'd gotten an email response—not a term sheet, but an email response—from Mark Cuban. But the business couldn't get enough traction; it fizzled after a few years just as companies like DoorDash and Instacart came on the scene. "We were before our time," said Ealy. "And we were young and had no idea what we were doing."

Delane and Ealy bonded in the Rocket Fiber office over their love of entrepreneurship. Ealy was a healthy eater, and Delane, never one to overthink his meals, would tempt him to join him in getting fast food. The office had a high-tech television connected to an Xbox, and Delane and Ealy would come back and play *NBA 2K* or *Call of Duty* during their lunch breaks. While the gaming setup got plenty of mileage from employees, its true purpose was to showcase Rocket Fiber's broadband to visitors. High-speed internet at the time was beginning to make online gaming more feasible, allowing many remote players to compete simultaneously with no lag. As Detroit's primary player in the broadband space, Rocket Fiber started drawing interest from people looking to get involved in the business of gaming. Hudson was overbooked one day in the fall of 2015, so he handed a meeting off to Delane and another colleague. The appointment was with a local millionaire whose son had become a rising pro gamer, which had sparked the idea to use Rocket Fiber's internet to participate in online esports tournaments. Delane asked the man question after question about the industry.

When he emerged from the meeting, it was clear something had clicked for Delane. "He came out of there so enthusiastic," recalled Hudson. "He very clearly was personally interested in it. From then on, he was always talking about esports."

Delane and the millionaire began discussing the possibility of building a franchised esports league, something that didn't yet exist. The league would be based in Detroit; players would live in Dan Gilbert-owned apartments, and teams would compete in arenas built within Gilbert-owned buildings that all relied on Rocket Fiber internet. Through conversations with various players within the space, Delane soaked up knowledge about esports like a sponge, growing ever more excited about the space.

The idea to build a league didn't come to fruition, but during his research, Delane learned that professional esports teams were being bought and sold for hundreds of thousands of dollars. Through the local millionaire, he met a pro gamer from Detroit, a twenty-one-year-old *Call of Duty* player named Jordan Cannon who went by "ProoFy" online. Cannon was the captain of a four-person squad that played the game for a living, sometimes winning thousands of dollars at a time for placing highly in sponsored online tournaments. The team had recently qualified for the *Call of Duty* World League—an accomplishment in itself, since doing so required finishing first in a handful of competitive tournaments.

Delane saw an opportunity: he could form an organization to house ProoFy's team, give it support, and help build it up in an effort to increase its value. But he would need more money. As one of his first calls, he reached out to Bryan Smiley, a Detroit native turned Hollywood executive whom he'd become acquainted with in recent years. Smiley, while back in the city for an event one day, had run into an old high school classmate who gushed about this local event organizer he'd heard about named Delane Parnell. Smiley connected with Delane, and their first phone call lasted three hours, spanning topics from tech—Smiley had previously tried to start a gaming company—to Detroit to Hollywood. It turned into a mutually beneficial relationship: Smiley had advice to give on how to move among powerful people, Delane had ideas, and both had deep networks of people worth knowing.

Now, Delane presented Smiley with the idea of investing in a *Call of Duty* team. Smiley was interested—Delane had only known about the space for a few short months, but it was clear he'd done his homework. "That was the magic about Delane," Smiley said later. "When he had a thing he wanted to do, he absorbed so much information about that industry—the players, the ups and downs or hurdles you have to face, the opportunity. He became an expert so fast. He could talk about that thing with such exceptional confidence and clarity and detail that you would have thought the guy had been doing it for thirty years."

Smiley agreed to invest. Delane drafted up some paperwork using the knowledge he'd gained at IncWell. He formed an organization called Rush Esports, came to terms with Cannon and his team, and officially became president and general manager of the *Call of Duty* squad.

At Rocket Fiber, meanwhile, the concept of a retail store was becoming less and less realistic. Delane and Hudson were having trouble making the economics work—in the best-case scenario, the store would break even; in the worst-case scenario, it would be an unnecessary financial burden on a startup trying to build expensive infrastructure. Hudson decided to shelve the idea. He and Delane discussed the possibility of moving Delane into another role, perhaps in sales, but deep down Hudson acknowledged it didn't make much sense. "Anyone who knew Delane and was being objective in their view of him knew that he was going to go do awesome stuff," he said. "So it was like, 'You need to go do awesome stuff. Go chase your passion and get after it.'"

Delane left Rocket Fiber and turned his attention to the *Call of Duty* team full-time. Managing four players in their early twenties quickly proved to be more than he'd bargained for. Delane found himself driving to the players' homes to wake them up for their 4:00 p.m. matches. The teammates would get into squabbles—about who had been talking to whose girlfriend, or about snarky messages they'd seen each other post online that they were convinced had to be about them. The role, at times, felt like a high-stakes babysitting job. After a few months, Delane started looking for potential buyers for the team. The esports organization Team SoloMid came in with a tempting offer. Delane pulled the trigger, and three months after buying the team, he and Smiley made a profit of $40,000.

Delane knew he wasn't done in the esports space. For his next act, he wanted to build his own company from scratch. Exactly what it would do still wasn't clear, but he did have one critical thing: a name. He'd thought of the moniker PlayVS, pronounced "play versus," months earlier. It was versatile, he thought, and could apply to just about anything he wanted to build in gaming. The $2,000 price tag on GoDaddy had scared him, but now he decided it was time. There was just one problem—the trademark was owned by another company building gaming software. After some negotiating, Delane bought the name and assets off its owners for $10,000. He snagged some similar domains for a few thousand more. Now he had a company name into which he'd dumped $15,000 of his own money. What he didn't have was a business plan.

As he brainstormed, Delane thought about his attempt to build an esports league while working at Rocket Fiber. He believed he could get there—starting with a platform on which gamers could compete against one another online and wager on the outcome. Delane researched and found that a few platforms were already trying to facilitate this, but their processes were clunky and required steps like submitting a photo of your screen to verify the result. He thought he could build something better.

Delane started setting up shop in a cafe every day where he researched the market and worked on a mockup of the product. Ealy, meanwhile, had taken an interest in what Delane was doing, coming to visit him in the coffee shop after work and talking through the idea. Through a connection, Delane eventually rented out some space in an ad agency for $1,500 per month. As he went all in on the venture, Ealy decided to quit his job at Rocket Fiber and join him. They bought some desks and chairs at Ikea and got to work.

Delane still needed a web designer. He dropped a note into a small but active Facebook group called Hackers & Hustlers, where people trying to break into Detroit's tech scene posted messages seeking work or talent. Fairly quickly, a handful of people all tagged the same person, a product designer in Detroit. It was a name with which Delane was already familiar.

THERE PERHAPS HAS never been a more perfect living embodiment of the adjective *chill* than Sean Yalda. Dark-haired, bearded, and usually wearing a long gold chain, Yalda's vibe was not unlike that of the lovable stoner in your favorite nineties movie. In the professional world, his likability was an asset—as was his talent for creating nice-looking websites. Yalda's path to joining the founding team of one of the world's premier gaming startups was, to put it mildly, circuitous. He found a number of passions at a young age. None of them involved schoolwork. Photography, coding, anime—if it allowed him to be creative and didn't require a classroom, he was into it. The son of two Iraqi immigrants, Yalda grew up in the Detroit suburbs and, as a teen, created a website for fellow fans of the animated Japanese show *Dragon Ball Z*. Through that, he met a group of fellow nerdy youths online, and they started making web pages dedicated to their favorite video games, with each title getting its own review, photo gallery, and list of crowdsourced strategies. Yalda, who had taught himself how to use Photoshop and develop websites in both HTML and CSS, took on the role of managing the projects. That left little time for studying. He fell a credit short of graduating, though his parents for years believed he'd earned his diploma—thanks in large part to his proficiency in Photoshop.

Yalda, like any responsible adult, decided to form a band with two brothers from town after high school. They rotated through a few names—the Volcano Brothers, Serene Green and the Secret Psychics, Vanguard Funk Militia—but settled on Deserae, an homage to their favorite local stripper. Yalda was a guitar player by trade, but the instrument was already spoken for, so he learned the electric keyboard. The band blended metal with rap, which the boys told people put them in the same category as the Beastie Boys or Rage Against the Machine. Strangely, though, they had trouble getting bookings. They didn't let that stop them from performing. The bandmates would go watch shows at clubs in town, then jump on stage between sets and start jamming. They'd blast through a song or two by the time anyone realized the takeover was unplanned. "Check us out, we're Deserae!" they would yell as a stagehand or bouncer forcefully dragged them off stage.

Soon one of the bandmates took a job fixing roofs with an uncle in the Iowa city of Glenwood, population five thousand. With little else going on in their lives, the others decided to come with him. The uncle agreed to buy the three of them a 1970s Dodge camper van to stay in. The roofing team, essentially a group of hailstorm chasers, would drive to neighborhoods that had just been hit by bad weather, knock on front doors—thick binders in hand—and ask to inspect for damage from the recent storm. Without fail, the homeowners were informed that their roofs were in need of repair. It was at best opportunistic and at worst predatory; the boss, an ultrareligious Christian, would close his emails to his employees with an earnest *Pray for hail*.

On weekends, the friends booked gigs in Omaha, drove the van the twenty-five miles into town, and played. If they didn't land a booking, they would set up on a street corner and jam. People sometimes told the three of them, with their dark curly hair, that they looked like the Jonas Brothers—so, naturally, they wrote a song about making it big and kicking the famed siblings' asses.

Yalda, lacking a computer or smartphone while living out of the camper van, kept himself occupied by reading. He got a card at the local library and checked out books on spirituality, like Ram Dass's *Be Here Now* and *Science of Breath*—a meditation guide written by a nineteenth-century Illinois attorney who suffered a mental breakdown, began studying Hinduism, and wrote occultist and psychic healing works under the name Yogi Ramacharaka. During one of his house visits, Yalda met a group of Mormon missionaries. He soon befriended them. When Yalda wasn't working, which was often, they came and hung by the van and shot hoops with him in the park nearby. They tried convincing Yalda to get rebaptized as a Mormon; "Thank you very much for the offer," he told them, "but I'm all set." Eventually, hail season ended and the gig came to an end. Deserae packed up its stuff and drove back to Detroit. "It was clear," Yalda said, "that I needed to find a real job."

Back in Michigan, Yalda started a website development consulting venture that, in a not-quite-subtle-enough tribute to some of his favorite musicians, he named Hendrix Floyd, LLC. He scored work by responding to listings on Craigslist. After replying to one ad, Yalda earned himself an interview with Rick Merlini, a local homebuilder who had made a few appearances on *Extreme Home Makeover*, a fact about which he was extremely proud. The man was built like an Olympic weightlifter and drank straight from a gallon jug of water he carried around. Yalda drove to meet with him at an office he had set up in one of his model homes in the suburbs.

"He was so buff and so assertive," said Yalda. "He was like, 'I want you to tell me what my website needs, and I'll tell you if you're right.' I said, 'Okay, well here'—I had printed out a ten-page heuristic evaluation of his website. He looked at it for a second, maybe read half a line, and said, 'So, you think I need this?' Then he just dropped the paper, said, 'I'll tell you what I need,' and went on for like an hour."

Merlini talked about his desire to have personality quizzes on the website—"Women love them," he insisted—and worked himself up to the point of turning pink in the face. At one point, he pulled out a copy of Arnold Schwarzenegger's *Encyclopedia of Modern Bodybuilding* and pointed to the table of contents to demonstrate exactly how he wanted his site set up. Yalda's door-to-door role had taught him how to deal with all kinds of personality types. *Just nod along, let him keep talking, and he'll give you the job.* Merlini continued to gush about his vision for the website. When he finally finished, Yalda said everything sounded just great. He got hired on the spot.

Yalda spent more than a year contracting for Merlini. Eventually, he tired of the role, went back to finding odd jobs on Craigslist, and took a side job delivering pizzas. Many of the companies he worked with were in their infancy. He was developing the startup itch, though he hadn't yet found a job fulfilling enough to satisfy it. When a Dan Gilbert–backed coworking space called Grand Circus sprang up in downtown Detroit in late 2013, Yalda made a point of attending all of its open houses and mingling with the staff so they would get to know him. The company offered a business boot camp that cost $5,000. Yalda didn't have the money. But the face time paid off. When one of the space's cofounders learned that the Michigan Economic Development Corporation wanted to sponsor one attendee with a great business idea, he called up Yalda and asked him if he had one ready to go.

"No," Yalda told him, "but I can write one. When do you need it by?"

"Tomorrow," came the reply.

Yalda borrowed his girlfriend's business textbook and flipped to the section on business proposals. He stayed up all night drafting a plan for a platform he'd been thinking about for some time. Essentially a LinkedIn for artists, it would serve as a place where people seeking photographers, musicians, and other creatives could connect with those looking for work. Yalda submitted the application by the 8:00 a.m. deadline and promptly passed out. He woke up and checked his inbox to find an email telling him he'd been accepted.

The course lasted three months. By the end, Yalda had parlayed it into a developer job for a startup called Click Click Car that was trying to bring the car leasing process online. He quickly became something of a poster child for Grand Circus. Whenever the staff were touring the space with a potential customer, they'd point to Yalda coding for the startup at his desk: "This is Sean. He was delivering pizzas three months ago—and look at him now!" The story was easy to tell, cleaner and simpler than one that included years of landing random, poor-paying design jobs through Craigslist. Yalda was happy to go along with it if it meant people in the startup world remembered him. Later, Grand Circus held a job fair–type event and asked him to speak.

"I essentially just said, 'Hey, three months ago, I was a pizza delivery guy. Now I'm making $40K as a front-end developer.' Then, I just mic-dropped it. I had nothing else to say."

Yalda caught wind of Delane's Starter Talks event at Ford Field while hanging in the space one day. Disappointed to find it was sold out, he located Delane's email address and reached out to him directly, offering to take photos of the event if it meant he could get inside. Delane took him up on it. On the day of the event, Yalda tracked him down, surprised to find that the guy running the show was five years younger than him. He took his photos and sent them along. Delane was pleased. The shots were good. It was a fair trade.

Neither thought much about the other until more than a year later, when the red notification number on Delane's Facebook page started ticking up as members of the Hustlers & Hackers group recommended Yalda for the design job. Delane reached out and asked him to lunch. Over sandwiches, he showed Yalda his deck on the esports industry and the problems other companies were running into as they tried to build wagering platforms. He thought he could overcome them by building a superior product. Yalda was intrigued. Every startup he'd worked for thus far had stagnated, and he'd often believed it to be the fault of incompetent or uninspired leadership. In Delane, he saw the opposite—he'd done his research on the industry and his passion was palpable. As the lunch wound down, Yalda invited Delane to his place to keep the conversation going. They went to Yalda's apartment and scribbled some thoughts on a dry-erase board about what the product might actually look like. The session went on for a few hours. By the end, Delane tried to convince him to agree to take the role on the spot. Yalda, at the time, had ditched the car startup and was working freelance with a handful of clients. He offered Delane ten to twenty hours per week. Sorry, said Delane—he'd have to get back to him.

Yalda awoke at 3:00 a.m. that night to his cell phone ringing. It was Delane. He wanted Yalda to work with him and was willing to let him come on part-time. "He makes me an offer right there," Yalda recalled. "Which was, in hindsight, a pretty terrible time for me to negotiate a contract. He's like, 'I want to know now, man!' Everybody else says, 'Take a day to think about things so that you know you're making the right choice.' Not him. He did not even want to allow for it. Once he made a decision, he wanted you to make a decision. That was the kind of personality he had, even at that young age. I realized this was just how it was going to be, and I felt like I had the patience to work with that. So I was like, 'All right, let's do this,' and I went back to sleep."

The next morning, Yalda came into the little office attached to the ad agency where Delane and D'Andre Ealy were waiting. Delane outlined for them what he sought to accomplish.

"I want a clean layout that incorporates elements of social media platforms like Facebook and Twitter," he said. "I want player profiles, a messaging tool, and a news feed. And I want it all in the next three months."

"That timeline is impossible," Yalda pushed back.

Delane wouldn't hear it. He knew what he needed done and when. Yalda started to suspect that while Delane possessed a great vision for a product, he didn't necessarily grasp what went into building it. "He was just kind of going in blind," Yalda said later, "but with complete confidence that he knew what he was doing."

Delane created a pitch deck he could show to potential investors and brought it to Smiley. The last investment had worked out well, so Smiley decided to roll the earnings from the previous sale into the new idea. He connected Delane with his contacts in Hollywood and some agreed to invest. Delane approached Hajj Flemings, who had missed out on the Rush Esports endeavor and wasn't about to let that happen again. He put in $10,000. In all, Delane gathered around $100,000 in seed money—enough for a few months of runway.

Using the new capital, Delane hired a few more engineers to help get the thing off the ground. The office would be buzzing until one or two in the morning. Delane practically lived there. "He wouldn't sleep unless he'd asserted every single idea or thought he had into the project and was completely depleted," Yalda recalled. "Then he would fall asleep, and he would still somehow get up earlier than everybody else." Using the startup's early prototype, Delane was able to secure another $250,000 in funding on top of the original hundred thousand.

Delane believed that the long-term success of the company was contingent on earning partnerships with game publishers, which would make the integration seamless for users in addition to providing the startup with much-needed credibility. And the best path to getting there, he was sure, was to create the market's easiest-to-use and most beautiful platform. Delane would discuss his vision with Yalda, who oversaw the outward-facing design, then sit next to him while he worked—a designer's nightmare. He got hung up on small details. "I spent a lot of time in the weeds of the product," Delane said. "In literally every inch of the product, from the size of a button to all of the functionality. And I tried to pack so much into it." Instead of focusing on getting a minimum viable product into the market as soon as possible, he pushed the team to build something robust. That slowed development time, which meant more cash burned before the platform even launched.

With funds beginning to dwindle, Delane email-blasted a press release announcing the platform's upcoming launch. He got a handful of pros with large Twitter followings to act as influencers, and PlayVS soon had three thousand people signed up. The team put the finishing touches on the platform, staying at the office until the morning's wee hours, shifting pixels here and there. The week of the launch, Yalda's phone rang again in the middle of the night. This time, the Delane that greeted him on the other line was frantic.

One of the engineers had accidentally deleted a table in the spreadsheet that housed the emails of everyone who had signed up.

The team rushed to the office to figure out the possible solutions. They called Amazon Web Services, which was hosting the PlayVS website, to see if the table could be restored. No luck. It was gone—months of work had evaporated in a few seconds. The team scrambled to manually restore as many of the signups as it could in the hours before the launch, but the damage was done.

The product hit the internet with a muted thud. Weeks passed; usership declined. The platform itself was operational and attractive, but it hardly mattered. No one was using it. There wasn't enough money left to start again. Delane had surrounded himself with talented engineers, but he hadn't created an operations team to secure partnerships, a support team to handle customer issues, or a marketing team to get the word out.

"So we built a better product than anything else in the market," Delane said, "and we had no strategy to get that product out there, no runway to make that product work. That was the worst company ever made."

Soon, Ealy left Detroit in pursuit of San Francisco's tech scene. Yalda followed a girl to Los Angeles, where he hoped to find more work. Delane, meanwhile, was left behind to try to figure out his next move.

4

THE KID FROM DETROIT

THE HOME WHERE Delane spent his formative years rests on a street called Burgess on the west side of Detroit, tucked between Seven Mile and Eight Mile Roads. Today the house sits empty, abandoned, the front yard mostly mud, the porch's wood banisters sagging with decay. The streets in this part of town are lined with decades-old oak trees that dwarf the homes. Many of the yards are overgrown with weeds. It's hard to tell whether some are occupied. This is one of Detroit's poorest neighborhoods, quite the distinction in a city that's notorious for them. Forty-five hundred people live in the census tract in which the Burgess house sits, a four-block-wide stretch that runs along Seven Mile. In 2018, two-thirds of the homes in the area were valued at less than $50,000. That same year, the median price of a house sold here was $25,000, and the median household income was just over $30,000. More than 70 percent of households with children in this neighborhood are led by women, due in part to the number of men who have been killed or incarcerated. Almost all the residents are Black.

Most of the houses in the Seven Mile and Burgess neighborhood were built in the early 1950s, when the Detroit metro area's population was surging in step with the thriving auto industry. The manufacturing boom, though, didn't benefit Detroit's citizens in equal measure. As historian Thomas J. Sugrue notes in *The Origins of the Urban Crisis*, 16 percent of the city's auto workforce was Black in 1960—despite the fact that Black people made up nearly a third of the city's population.

With no federal laws forbidding discriminatory hiring practices at the time, plant managers were left to develop their own policies, which in many cases meant shutting Black people out of jobs. Some facilities, like General Motors' plants in the suburbs of Livonia and Warren, employed fewer than 1 percent Black workers. "We are not employing Negroes," stated a Chrysler official in 1954. "We may employ a few when the situation becomes desperate enough."

Of course, getting a job was only part of the battle. Black people in Detroit in the 1960s were often charged higher prices than whites for the same homes, according to a report in *Michigan Historical Review*. At least one brokers association had a secret scoring system for determining housing applicants' eligibility, with points awarded based on the person's clothes, accent, education, and whether their "way of living" could be considered "American." Asian, Mexican, and Black candidates were immediately disqualified. These various forms of systemic oppression conspired to ensure that Black families in 1960s Detroit were nearly three times as likely as whites to live in "dilapidated or deteriorating" homes.

Throughout the fifties and sixties, the Big Three manufacturers relocated many of their operations to the suburbs, where the land they needed for massive plants was cheaper and more readily available. The suburbs also happened to be where a higher proportion of real estate was designated for whites, further sealing off Blacks from much of the wealth that the automakers pumped into southeastern Michigan. Resentment over discrimination and poor living conditions had been simmering for some time when, in 1967, a police raid on a Black-owned after-hours club in Detroit escalated into four days of rioting. Forty-three people died; more than a thousand buildings burned. In the aftermath, President Johnson assigned a commission to analyze the roots of the upheavals as well as their potential effects. "Our nation is moving toward two societies, one black, one white—separate and unequal," the group wrote in its 426-page report. "Reaction to last summer's disorders has quickened the movement and deepened the division." The analysis proved prescient. White flight to Detroit's suburbs quickened in the ensuing years and Black families were left behind in a metropolis that now had fewer jobs to go around. Tax revenues plummeted, hampering the city's ability to repair its infrastructure. The slow, decades-long rot of urban Detroit was underway.

This was the world that Juandali "Terri" Parnell, the youngest of two children, was born into in 1969. Terri's parents split up when she was young. Her father settled down with a new woman in California; her mother remarried a man named David Thompson and moved into the house on Burgess in the 1970s. Together they had three kids: Courtney, David II, and Olivia, or Libby, as everyone called her. In the seventies and eighties, the Burgess neighborhood was middle class and tight knit. Children would walk down the street to buy candy or stroll into a neighbor's home uninvited and stick around for dinner. One day in 1985, with their mother out running errands and their older sister down the hall, young David and Libby played with matches in one of the bedrooms, lighting the wicker strands sticking out under the bed frame on fire and watching them burn out. One time, the flame didn't extinguish. The bed frame caught fire, then the mattress, and soon the kids were all running to a neighbor's for help. By the time the fire department arrived, the flames had completely engulfed the house. It was mostly destroyed. The family spent six months rotating between relatives' spare bedrooms and couches while the home was repaired. The moment would stick with Libby through the ensuing decades. The incense-like smell of the burning wicker. Racing to the house down the street.

The flashing red lights of the fire trucks. It was the last time she ever played with fire.

Most of the other memories of growing up on Burgess were pleasant. Everyone knew everyone. Residents looked out for one another. "The street was a community," Libby said. "It was like a big family. We knew where we were welcome, and that was most places."

When the youngest generation of Parnells and Thompsons grew up and started having kids of their own, the house began to fill, a new generation squeezing into the small home's three bedrooms and basement. Beyond those walls, though, Detroit was in decline. The city's homes were losing value. The population was tumbling. Downtown was marked by a growing number of abandoned buildings, damaged roads, and other signs of urban blight. As the national unemployment rate climbed in the late 1980s, Detroit felt it harder than the country as a whole. By 1991, Detroit's jobless rate had reached a staggering 18 percent. Crime rates soared. On Burgess, parents lost their jobs; families, unable to keep up with their rapidly climbing mortgage payments, lost their houses. New residents moved into the now-inexpensive homes, folks who didn't have the same connection to the neighborhood and its people. The social fabric began to tear. Area institutions were shuttered, and children were left with fewer safe places to spend time together once the school day ended.

"As a kid," said Libby, "I could walk to the bowling alley, or the YMCA on the corner, or the skating rink. Those started closing. The local grocery store, Farmer Jack's, closed. Major businesses that made the neighborhood the community it was were gone. There wasn't anywhere to go. So you saw that shift. And in the surrounding blocks in the neighborhood, you saw this younger generation where drugs were the easiest way of life."

While living in the house on Burgess in the early 1990s, Terri started dating a guy named Charles, whom everyone called Chucky. He treated Terri well and became a friend to the family, coming over for dinner or to celebrate birthdays. Chucky and Terri got pregnant and gave birth to a boy, whom they named DaeLon after one of the neighbors on Burgess. When DaeLon was just a few months old, though, Chucky grew sick. He'd been quietly fighting sickle-cell anemia. The disease progressed quickly, and Chucky's health deteriorated. When he died, Terri was left devastated, a single mother. Her family helped out, taking turns watching the new baby—even her youngest sister Libby, barely eleven years old, would babysit after school. Soon, Terri started seeing a man named Anthony Robinson. Robinson was one of the biggest drug dealers on Detroit's west side. He had a lot of money and a lot of real estate. With one-year-old DaeLon at home, Terri found out she was carrying Robinson's baby. A few days after she told him the exciting news, just before Christmas of 1991, Robinson was shot and killed by a rival drug dealer.

Terri gave birth to a boy eight months later. She named him Delane, after Delana, a friend across the street whom she'd known most of her life. Terri's older sister had three kids of her own who lived in the house on Burgess while she and her husband in the Army were stationed in Germany. That meant that the house was occupied by ten people on most days. Terri, still just twenty-three, was struggling with the costs of raising the children. She would have a job for some time—sales jobs, administrative jobs, at an auto dealership—then quit to try something else. On many days, the responsibility fell on Libby, ten years her junior, to watch the children. Her younger sister started to feel resentment and told her about it. "Your decisions," she would tell Terri angrily, "are impacting my life."

Terri sought out other solutions. She shuttled Delane from home to home, sometimes dropping him across town to spend the day with her grandmother and aunt Belinda. Mostly, though, he stayed with Terri's friend Rhonda, who lived in the Jeffries Projects, a housing development off the highway in the heart of Detroit. Delane spent his weekdays with the woman, believing for years she was his aunt, and his mother would come by on weekends. Terri was a good friend to Rhonda—she hadn't gotten a proper education, so Terri taught her to read and write. But Terri's love for her friend blinded her to the signs Rhonda had started smoking crack. The addiction continued to fester even as Delane spent many of his early days in Rhonda's apartment.

The Jeffries Projects were a conglomerate of thirteen affordable city-owned high-rises and row houses. They were also the site of frequent drug deals, robberies, and murders. A series of front-page *Detroit Free Press* stories in the eighties illustrated the extent to which the courtyard between the complex's towers and the adjacent service road had turned into one of the city's most dangerous drug havens. Dealers as young as eight and nine years old would sell drugs to customers in cars, sometimes sprinting at the vehicles and throwing themselves onto their hoods to beat out rival dealers. Kids in the projects jumped rope while singing the names of popular heroin brands. On nights with especially active gunfire, some lower-floor residents resorted to sleeping in the halls—popular hangouts for junkies—to remain farther from the windows. "Don't forget to duck, Grandma," one visiting nine-year-old reminded his grandmother when he left her apartment. By the time the buildings were slated for demolition by the city in the late 1990s, Delane had spent much of his developmental years at Rhonda's.

"That environment was a big part of his foundational growth, his learning," said Libby years later. "I set a fire at age five and I vividly remember it. By that age, you know the world around you. You might not understand why things are the way they are, but you know that this is your world."

With Rhonda's apartment no longer an option, Terri started bringing Delane to spend more time with her grandmother and aunt. He moved from home to home with few complaints, quick to adapt to the new surroundings each day. As a grade schooler, he was inquisitive, sharp, strong minded. "He was a talker," said Libby. "He always liked to get the last word." More than anything, he was competitive. He learned to play Monopoly at a young age and would often challenge his family members to play against him. He liked building properties, collecting money. His young mind soon understood how that could translate into the real world. Terri and Libby would take videos of him.

"What do you want to be when you grow up?" they would ask.

"I want to be a billionaire!" he'd reply.

When Delane was eight, Terri brought him in to live with her full-time. Being under the same roof as his immediate family was a new experience, though not necessarily an easy one. An unmistakable sense of distance had developed over the years spent mostly away from his closest relatives. There were fights and arguments, uncomfortable moments. "I didn't really have a relationship with other people in my family, including my mom or my brother," said Delane. "Like, of course, we're family, and we love each other, but we've never done the work to get to know each other, and that's strained our relationship."

As he spent more time around his family, Delane grew close with Terri's cousin, Juan Raybon. Years earlier, Terri's brother

David had suffered an asthma attack in the house's stairwell and died in front of DaeLon. The tragedy left Juan as one of Delane's only older male family members. For his younger relatives, Juan blurred the lines between uncle, cousin, and big brother, though they all referred to him as their cousin. They dubbed him the Outdoorsman due to his love of hunting and fishing, and he would often take them along on day trips. Once when Delane, DaeLon, and their cousins were young, Juan drove them all to a lake to go ice fishing. While the rest of the kids spent most of the time staying warm in the car, Delane remained outside to drill holes in the frozen lake and bond with his older cousin. Delane didn't even particularly like ice fishing. It just gave him an opportunity to spend a few hours with someone he admired.

Juan took Delane under his wing. Using the initials of his full name, Delane Antonio Parnell, Juan nicknamed him DAP. Soon both of Juan's houses in Detroit had a spare bedroom for his younger cousin. Libby was happy to see the relationship blossom. Juan had always tried to act like a parent to her, even though he was only a few years older. "I was like, 'I have my life together, thank you,'" she recalled. "But now Juan had someone to pour all of his wisdom and guidance into, someone that wanted it. And Delane had that father figure."

What Delane didn't know at that age was that Juan was also one of the more established drug dealers in Detroit. It was something of a family secret. Juan gave off the appearance of someone successful through legitimate means. He was smart, kind, big-hearted. In many ways he was the glue of the family, the one who organized get-togethers, including cookouts every summer to celebrate the cluster of birthdays in late August and early September. In one of his homes he'd built a recording studio that he occasionally rented out. One day he took Delane into his studio, laid down a beat, and helped him record his first rap:

D-A-P
Y'all can't see me
I stand about five feet
Got big dudes behind me,
So go ahead and try me
Y'all find out why the whole world call me
D-A-P

The lyrics were truthful. Delane had powerful people in his corner from a young age. Being related to Juan gave him an instant level of respect, as did Terri's entrenchment in the neighborhood; having spent most of her life in the house on Burgess, she knew all the families and they knew her. Many of her local friends were the parents of the kids who now ran the streets, the people whom Delane now started spending time around.

Delane came to find out from his family that his father had been killed by a rival dealer. It was a targeted hit; a dispute over power. Meanwhile, he had never gotten to see what his father looked like—Terri always told Delane she had lost the few photos she had of him in a house fire. But people who had known Robinson likened Delane to him. They would tell him he looked like his dad or carried himself the way he did. It was clear to just about everyone in the Burgess neighborhood that Delane was sharp. He got good grades in school, was quick with a joke, and could hold his own among any crowd. He had clear value. "If you're looking at Delane from a street perspective," said Libby, "you see not just a smart kid, but someone who has his wits about him, too. He understands business. He has book sense and street sense. So that's appealing. You want that kid."

For anyone observing Delane around that time, spending most of his days around those in the game, the blood of two of Detroit's most prominent drug dealers in his veins, it probably looked like his fate was sealed. "Back then," Delane said years later, "a lot of people would be like, 'Delane's going to be the biggest drug dealer Detroit's ever seen.' That was just what they assumed."

5

FATE ON THE

DANCE FLOOR

DELANE STROLLED DOWN to the lobby of a hotel in balmy Miami. It was 2015, and he was in town for the Black Tech Week conference, a several-day event geared toward Black professionals in the tech and startup worlds. He started chatting with a group of fellow attendees, and the conversation turned to rap music. One of the more opinionated voices on the matter—besides Delane's, of course—was that of Marcus Carey, a young man working in private equity in New York City. It quickly became clear, as the group discussed their favorite artists and albums, that Delane and Carey had very different taste. The pair started dominating the discussion. The others in the group slowly broke off, but Delane and Carey continued their debate, making points and counterpoints for nearly an hour on everyone from Meek Mill to Big Sean to Kanye. Eventually, they parted ways and went to their respective rooms, Delane shaking his head to himself. *Man,* he thought, *I hate that guy!*

The two crossed paths several more times as the week wore on. Delane at the time was working at IncWell, and Carey had dreams of breaking into venture capital to get closer to the startup world. As it turned out, the two had much more in common than their career ambitions. One year apart in age, they'd grown up just a few miles away from each other in Detroit. Beginning when Carey was twelve, his parents had sent him off to caddie at a nearby golf course during the summer. While he made money and did well in school, he watched many of his childhood friends go down unfortunate paths. Carey, meanwhile, ended up taking the college route, attending Howard University and earning a degree in finance. Now he was considering ditching Manhattan and heading west. Delane and Carey exchanged phone numbers. Slowly, they grew to like each other. Both of them had made plenty of new contacts in their first few years out in the real world, but neither had made many new true friends they could confide in, friends who truly understood one another's experiences. "Before I knew it," Carey said, "it was maybe a month or two later and we were on the phone every day, trying to brainstorm ideas, talking through tech stuff. We both just were enamored with the space, enamored with ideas, and wanted to talk through it all the time. Neither one of us had prior friends that we could jam with like that."

Carey landed a job as an analyst at Silicon Valley Bank's venture capital arm a few months later and made the move across the country. Delane, meanwhile, plugged away at his video game wagering idea. After the startup crashed and burned, he was plotting his next steps when, in January 2017, Hajj Flemings told him about an event in Detroit he was helping to organize. Called Culture and Code, it was part of a series put on by a group including Troy Carter and Suzy Ryoo, investors with the Los Angeles–based Cross Culture Ventures. Carter had made his career in the music world—managing for artists like Nelly, Eve, John Legend, and Lady Gaga—before cofounding the VC firm and bringing Ryoo on board. Now, as the pair sought to expand their reach outside of California, they were holding meetups in Miami, Atlanta, and Detroit, cities with oft-overlooked startup scenes.

Delane secured a ticket to one of the events with Flemings's help, a dinner at a trendy new restaurant in midtown Detroit. At the end of the meal, Carter and Ryoo asked the three dozen guests to take turns standing up and introducing themselves. Delane rose for his turn. He revealed some of his life story and spoke of his aspirations of building a tech company.

At the other end of the room, Carter and Ryoo glanced at each other, looking, as Ryoo would later describe it, like human versions of the heart-eyes emoji. She had grown up frequenting PC bangs—gaming cafes in which guests compete against one another—as a teen while visiting family in South Korea. "Let's keep in touch with him," whispered Carter, who, having grown up in a West Philadelphia home torn apart by violence, saw some of himself in the kid. The pair chatted with Delane after dinner. They all vowed to remain in contact.

Delane, at the time, was facing a choice. He could keep trying to build an esports company in his home city, or he could pick up and move to a place like Atlanta or Los Angeles, two cities with high concentrations of game publishers. He was still debating this choice a few weeks later when he received an email invitation. Cross Culture Ventures was helping to run an event space at the SXSW festival in Austin called the Culture House. The invitation promised good company along with "biscuits 'n brisket" at the noon event—an odd time for a party under normal circumstances, but not at SXSW, where founders, investors, and tech nerds cram-pack their schedules with meetings over coffee, beer, and kombucha. The idea for the Culture House was to curate a guest list that looked different than the usual VC-slash-tech-startup party. "A lot of times I'm invited to things by venture funds," Ryoo said later, "and their community looks a certain way. They don't spend the extra time or energy to look at their own network and think to decisively invite more women, more people of color. Culture House was flipping that on its head."

Delane was intrigued by the invitation, but he had no plans to travel to Austin. That didn't sit well with Carey, who would be traveling to the festival to try to network and drum up interest for a new business he'd cofounded called Homage Hospitality, a boutique hotel company that infused its spaces with elements of Black culture. He and Delane hadn't been in the same city in a while. The conference seemed like a good opportunity to catch up, and the party at Culture House sounded legit. Plus, it could be good for Delane, whose career seemed to have hit something of a crossroads.

Carey and Delane chatted on the phone one day, Delane pacing up and down the driveway in front of his townhouse as he often did during long calls. Carey was blunt with him in the way only a best friend can be.

"You've got to come to Austin," he said. "What other plans do you have for those days? You're not even doing shit. Get out here."

Delane relented. He booked a flight and told Carey he'd meet him at the party.

A few days later, in a swanky house on the outskirts of Austin, Carey stood downstairs waiting for his friend. The early afternoon sun shone through the floor-to-ceiling windows of the living room, where a deejay in a booth spun hip-hop tracks. A hundred people mingled and noshed on the buffet, the air sweet with the smell of barbecue and freshly baked bread. From the street, the house appeared nondescript and somewhat ugly, a modern-looking structure with a white paint job and a single leafless tree near the entrance.

Delane reached the door and flashed the doorman the invitation on his phone. He stepped inside and immediately felt the vibrations from the bass in the other room. The floor was packed like a subway during rush hour. He scanned the floor and didn't see anyone he knew. He turned the corner, and across the room Carey stood hovering near the bar. Delane headed toward him.

He never made it there. From across the crowd, Ryoo spotted Delane, hustled over, and intercepted him.

"Come with me," she shouted over the music. "There's someone here you should talk to." A moment later, she was guiding Delane in and out of groups of people and toward the back of the house. There was Peter Pham, all alone in front of the deejay booth, partially hidden underneath his trademark cowboy hat, moving in rhythm with the music bumping from the speakers.

Ryoo interrupted his solo dance and introduced him to Delane.

"Good to meet you," Pham said and extended his hand. Ryoo left them alone. Delane glanced around the packed room. In a sea of people making conversation while eating food off small paper plates, Pham was the only person dancing. He swayed with the rhythm, jerked his body and grinded provocatively. While he and Delane got to know each other, Pham never stopped moving. *This,* Delane thought to himself, *is fucking weird.*

Pham, it turned out, was growing infatuated with the esports space. A few months earlier, his alma mater, UC Irvine, had finished building an esports arena on campus, making the Anteaters the first college team with their own stadium. It had become clear to Pham that his firm Science needed to get involved in the industry in some way. The partners at the startup incubator had spent the past year thinking about the kind of esports company they could help build, invest in, and bring to market—but they hadn't yet settled on a concept or found an entrepreneur compelling enough. "Everything kind of aligned," Pham said later, "to have Delane introduce himself in that moment."

Delane told Pham about the *Call of Duty* team he'd built and sold as well as his efforts to develop a wagering platform. Pham nodded along, his body's rhythms shifting whenever the soundtrack did. At the end of the conversation, Pham, who believed society had advanced past the need for business cards, exchanged email addresses and phone numbers with Delane. They parted ways and Delane went off to seek out his patient friend, now surrounded by a group of people near the bar. He told Carey about the conversation. Not long after, they had moved on to other topics.

"We pretty much forgot about it," recalled Carey. "It's not like we left the Culture House and Delane was talking about Peter all day. You tend to discount it a little bit in your head as a Black entrepreneur and think, 'Oh, you know, maybe they're just talking. They're in a good mood, there are drinks at the party, and they're just talking.' There were other people talking big talk that day, saying, 'Oh, yeah, we'd like to fund Black entrepreneurs,' and then they kind of ghosted after. So I think there's always a little bit of you that says, let's see if they're blowing smoke or not."

But Delane hadn't even gotten around to his usual followup email when his phone rang the next day. From the other line, Pham asked if he was interested in talking some more to see if they could find an idea worth incubating at Science. There was a ton of potential in the bustling and massive world of esports, Pham thought—they just needed to find the market need. Delane was all for it. Pham looped in his Science cofounder Mike Jones, and the three started a high-level conversation about the industry. They briefly discussed a few ideas, but nothing stuck.

A few weeks later, Pham and Jones received an email from Matt Mazzeo, an investor at the venture firm Lowercase Capital. Mazzeo had been familiar with Pham and Jones for a long time from investing circles, and he had an idea. Almost all the infrastructure that existed in the esports world—the governing bodies, the weeks-long tournaments, the championships in packed arenas—was focused on the pro level. That stratosphere only serviced a few thousand players worldwide, the fraction of one percent of the gaming population who got paid to play. The other 99.99 percent were mostly on their own. Whereas baseball had Little League, football had Pop Warner, and just about every sport had middle and high school teams, esports remained unorganized below the pro level. The handful of startups that did service the high school space were more competition organizers than tech companies, and none staffed much more than a dozen people.

"Nobody was approaching it in a way that would scale," recounted Mazzeo. "There was a chance for a new player to come in and build that ecosystem, from creating software that would handle all the things that went into running a league to distributing the games through partnerships with the publishers and the schools. It felt like a wide-open opportunity."

Mazzeo, at the time, knew his role at Lowercase was about to end. The firm's founder, Chris Sacca—the famed VC who bought into Uber, Instagram, and Twitter in their early days and made deals on the show *Shark Tank*—was planning to shut down the fund and retire from investing at the ripe age of forty-two. Mazzeo believed the high school gaming concept was a winner. He passed it along to Pham, Jones, and the team at Science, who he knew had been in touch with an esports-savvy entrepreneur looking for his big idea. "I don't ever want to be the kind of person that just sits on an idea, regretting that they never got around to it," Mazzeo said later. "I would much rather share ideas as widely and broadly as possible with friends and find ways to work together on those opportunities." (He would go on to find that opportunity when he invested in PlayVS's Series A.)

Delane wasn't in love with the concept at first. He still believed his wagering platform could work with better execution.

He had trouble visualizing what a high school esports platform might look like and had doubts about its potential for growth. "No one had done anything like it before," he said. "So I thought, 'Well, if it's never been done, maybe it's for a reason.' You never think you could be the one to do something that hasn't been done before."

Still, he began researching the topic fervently. Over the next few months, he agreed to take a handful of trips out to Southern California to meet with the Science team. He called up Sean Yalda a few days before one of them. Yalda had started dating the young woman who had drawn him to Los Angeles and had been finding interesting work in his new city, building a website for an awards show and working on an interactive music video for the band Foster the People. Delane asked him one day if he wanted to come with him to the Science office to meet with the firm. Yalda agreed. When they got there, Yalda and Delane took their seats in a conference room. Soon the chairs filled with two dozen members of Science's portfolio companies as well as the firm's staff and partners, all of them pointed toward the two kids from Detroit.

Delane had severely underplayed this. This was a pitch meeting.

Yalda's heart rate barely even had time to tick up. Soon Delane was speaking to the room about his vision for building a high school esports company. He and Yalda took turns discussing their previous experience trying to build within the space and the hustling they'd done to get to this point. They fielded questions from the partners and startup founders. As the meeting reached its end, the Science partners informed Delane and Yalda that they wanted to incubate the esports concept.

Yalda exhaled. "I kind of went into that blind," he recalled, "but it worked out really well."

Delane and Yalda came out of the Science building stoked. Walking down Santa Monica's tree-lined Second Street, Delane presented him with a proposition. Yalda had gained his trust during their time building the wagering platform. Their personalities meshed well: Delane the hard-driving tech visionary; Yalda the laid-back, talented designer whose feelings weren't easily hurt—and who, in turn, wasn't afraid to tell Delane what he thought.

Standing on the sidewalk, Delane asked Yalda if he wanted to be his cofounder.

"But you've got to be all in," he told him. "You need be willing to sacrifice everything to get this company to a billion dollars."

Yalda thought for a moment before speaking. He was happy in his relationship. He was enjoying life in Los Angeles, and he liked having the freedom to pursue his artistic hobbies on the side. "I'm, like, 90 percent happy," he told Delane. "I don't need to put that at risk to get the other 10 percent."

Delane appreciated the honesty. As he and Yalda drove through Santa Monica, they came to an agreement: Delane would try to start this thing on his own, and he would give Yalda a call if and when it got off the ground.

Back home in Detroit, Delane continued to weigh Science's offer. All the late nights, the saving, the conferences, the networking—this was the kind of chance he'd been working toward for years. But there was still a major hangup. Science would only accept him if he would work from its office in Santa Monica. That was a long way away—from his girlfriend, Ashley, and from the only city he'd ever called home. He'd always wanted to be able to build something successful in Detroit. Throughout the next few months, Delane struggled with the idea of leaving. He spoke about the dilemma with those whose opinions he respected most, including Bryan Smiley, who was a decade removed from migrating to Hollywood from Detroit himself.

"This is something that's very true for a lot of young Detroiters," Smiley said later. "There's this strong desire to stay and help build your city. Delane and I used to get in these debates about his desire to stay and build a company in Detroit, to help bring his city back and be a part of its transformation, which I deeply respected. But I told him there would be great opportunities for him socially to advance his business goals here in LA. You can have dinner with anyone from an NBA star to a famous actor to some of the VCs that at that time were flooding into the city. He knew he would be better suited to be surrounded by people like that. So it was a constant tug."

Pham shared a similar sentiment, though he took a less empathetic approach with Delane. "Look," Pham told him on the phone one day, "you can be a millionaire in Detroit, or you can be a billionaire in Los Angeles. You get to choose."

As the calendar flipped to June, now three months since the encounter on the dance floor, Pham pushed harder for an answer. Delane knew he couldn't put off a decision much longer. He scheduled a meeting with Detroit Venture Partners as something of a last resort. He visited the firm's office, where he again met with Jake Cohen, the partner with whom he'd once applied—unsuccessfully—for an assistant position. This time Delane told Cohen about the high school esports concept. He explained that Science had offered to incubate the business, but that he wanted to be able to remain in Detroit. Deep down, he hoped Cohen would tell him to stay, that the Dan Gilbert–backed fund would open up its checkbook and help him build the company in Detroit. But that didn't happen. Cohen told Delane the opportunity in Los Angeles was a great one, that having support from

Science was too good a chance to turn down. Delane left the office disappointed.

One Wednesday afternoon, Delane's phone rang. It was Pham. He couldn't wait any longer. The business concept, he believed, was a good one, and Science was going to pursue it, whether it was with Delane or someone else. "You're either gonna build this company or you're not," Pham said. "But you can't keep wasting my time."

"Okay," Delane replied. "I'm in."

"Great," Pham replied. "Let's start on Monday."

THERE WASN'T EVEN time for the dread of telling Ashley to set in. She'd support him like always, Delane knew, but the conversation wasn't going to be easy—the whole long-distance thing sounded nearly impossible. Delane sat her down in the townhouse they shared and told her that he'd made his decision. "I'll give it a year," he said. "If it doesn't work, I'll move back home and try something else."

He'd hoped for Ashley's response, but didn't quite expect it.

"I'm coming with you."

It was now a race against the clock—the couple had just a few days to transport their lives across the country. First, they needed to find a new place to live. Delane knew almost nothing about Los Angeles's sprawling geography, even after a few visits. He talked to Matthew Haag, a friend and founder of the gaming company 100 Thieves who was living in the city, and asked him for advice on where to live. Haag's neighborhood of Playa Vista, he told Delane, was conveniently located just down the beach from Santa Monica. But Delane would need something by this weekend. Haag told him to call his apartment complex's office and drop his name.

A few hours later, Delane had secured an apartment, no credit check required.

The next forty-eight hours were a whirlwind. Delane broke the news to his mom, his brother, and the rest of his family. Nobody was shocked—they'd suspected something like this might happen for a while. The couple rented a U-Haul, loaded in their furniture—a bed set, two couches, two dressers, two TVs, a treadmill, assorted trinkets—and spent a sweaty summer day driving all over the greater Detroit area and dropping them off with family and friends. They negotiated their way out of their apartment lease, dropped two cars and a motorcycle back at the dealership, stuffed some clothes and toiletries into their suitcases, and bought a pair of one-way tickets to LAX.

On a Saturday afternoon in June, Delane and Ashley hugged their families goodbye. When their ride dropped them at the gate, they left with their belongings: Ashley's purple suitcase and Delane's black one. This was everything they'd be bringing with them to start their new life in Los Angeles.

Neither of them slept on the five-hour flight over green plains, snowy mountains, and sandy desert. When the plane started its descent over California, Delane asked Ashley from the middle seat to pull up her window shade. They both stared out at the rolling expanse of twinkling orange lights stretched to the horizon in all directions, a brand-new level to try to conquer. As the plane slowly lowered toward the ground, Delane sat back in his seat, alone in his thoughts. He suspected it would be the last time he'd be able to truly relax for a long, long time.

6

HIGH SCHOOL LEGENDS

BENJI SAT AT the computer at the end of the row, tapping on his keyboard. Up on his screen, a sword-wielding character took a few steps forward, then lurched back. Coach Magoffin came over and stood behind him.

"You can move up a little at a time," he instructed. "Just make sure you can get back to safety if you have to."

Benji poked a few keys gently, inching his champion forward again. When the enemy appeared, he took a few swings with his blade, then quickly scampered back. Magoffin nodded in approval.

On their side-by-side computers down the row, Justin and Isaiah stared intently into their monitors. Their characters were starting to push behind enemy lines. The colorful images on the students' screens weren't of the double-take-causing realistic quality of some modern video games. Instead, the graphics looked something like a modernized version of the nineties game *Zelda*, an aerial view of characters navigating a world of green grass, brown boulders, and steep cliffs. Each player's champion sat in the center of his own monitor, committing different attacks and defenses as the boys smashed away at their keyboards. Some emitted blue flashes of light, others red flames. Widgets at the top of their screens tracked the elapsed time since the start of the match, plus the players' kill counts and remaining health. Classic video game stuff.

League of Legends, or simply *League*, falls into the popular genre known as multiplayer online battle arena (or MOBA). That's a fancy way of saying there are several players on each side and both teams want to be first to achieve an objective. In *League*, that objective is to try to infiltrate and destroy the other team's base, or Nexus—essentially capture the flag in video game form. The board is split into three lanes (top, middle, bottom) that can be used to approach the opponent's Nexus. Five people play on each team. To the untrained eye, their roles appear indistinguishable, much like they would to someone watching basketball or soccer for the first time, but each player has unique responsibilities. The top laner serves as the attacker, operating mostly alone and attempting to blaze a path for teammates. The mid laner is a well-rounded jack-of-all-trades, sometimes playing offense and sometimes defense. The bottom laner, or bot, hangs back and kills minions to build up the team's strength. The jungler explores the map freely and picks fights with the opponent. The support is the glue of the operation, coming to the aid of others as needed—the ultimate team player. Before each match, *League* players choose from among nearly 150 different champions, each of which have their own skillset that makes them best suited for certain roles.

"Meeks," said Isaiah, now slashing through the vegetation, to his teammate in the support role, "when I say go, I need you to come to me."

"K," replied Meeks quietly, not instilling much confidence that he was fully paying attention.

A moment later, Isaiah yelled out. "Go, Meeks, go! Go! *Gooo!*" Meeks didn't go. The ambush didn't work.

Magoffin stood cross-armed and emotionless behind his team. "Boys," he announced, "we've got to work on our communication."

The match was a massacre. It ended so abruptly and with so little fanfare that to an untrained observer it looked more like a technical malfunction, all four monitors suddenly snapping to bright blue desktop wallpaper. The boys stared ahead, blinking in the cool glow. They pulled off their headsets. For the first time all afternoon, the room was silent.

"Seventeen minutes!" Isaiah finally cried out. "We just lost in seventeen minutes!"

Justin shook his head. "That's gotta be a record."

"It wasn't that bad," Coach Magoffin assured his team. "You were overmatched."

"I've never lost in seventeen minutes," Isaiah said. "Ever!"

The other boys chuckled, Justin included. He and Isaiah were best friends; Isaiah lived with his grandparents in a small house next to the trailer where Justin lived with his mom. The boys stuck together as much as possible. Like teenage pals do, they often butted heads. Magoffin had instructed them not to play *League* with each other outside of school for the sake of the team—the emotions sometimes carried over from home to school, and that wasn't good for anyone. (The previous night, Justin admitted, they'd broken that rule; Justin had gotten too aggressive toward the opponents in the game's chat feature and as a result was banned by Riot Games from using it for his next twenty-five matches. "I was defending his honor!" he said, pointing to Isaiah.) After one too many blowups in the computer lab, Magoffin had printed and laminated a sign reading *DON'T BE TOXIC*. It sat on a metal bookshelf behind the computers. If one of the students got too hostile, any of their teammates could grab the sign and hold it over their computer to silently prove a point. More often than not it was Magoffin who did it.

The coach tried to regroup his players. "Let's shake that one off," he boomed.

Match days meant two games held back to back—hopefully, a chance to apply to the second competition anything they might have just learned from the first. As the boys scrolled through the character selection screen, Justin announced that he was switching to a new champion he'd seldom used. The move didn't make sense to Isaiah.

"Troll," said Isaiah. "You're a known troll."

"Dude, you're a troll," said Justin. "You live under a bridge and you're covered in warts."

The boys collectively decided Benji should play as Garen, a character with a lower learning curve. A simple man's pick, as Justin called it: his best use was to spin in circles with a giant sword and he could sustain a lot of damage without dying. Now Benji sat staring at the selection screen, struggling to find Garen even though the champions were listed alphabetically.

Justin observed from the next seat. "Go left," he commanded. A small clock in the corner of Benji's screen counted down from ten. "Left," Justin said with increased urgency, a layer of his hair damp at the hairline. "Left left left left!" He jumped out of his chair and rushed toward Benji's computer. The clock hit zero. Benji was stuck with a different champion. He stared wide-eyed, glancing from the monitor to Justin and back again. Isaiah's head dropped into his hands. Justin could only laugh. An inauspicious start to the second match.

Twenty minutes in, though, it was clear things had changed. For one, the undermanned squad had already survived longer than the first time around. It now had an audience, too, as a pair of boys had come in from the hall and sat at a table behind them to watch. The communication had improved.

"Meeks, I'm gonna need you to come to me, okay?" Isaiah asked. Meeks muttered in agreement. "Ready, Meeks?" Isaiah yelled. "Now come! Come, Meeks!"

This time Meeks did as his teammate asked. He rushed his champion up to his teammate's side and unleashed a barrage of attacks. The cover lasted just long enough to let Isaiah slip past the enemy.

"Good job, Meeks," said Magoffin, watching the kid's screen from over his shoulder.

Justin, meanwhile, was uncharacteristically quiet, exchanging instructions with his teammates as needed but devoid of his usual running in-game commentary. He peeled off his headphones and flagged down Magoffin. "Put on my headset for one second," he said. "This has me so hyped." He handed the piece of equipment to his coach, who put one of the earpieces to his ear and listened. Justin, it turned out, had discovered a trick for keeping a sense of inner calm while he played.

"Dude, it's like Beethoven," Magoffin said. "Or Hans Zimmer or something."

"It's got me crying," replied Justin, taking the headset back and strapping it on to reenter his zone of Zen. "It's so beautiful." Coach Magoffin raised his eyebrows but withheld the sarcastic comment that would usually follow. Anything that kept Justin even-keeled was a good thing, and there was no reason to mess with that.

The two teams pushed into each other's territories. Hiding was no longer an option. Benji was starting to panic, moving his champion in circles and firing off attacks blindly.

"If you're in a fight, use your *R*," Magoffin instructed him, gesturing toward the keyboard.

"I need you over here, Ben!" shouted Isaiah. Benji sent his champion running in his direction. Within seconds, they were in the midst of an all-out brawl, flashes of light pulsating across both their screens. Justin suddenly hollered. A message appeared across the monitors: *Your team has stolen the Ocean Drake!* The thievery in question involved a very valuable dragon.

"So you're telling me there's a chance!" exclaimed Magoffin.

The thirty-five minute mark arrived. Fighting shorthanded against a capable adversary, the boys now had survived for longer than the length of an average match. Magoffin texted his wife to tell her he'd be home later than expected. He glanced at Benji's screen and pointed out a safe haven in the shrubs where he could run and hide. A moment later, the coach instructed him to charge. Benji did as he was told. Isaiah and Justin whooped and cheered. They were on the offensive. They fought valiantly for a few minutes of chaos before the shouting settled down. There would be no miracle today. The match had ended, but it had been far more respectable this time around.

"It's okay," Isaiah reassured his teammates. "We played out of our minds."

"Forty freakin' minutes, holy smokes!" Magoffin yelled. He high-fived Meeker, then turned to Justin. "Would you say you're pleased?"

Justin paused. "No."

"That's right," said the coach. "Never settle!" He bent down in front of his laptop and refreshed his browser. The Massachusetts standings now showed Mahar at two wins and two losses, but the tiebreaker algorithms that factored in schedule difficulty and overall gameplay put them at seventh in the state out of thirty-six teams. The band of outsiders was improving.

That night, Isaiah logged into the team's private chat on Discord, the messaging platform used widely by gamers. He posted a message:

great games today guys! love ya all!

Justin's reply:

known troll.

•   •   •

JUSTIN VISITED THE teachers' lounge the next day to eat lunch with Magoffin, as he often did. They talked *League* strategy. Benji, for one, was going to need to take on a more aggressive role. That would mean using a champion that could attack from long range and cause damage to the opponent without making himself too vulnerable. Justin settled on Dr. Mundo, a muscular purple brute that hurled a meat cleaver. It was only mildly effective compared to some other champions' attacks, but at least it could be accomplished from a distance.

At that afternoon's practice, Isaiah agreed to play Benji in a one-on-one match to help the younger player hone his tactics. They sat down and started to battle. Each champion in *League* had a variety of attacks, all of which were performed by pressing a corresponding key on the keyboard. The primary move, which in Dr. Mundo's case meant launching and catching his blade like a boomerang, used the Q key. Benji ran in circles onscreen and continually chucked his weapon at Isaiah's champion. After a while of this, Isaiah encouraged him to attempt something new.

"Try using your W," said Isaiah.

"How do I do that?" asked Benji.

"Press W," said Isaiah. Both boys laughed. The apprentice was still learning.

Meeks sat at one of the computers and next to him plopped Justin, dressed in his navy blue and maroon Mahar esports jersey. The team had some extra money in its budget, and Magoffin, believing his players should feel like they were part of a real team, let them assist in designing a uniform. They opted to replace the school nickname of Senators with Disruptors. The jerseys featured a D on the sleeve and each kid's gamer nickname on the back—*Boltzzzy* in Justin's case. The boys wore them to school on match days and randomly throughout the year.

Now Magoffin toyed with Meeks's computer. He programmed it to record the match so they could review it afterward and see where Meeks could improve. He sat down next to Meeks, coaching him while he competed against Justin. After a few minutes of head-to-head clashing, the boys decided to play one big match, throughout which Justin and Isaiah shouted tips at their younger counterparts.

"Be careful, that takes away some of your health."

"Try using your *R* more."

"Don't let him bully you! Fight back!"

Suddenly, Meeks's champion broke through and got a kill.

"Oh man, Meeks," Isaiah yelled, "that was god-like!"

Meeks plugged away, all business.

"Don't get too close to Mordekaiser," Magoffin warned Benji, who, looking genuinely afraid, turned his character around, and ran him in the opposite direction. It was too late.

"You got too close, didn't you?" the coach asked rhetorically.

"I didn't even get that close!" yelled Benji.

"He doesn't have to be that close to you to kill you," replied Magoffin. "He's a multidimensional being!"

Across the room, three members of the *Rocket League* team prepared for a scrimmage that Magoffin had set up against a school from Georgia. This had become a common practice in the high school esports world: coaches would post a message in Discord proclaiming the skill levels of their players—*Team of one diamond, one gold, one silver looking for an opponent at 3:30 on Wednesday*—and try to find suitors of similar abilities, a way of giving the kids the chance to exercise their teamwork on nonmatch days. The three-versus-three game took place in a simulated arena, with each player using a futuristic race car to try to knock a giant soccer ball into the opponent's net. The game was fast paced, vehicles flying through the air and rotating midflight, occasionally aided by orange flames shooting from their exhausts. Mahar had two *Rocket League* teams. Both were good—the better of the two ranked second in the state. Today, that team's three boys had essentially guaranteed their coach a clean sweep in the three matches they'd play, and Magoffin demanded twenty pushups if they lost one. The boys competed in the first of the five-minute contests, playing on Xbox controllers connected to their PCs via Bluetooth. When the match concluded, they had been shut out, 2–0. The three students rose from their chairs, sunk down to the ground, and started counting off their reps. The smallest boy, a seventh-grader, finished only three before announcing he couldn't go on. Magoffin placed his foot gently on his back and told him to keep trying. The boy giggled, squeezed out one more, and collapsed on the ground in surrender.

The idea of Kyle Magoffin becoming the coach of an esports program would have seemed absurd right up until the moment it happened. Growing up in Connecticut, he played traditional high school sports like soccer and volleyball, the latter of which he continued at Springfield College in Massachusetts while studying physical education. When Mahar Regional had an opening for a PE teacher, he applied and landed the job. Early on, a young woman named Alyssa in the school's HR department caught his eye. He spotted her while out with some coworkers the night before Thanksgiving. They started chatting, he bought her a drink, and by the end of their conversation he had saved his number in her phone as *Sexy as fuck*. Several years later they were married in a beautiful outdoor ceremony in the Berkshires.

Magoffin eventually took a gig coaching special teams for Mahar's football team. The roster was small—just forty kids, with many playing both offense and defense. Magoffin had never played in an organized setting, but he'd watched plenty of Buffalo Bills games since the late 1990s, which was to say he'd developed a pretty good idea of what not to do. He flourished in the role, connecting with the kids in a way that impressed his head coach and the school's administration. He soon took on some more coaching gigs and was named the chair of both the physical education and health departments.

Soon after, Magoffin convinced Justin to pitch an esports team to the school's administration, but he himself had to face a reality: he knew nothing about *League of Legends*. He found a Reddit thread on how to practice specific in-game skills and started reading up on strategy in online gaming forums. He sat in front of his laptop for hours after dinner watching tweens narrate as they played *League* on YouTube. One Saturday night, while he and Alyssa tried to decide on a movie to watch, Magoffin suggested a two-hour documentary about esports. She relented, earning an accolade for her Wife of the Year nomination.

Balancing football and esports duties was tricky. The coach would stay in the computer lab for the hour between the end of the school day and the start of football practice—unless it was a match day, in which case he stuck around and the football team started without him. The esports squad got off to a respectable start, winning just as often as they lost. Soon the school began including the team's results in the morning announcements, mixed right in with those of the football, soccer, and field hockey teams. The program got coverage in the local papers. The athletic booster club gifted the program a set of ergonomic gaming chairs. Other students took notice. Mahar had a fierce football rivalry with the nearby town of Athol that spanned more than a century. At practice on the eve of the big game, Mahar's starting running back approached Magoffin on the sideline with an urgent question.

"Coach," the boy asked, "is it true you might be creating a *Rocket League* team?"

Magoffin ignored the inquiry. "Go back to tackling drills," he told the boy. Privately, though, he had a realization: *This is getting huge.*

Magoffin started to detect the changes in some of his players as the first season wore on. They were more upbeat. They were performing better in class. The shift was perhaps most apparent in Justin. For starters, he was actually showing up. Mahar, like most high schools, had a rule that students needed to be in class to attend that day's practice—and had to attend a certain number of practices to be eligible to play in matches. Truancy was no longer an option if he wanted to compete. Not surprisingly, going to class did wonders for his grades. By the end of the semester, his smattering of D's and F's had transformed into a respectable collection of B's and C's. He started thinking about college and potential career paths in gaming.

So after Justin didn't show up for Magoffin's morning advisory block for the second time one week, the teacher asked him about it the next day.

"Is everything okay, Justin?"

"I'm fine," he said. "My mom hasn't been around to give me a ride and I didn't feel like walking the three miles to school."

"I'll make you an offer," Magoffin countered. "If you ever need a lift, all you have to do is text."

Soon Magoffin was swinging by the trailer to get him each morning and dropping him off after practice. The car rides became ten-minute therapy sessions. Justin had always been prone to bouts of sadness. There were still some days he would text Magoffin and tell him he wouldn't be making it into school, then lie in bed until the afternoon. Those were the bad days. On the good days, which now greatly outnumbered them, he'd ride with his coach and talk strategy for the upcoming match.

Much of the work that went into succeeding at *League*, like in any sport, took place before the game even began. A team needed to decide which of the five roles each player would assume, then choose the champions best suited to those positions and to the aptitudes of the humans commandeering them. Gamers needed to know one another's strengths and shortcomings. They needed a system for efficiently barking out orders during live gameplay and telling each other when they'd need backup and where. "Most of our mistakes are made when nobody's communicating," said Justin. "Communication is huge. I'm a big stickler for it."

The practices were more than just a time to play video games—they were an essential step toward the goal of winning. Though Magoffin was the coach, he'd designated Justin as team captain and more or less let him call the shots when it came to game planning. He knew it wasn't in Justin's nature to be a leader. He was quiet in class. He wasn't involved in any other sports or clubs. The kid could barely maintain eye contact when meeting someone for the first time. In his new role, though, Justin found himself standing in front of his teammates at the computer lab's touchscreen monitor before matches. He pointed out the opposing school's players and their stats, scribbling notes on the screen about who should take on what role that day and which champions should be banned. Magoffin mostly stood off to the side, observing, letting Justin have the spotlight.

Other teachers and staffers at Mahar noticed the changes in Justin and his fellow players. Some administrators believed the team wasn't just a nice new addition to the school's offerings—it was nothing less than a lifeline.

"I think there are kids who would have dropped out of school if it weren't for this team," said Mahar's co-principal Scott Hemlin, who admittedly knew almost nothing about esports until the day Justin pitched it to him. "They finally feel like they belong."

Magoffin soon decided to give up his gigs coaching football and track to focus on esports. Esports, he believed, was too important to not dedicate his coaching energies to it completely. "Before this," he said, "these kids were getting home from school, throwing their backpacks down, going in their room, putting on their headsets, logging in, and playing. Now we're giving them a spot to do that after school with adult supervision. These kids might have gotten made fun of for being gamers in the past, but this has given legitimacy to their passions, and the other kids realize it."

That newfound legitimacy played out in the weeks after the team launched, when students who had nothing else to do after school began visiting the computer lab and watching his team play. Some hoped to pick up a few new skills of their own. Some just liked the excitement. And it wasn't just gamers. When kids from the football and basketball teams had time to kill between the day's final bell and the start of their own practices, they came down to root for the boys while they competed in their *League* matches. The dynamic was flipping. The group of self-proclaimed loners and outcasts was becoming the center of attention. At Mahar Regional, esports had become a spectator sport.

7

BIG DEAL

DELANE AND ASHLEY sat in a dingy hotel room surrounded by bagged snacks and bottles of water. The roar of jet engines filled the room every few moments. The administrative office at their new Playa Vista apartment complex had been closed when they'd arrived in Los Angeles, so they'd booked a cheap room a short cab ride from the airport. They were amazed to find a twenty-four-hour supermarket, something they hadn't encountered at home, right next door. They'd stocked up on junk food and settled in for their night in the loud, musty room.

The next morning, a Sunday, they called the complex's office. It was open—*thank God*—so they loaded their suitcases into the trunk of an Uber and rode across town to the apartment where they would start their new lives. The couple's first order of business was setting up the living quarters. They opted against buying couches or a television, not wanting to overdo it in case their time in Los Angeles was short lived. Instead, they converted the living room into a mini-office with a standing desk and whiteboard. They bought an air mattress from Walmart—a stopgap until the real one they ordered online got delivered—and laid it down on the bedroom floor. In the coming days, Ashley would secure an administrative role at a nearby hospital. "Man, it was an incredible time, to be honest," Delane said later. "I wish that I could go back and relive that moment, doing something that risky together."

When Delane strolled into the Science office for his first day Monday morning, the partners showed him to his work station:

a humble wooden desk in the corner of the second floor with a stack of Post-it notes. This was where he would begin to work on his new venture, which he'd decided—again—to call PlayVS. He loved the name, after all, and didn't want to see the thousands of dollars he'd already spent on it go to waste. (The silver lining to the gambling platform failing so quickly was that it barely had any digital footprint, so the moniker remained clean.) To personalize his workspace, Delane installed the oversized monitor he'd brought with him, then printed out some photos and taped them above his desk. One was a screenshot of the original Google homepage—not all that aesthetically distinct from the modern version, but still a reminder of the $700 billion company's humble beginnings. Another was a photo of Jay-Z and Sean "Diddy" Combs. Their music had served as the soundtrack to Delane's childhood, and he'd hung their likenesses on the wall of his bedroom on Burgess. The two hip-hop stars also served as motivation. Both had grown up without their fathers in drug-ridden environments, fought their way to massive success, then held the door open for other Black men and women behind them. They were reminders of what was possible.

Science assigned an asset manager named Talia Rosenthal to serve as Delane's day-to-day contact within the firm. The Oregon native had worked in venture capital in Singapore for a few years before coming back to the States. Her role at Science entailed working closely with the company's startups and guiding them through their business strategies, fundraising, partnerships, and even daily operations. Delane and Rosenthal had a critical first task: try to figure out the best point of entry into high school esports.

Delane had decided to take an approach far different than the one he employed while building the gambling platform. That startup's software was slick, but even if its launch hadn't been a disaster, it might still have been doomed; the company didn't have partnerships with any publishers or organizations that could help it scale. With his new startup, Delane decided he would put less early emphasis on the product and more on developing crucial business relationships. He reached out to youth organizations like the Boys & Girls Clubs of America, thinking that an alliance with the nonprofit could help get PlayVS's still-hypothetical product into students' hands after school. He talked with colleges and universities that had created esports programs and asked them about their scholarship offerings, considering whether they could be used to entice high schools to create teams. He spoke with decisionmakers at game publishers. Delane sought out conversations with absolutely anyone who had an informed opinion on youth esports. When visitors came to meet him at the Science office, he would lead them through the firm's second floor and into a conference room. "My team sits over there," he would say and gesture toward his desk, near which employees from several other startups worked. It technically was true, though the guests had no idea the "team" in question consisted only of Delane.

As Delane learned through his conversations, some game publishers that had already established a presence in the college space, like Riot Games and Activision Blizzard, were now considering trying to build high school leagues of their own. This was doubly bad news for him—not only did it mean he was up against massive competitors; it also didn't bode well for the possibility of the publishers licensing their intellectual property to PlayVS, which the startup would need if it wanted to offer their hugely popular games on its platform. Two months in, the high school esports concept felt like more of a long shot than when he'd arrived in Los Angeles. Delane had talked to hundreds of people, was working nights and weekends and practically living in the office, and had almost nothing to show for it. The Science partners had even begun floating the idea of a pivot, casually presenting him with entirely new potential business concepts and introducing him to players in other industries.

Delane and Rosenthal had recognized fairly early that the most surefire way to crack into the high school gaming market was through the NFHS, which had the ability to declare esports an officially sanctioned sport and recommend that states' governing bodies adopt it. It was the real-world equivalent of a cheat code: a partnership with the organization wouldn't just give PlayVS an avenue into the difficult-to-access demographic it sought; it would also provide the startup with leverage over publishers and defensibility against competitors.

Unbeknownst to Delane and Rosenthal at the time, the century-old NFHS had been seriously discussing esports internally for the previous year and a half. After-school esports clubs had been springing up across the country, and a handful of state associations were pushing the organization to declare esports an official sport and help them run their competitions. A recent Pew study had found that 72 percent of teens played some form of video games, including 84 percent of boys. The NFHS's own research ascertained that more kids were playing video games than were playing traditional sports. At the same time, millions of students across the country weren't involved in any sort of after-school clubs or activities. These concurrent realities had turned Mark Koski, at the time the NFHS director of sports, events, and development, into something of an esports evangelist. He saw sanctioned esports as a way of taking kids who were playing video games anyway and placing them within their schools' walls under the supervision of an adult. "We looked at it as a way to get more students involved," said Koski. "As long as students are in the education setting between the hours of 2:30 and 5:30 every day, we believe that's a positive thing, as opposed to them playing by themselves at home without the team and education aspects." The

NFHS had spoken with a handful of gaming companies over the past eighteen months about building the online infrastructure for high school competitions, but nothing had stuck.

One day, Delane held an exploratory call with leadership at the German firm ESL, one of the largest esports companies in the world, which had found success hosting cash-prize tournaments in games like *Halo*, *Counter-Strike*, and *Mortal Kombat*. ESL had been in contact with a company called PlayOn! Sports that broadcast high school competitions online in any sport from basketball to diving. PlayOn and the NFHS a few years earlier had partnered to form the NFHS Network, a for-profit company that streamed thousands of high school games and matches each year. High schools didn't quite fit within ESL's business, which was focused on pro competitions, so the company agreed to introduce Delane to the NFHS Network.

"I don't think they thought much of it. They were just trying to be helpful," recounted Delane. "But I also don't think they knew exactly what they were giving us at the time, because if they did, they wouldn't have given it to us."

Delane exchanged friendly emails with David Rudolph and Robert Rothberg, two executives at the NFHS Network. They soon looped in Koski, who had recently taken on a role as CEO of the NFHS Network in addition to his NFHS duties. The whole arrangement was confusing, but the important thing to Delane was that he now had an in with the NFHS. Not wanting to scare the NFHS folks off with an immediate pitch, Delane instead offered himself up as an expert on the subject of esports. *How can I help? What do you want to learn about the space?* He and the organization began holding occasional phone calls to talk about the esports industry in general.

Delane was tantalizingly close to a breakthrough. Here he was, talking to the organization that could help him blow this whole thing open. But it was starting to feel like the relationship was stagnating. One day, he decided to go for the kill. He emailed the NFHS folks and asked if they could make time to chat about what PlayVS was building. They agreed.

A few days later, Science's Mike Jones and Rosenthal sat in with Delane as he gave his pitch over speakerphone as to what his startup could offer the NFHS: essential gaming infrastructure built with software and, eventually, partnerships with publishers.

"How far along is PlayVS with its software?" the NFHS people asked from the other end of the line. "Do you have a product ready now?"

"We do," Delane told them. "We have a demo ready to go. Let me fly out there and show it to you all."

"How about at our headquarters in Atlanta next month?"

"I'd love that," said Delane.

Rosenthal had been in the trenches with Delane. She knew as well as anyone that PlayVS's product didn't actually exist.

"I looked at him when the call ended," she recalled, "and said, 'What are you talking about? We have a pitch deck. We understand our strategy. What is this demo that you speak of?' He was like, 'Just don't worry about it.'"

The race was on. Delane scrambled to sketch a wireframe (essentially a blueprint of the platform) using design software. He reached out to Sean Yalda and Dawid Loubser, an engineer in Johannesburg who had done some work for him on the wagering platform, and asked them to help bring the mock-up to life. They spent the next few weeks working under contract and building a product demo, collaborating with Delane to make sure everything on the front end was well designed and functional, which helped give the appearance that it was further along than it was. One day in November, a month after Delane gave his pitch over the phone, Delane and Peter Pham hopped on a plane to Atlanta along with the completed demo. They met in a conference room at the NFHS Network headquarters with Koski, Rudolph, and Rothberg.

The NFHS at the time was evaluating about a half-dozen companies as potential partners to help it roll out high school esports, from upstarts like Electronic Gaming Federation to publishers like Riot Games and Activision Blizzard. All were larger and more established than PlayVS. When Delane and Pham walked in the room, the organization was fresh off a meeting with Super League Gaming, a three-year-old company backed by nearly $30 million in VC money. The group had been impressed with the company's proposal—a fact that Rothberg made sure to communicate to Delane and Pham as soon as they sat down. Things already felt tense. Delane opened his laptop and dove right into his demonstration.

"So," he began, "here's how a student will log in and view their schedule and the opposing team's roster. Here's where they click to drop into a lobby, and when all the students are in, the match begins. When it ends, the relevant data gets sent to PlayVS, and we'll present it to the players like this." The NFHS folks seemed receptive. Delane had already thought through even the most granular details. What was supposed to be an hour-long meeting went on for three, Delane and Pham discussing the product and their greater vision for high school esports.

Then, toward the end of the conversation, Koski and company casually dropped a bomb. "We expect to make our decision in about a year," he said.

As their Uber back to the airport weaved through traffic to catch the return flight, Delane felt deflated. A year was a long time to wait, especially with a favorable outcome far from guaranteed.

Koski, Rudolph, and Rothberg, meanwhile, discussed what they'd seen and heard. They liked that PlayVS didn't look at high schools as some additional revenue stream—it was focusing its efforts exclusively on the academic level. They were impressed with Delane's knowledge of the space, and they liked that he shared some of their most fundamental philosophies, like not offering first-person shooter games and creating a no-cut sport open to any student who wanted to play. They knew the startup was small, though perhaps not quite *how* small, but they also knew it had the support of Science, the firm behind the recent fast success of Dollar Shave Club and DogVacay.

"We generally take things very slow at the NFHS, and we vet thoroughly," Koski said later. "We're going to be rubber-stamping something for 20,000 high schools, 16 million students, and a million and a half coaches. We knew, through talking with Delane and Peter, that they had it together. It made the process a lot shorter than I would have ever expected."

Two weeks after the meeting, Koski called Delane. The NFHS, he told him, was interested in partnering with PlayVS.

Delane was ecstatic. But that was only step one. While the NFHS had the ability to approve of high school sports and activities, the decision as to whether to actually adopt them was left up to the athletic association in each individual state. The NFHS held its winter meeting each January, a four-day event at which administrators and athletic directors from across the country convened. This year, the conference would be in Scottsdale, Arizona. Delane was going to have to come and pitch the idea of adopting esports to all fifty states.

A FEW MONTHS before he decided to move to Los Angeles, Delane grabbed coffee with someone to whom Suzy Ryoo had introduced him. Ryoo had recently become acquainted with a young man named Laz Alberto, a twenty-four-year-old with a passion for all things esports who was working as an analyst at LA's Lowercase Capital. Ryoo's assumption that the two would be compatible proved accurate. During one of Delane's trips to visit Science, he reached out to Alberto to see if he wanted to meet. It quickly became clear during their conversation in the cafe that they shared similar mindsets. They both loved the tech space and dedicated much of their time to learning everything they could about it. Alberto at one point started to explain to Delane what kinds of companies Lowercase invested in.

"Don't worry. I know everything about you guys," Delane said, then proceeded to rattle off much of the fund's portfolio.

Alberto was impressed and intrigued. "It was cool to talk with someone else who was just as genuinely curious about the tech world," he said later. "Whenever I saw someone who had been at all successful in that space, I wanted to meet them and know them. I saw a similar spark in Delane. We were both just kind of hustling to build relationships."

Months later, after Delane settled down in Los Angeles, he called up Alberto again. As Delane explained what he was up to with Science, the business concept sounded jarringly familiar to his new friend. Alberto's boss at Lowercase had been Matt Mazzeo, the VC who had conceived of the high school esports idea that eventually became PlayVS. Alberto had helped him research the topic, and together they tried to find a startup in the space that they felt was worthy of an investment. They never did, and Chris Sacca soon retired and shut down the fund, which was when Mazzeo had decided to pass the idea along to Pham and the guys at Science, who then passed it along to Delane. Alberto had never known what, if anything, had become of the concept, and Delane never knew its true origin—until this moment, on the phone with each other, when the two suddenly discovered their paths had intersected in a way they'd never realized. With Lowercase now closed, Alberto was looking for work. He wanted to stay in venture capital.

"Why don't you try to get a job at Science," Delane asked him, "where you can help me pursue this idea that you once found so interesting?" Delane put in a good word for him, and the same month Delane and Pham flew to Atlanta to meet with the NFHS, Alberto began a job as an asset manager at Science. He was quickly assigned to work with PlayVS.

One of Alberto's first tasks was to help Delane prepare for his presentation at the NFHS Winter Meeting, which was to be held January 3 through 6 at the succinctly named JW Marriott Scottsdale Camelback Inn Resort & Spa. Talia Rosenthal had a conflict—she and her husband were spending the week on vacation in Morocco—so Science arranged for James Hicks, another asset manager, to pinch hit. "He was an older gentleman," Delane said later, "so he sort of served as the adult in the room." Which was true, but only relatively speaking—Hicks was thirty-four. He hadn't been particularly hands-on with PlayVS to that point, so he spent much of December becoming more familiar with Delane and taking a crash course on the high school esports space. He, Delane, and Alberto spent the weeks leading up to Christmas studying the structure and politics of the NFHS and working on the messaging Delane would deliver to the organization and the state athletic associations.

The day after New Year's, the trio, plus Hicks's wife and their baby, flew to Arizona. They arrived at a campy but scenic Western-themed resort outfitted with cacti, palm trees, fountains, views of the nearby mountains, and life-sized busts of cowboys and Native American warriors. The grounds teemed with high school athletics folks, most of them older former teachers dressed like they were about to play eighteen holes at a country club. Standing in the lobby, Delane and Alberto had a realization: they'd severely underpacked. As per the itinerary, they'd each brought a suit for the next evening's cocktail hour, but otherwise their suitcases were filled with their usual startup garb of T-shirts and hoodies. The pair dropped off their bags, jumped into an Uber, and headed to a discount store, where they stocked up on button-downs, polos and khakis.

Hicks and his family retired to their room that evening. Delane and Alberto, meanwhile, ventured down to the outdoor hot tub to try to relax before the big few days ahead. Most of their interactions to that point had revolved around tech, esports, and PlayVS, but the two didn't know much about each other's personal lives. Alberto had heard about Delane's journey in general terms—the projects in Detroit, the single mother, the cell phone stores—but hadn't heard how they all connected. As Delane talked, Alberto began to gain a more complete picture of who this person was and what motivated him to be great.

"I had believed Delane would be successful from the first time I met him," Alberto said. "But when we talked about his background and how that played into what he was doing, that was when I knew he was a generational founder, and that his story was worth knowing, and, in my case, worth being a part of in some way."

Alberto shared some of his life story, too. Both his parents' families had emigrated from Cuba and settled down near Los Angeles. They met at a neighborhood function and were later married, and Alberto's father went on to launch a construction business. The couple sent Alberto to study business at the University of Southern California, making him the first on his father's side to go to college and one of the first on his mother's. "For my parents to get here and get to this point was challenging," said Alberto, "and that created in me a kind of intrinsic motivation and sense of responsibility to be the person that they set me up to be. So I worked hard, if nothing else, for them—to live out the story that they set in front of me." During Alberto's senior year, his mother was diagnosed with breast cancer. He made the drive from campus to his family's house in Orange County nearly weekly to take her to chemotherapy or to simply be present. She eventually beat the disease, but the experience reoriented his way of thinking about what was important and what kind of work really mattered—and led him to want to make sure he could always provide for his future family should he ever be faced with a similar crisis.

The next day marked the conference's first full slate of activities. Alberto, Hicks, and Delane spiffed up in their respective rooms before meeting in the hotel lobby to head to the welcome reception. "It was our first time ever seeing each other in suits," Hicks recalled. "We all got a kick out of that." They mingled with the crowd all across the grounds, introducing themselves to anyone they came across as a means of trying to build relationships with the key players in various states. They wrote down the name of any executive who seemed even remotely interested to follow up with them later.

"The median age was probably like sixty-five—imagine ex-gym teachers, wrestling coaches, heavy mustachioed men," recounted Hicks. At one point, he found himself chatting with a younger female athletic director, explaining who he was and why his group was there. "She said, 'I'm looking forward to this. We've had challenges before with controversial sports, getting them acknowledged and certified.' In my mind, I'm thinking, *Was this like skeleton luge or something super dangerous?* So I asked for an example. She said, 'We had the hardest time with boys' soccer.' I was like, 'Boys' soccer!' She's like 'Yeah. There was a good amount of state athletic directors who thought All-American boys should only play football and therefore they should not acknowledge boys' soccer as a sanctioned sport.' I remember thinking, *We're fucked. Men's soccer is the most popular sport in the world. If boys' soccer is an issue, there's no way they're going for video games.*"

Hicks decided not to tell Delane and Alberto about the interaction until after the trip was over. After the day's events wound down, the trio met in the lobby to discuss Delane's big pitch the next day. They'd gleaned what types of questions the educators had about esports through their random interactions. Together, with their laptops and notebooks spread across a coffee table in the lobby, they honed the presentation, adding and removing sections, changing a word here or a metaphor there. Eventually, Hicks went up to bed. Delane and Alberto continued to work into the night, the table filling with soda cans, bottles of water, bags of vending machine chips, and Styrofoam containers of hotel-bar chicken wings as the hours whittled away. A little after 2:00 a.m., while Delane rehearsed the presentation with headphones on, he had a jarring thought: *What if the associations wanted details about PlayVS's pricing structure and projections as to how quickly the product could scale?* He wouldn't have an answer—the startup hadn't yet decided on a fee or mapped out any growth goals. Delane whipped out his phone, scrolled to Talia Rosenthal's name, and pressed the FaceTime button.

In her hotel room halfway across the world, Rosenthal was getting ready for another day in Casablanca with her husband when she noticed the missed calls on her phone. There was a follow-up text from Delane in all caps: *I NEED TO TALK TO YOU NOW.* Rosenthal FaceTimed him back.

"Yes?" she asked.

"The NFHS is going to want to understand our structure, to know if this thing really scales," Delane said in a huff. "Do I give them figures up front? Do I tell them how much they're going to make right now?"

"No, definitely not," she replied, her husband looking on. "We haven't modeled this out yet. We don't want to tell them anything that we might need to backtrack on."

"We need to figure this out *now*."

"I think that you can get around it," she told Delane. "Massage your presentation in such a way so you don't give them all of the information yet, and we'll talk to them in more detail later. I know it's tempting to give the organization numbers, but what if PlayVS fails to reach them? The last thing we want is to sign a deal with the NFHS and then fall massively short of our promises. This relationship is supposed to be built for the long term."

Delane calmed down, reassured that Rosenthal—an expert on early-stage companies—thought it acceptable for him to work around the question if asked. He hung up and let the couple go to breakfast.

Soon the sky started to lighten over southern Arizona. Delane and Alberto wouldn't be sleeping tonight. They put the finishing touches on the presentation and went up to change into their newly purchased button-downs. When Hicks came downstairs, he found the pair back in the lobby, the same place he'd left them hours earlier. Soon, the attendees, rested after full nights of sleep, started making their way to the ballroom.

It was go time.

Delane, Alberto, and Hicks went in and took their seats. When Delane's turn came to speak, he stepped up to the podium brandished with the NFHS's insignia and, there in front of more than a hundred administrators and athletic directors, gave a presentation about bringing esports to America's high schools. He spoke about the popularity of competitive gaming, particularly among the teen demographic. On the projection screen, he showed clips of thousands of spectators packed into arenas watching *League of Legends* tournaments. He pulled up the demo of PlayVS's software and explained how simple launching esports would be for any school that wanted to.

When he concluded, the audience broke into applause. The first phase was complete. The next was to attend a more intimate meeting—another pitch followed by a question-and-answer period with the NFHS Network board, a group that also included several state association executive directors. These were the ones whose opinions mattered most; they would ultimately decide whether or not it was time to adopt esports—and if they thought PlayVS was the right company for the job.

Alberto and Hicks sat down at a table facing the audience in the front of the conference room, the rest of the desks in a U-shaped formation around them. Standing beside the table, Delane delivered another presentation, this time diving into the specifics of how the software would work and what the states would need to do to get started. When he finished, the floor opened for questions. They were immediately barraged. Some administrators wanted to know more about how season schedules would be created. Others asked about the nature of violence in video games, or about the sport being coed. When time was up, the three men rose—only to be blocked off by the administrators. They weren't finished with them yet. Alberto, Hicks, and Delane stood a few feet apart, each fielding inquiries from the handful of educators gathered around them, always keeping one ear out for their comrades. When one of them heard another get stumped, they'd jump in and help out.

100 million viewers last year . . .

No publisher deals yet, but we expect to soon . . .

After what felt like a lifetime of rapid-fire questions and answers, the attendees mercifully dispersed to get to their other meetings. The trio had survived.

Afterward, Delane and Alberto wandered out to the patio and sat by the fire pit, waiting to hear from Koski and the NFHS folks about how they thought things had gone. They ate quesadillas and talked for hours under the clear desert sky as light gave way to darkness. Close to midnight, Delane's cell phone rang. The NFHS executives wanted to meet with them. They came out one by one to join Delane and Alberto on the patio. When everyone had arrived, the group delivered the news. The NFHS wanted to officially partner with PlayVS and was ready to sign the paperwork. The deal would be exclusive, meaning the NFHS couldn't partner with another esports startup for at least five years.

A weight lifted off Delane's shoulders. He, Alberto, and the NFHS folks strolled to a rented villa and celebrated. The wine flowed. Everyone toasted their new partnership, the one that would deliver officially sanctioned esports to high schools. The tiny startup from Santa Monica had done it.

Hicks arrived at breakfast the next morning with his newborn to find Delane and Alberto beaming over eggs and hash browns. Delane gave him the good news.

"He was psyched," recalled Hicks. "Like he was shot out of a cannon."

After four days and three nights of running on pure adrenaline, the trip had been a success. The motley crew boarded their flight together and flew home, the Hickses bouncing a baby between their two laps, Delane and Alberto sleeping harder than anyone else on the plane.

THERE WAS ONE minor detail that Delane and Science had overlooked ahead of PlayVS signing a contract with the NFHS: the company technically didn't exist yet. When the group returned to Santa Monica, Delane filed online to incorporate the startup, waited several days to be approved, then finally inked the contract with the organization.

The NFHS had said from the start that it wanted to launch esports as soon as possible, but that it would allow PlayVS to determine what kind of timing was feasible. Since schools tend to adopt new activities at the start of the school year, the options were to either launch in nine months or wait until the following year. To Delane, that was no choice at all. The first season of high school esports would come online in the fall.

It was time to start building a staff. Delane reached out to Dawid Loubser, the engineer in South Africa with whom he'd worked on the wagering platform and the product demo for the NFHS meeting. Loubser had spent the past several months coding with a pair of younger engineers for a project that, serendipitously, had just been put on hold. Delane hired him as a contractor, giving him the title of chief technology officer, and brought on his two fellow engineers as well. He reached back out to Sean Yalda, following through on his promise to loop him in once the company had some traction. When he accepted, Delane sent him an enthusiastic form email that began with *Welcome Player One!* Yalda showed up on his first day at the Science office to find a desk with some office supplies and an Atari shirt waiting for him. "It was really cute," Yalda recalled. "I was like, 'He's taking this really seriously.' He was already trying to put in some culture and everything. Even though, low-key, I knew him already for years, so he didn't have to do any of that, but I appreciated it."

Delane paid each employee using a combination of equity in the company, back pay that would be issued once the startup had capital, and small salaries from his own pocket and the less than $50,000 in seed money left over from the wagering startup. When he'd arrived in California, Delane had reached out to all the betting platform's investors to ask if they wanted their investments back or preferred to roll them into his next venture. Almost all had stayed in, earning each of them a spot on PlayVS's cap table. ("That might go down as one of the best venture returns of all time when it's all said and done," Delane said later.) Delane called up Bryan Smiley to deliver him some news. He was naming him the company's cofounder.

Smiley was surprised. "Did I feel great about the cofounding title? 100 percent," he said later. "It's something that I can leverage today. But he gave me a title that I didn't necessarily deserve. I was a friend and advisor. I was somebody who had his back, and I had a little bit of money to help out. That's what I was. He gave me a lot of shares, more than I was entitled to." Smiley wouldn't have a day-to-day role with the company, and most of the staff would never meet him. But for Delane, it was about doing right by someone who had believed and invested in him since day one.

In the Science office, Delane would often cross paths with Darondo, a stocky French bulldog that belonged to Mike Jones's assistant. Delane liked the pooch and would take breaks to play with him—and even made time to attend his birthday party. When it came time to design a logo, he paid a designer he found online seventy bucks to draw the dog with headphones on alongside the company's name. Delane never particularly loved the insignia—it was hard to tell what kind of creature it was, and it didn't mesh well with the font—but it stuck. For a color scheme, he chose orange, a tribute to two of his favorite startups, the digital coupon company Honey and Eventbrite, which he'd used to monetize his events in Detroit.

Many of Delane's first days as CEO were spent on the road, often with Laz Alberto. Soon after the Winter Meeting, the

NFHS and PlayVS organized a symposium for executive directors across the country to fly into Atlanta and spend a few days learning more about esports. Representatives from more than twenty states came in and toured the headquarters of Hi-Rez, the publisher of the popular game *Smite*. There the educators learned about the creative and technical processes behind the making of video games and the types of roles available to students who chose to pursue careers in gaming. Other times Delane and Alberto visited with game publishers on their own or met state administrators on their turf as they tried to sell the educators on esports.

All the time on the road left Yalda alone in the office for many of his early days. As his first task, he took it upon himself to try to compile a list of every high school in the country, thinking it might be useful for the company down the road. He pulled data from the Department of Education and a public website he'd found and organized them in a spreadsheet, including each school's size and contact information. He played video games in the office—just research!—to get an idea of what statistics would be useful for students and coaches to receive regarding their gaming performances.

Delane decided in March to bring on another employee to keep Yalda company. James Kozachuk was a lifelong gamer who grew up playing *StarCraft* and the war strategy game *Age of Empires*, entering tournaments as a kid and sometimes winning thousands of dollars. He developed carpal tunnel in his later teenage years and decided that, just perhaps, it was time to stop playing so much. While attending the University of Central Florida, he started organizing small tournaments for his classmates to compete against students at different schools. He soon connected with the High School Starleague. Founded by a pair of high school students in 2011, the organization was one of the earliest attempts at establishing high school esports. It was also fairly informal—the staff were volunteers, entry cost $3 to covers server expenses, and teams were student-run and mostly played from home. Given the nature of teenagers, this meant it was common to sit down for your match and find your opponent had ghosted. Still, thousands of students across the country participated. Kozachuk spent a year and a half helping to run the league before it eventually folded.

"It didn't really turn out to be much," said Kozachuk, "but it put that seed in my head that high school esports was going to be really big."

Having a front-row seat to the way the Starleague operated gave Kozachuk a working thesis. He knew that research on the relationship between video games and schoolwork showed that the more time a student spent playing games, the lower their grades tended to be. But observing the kids play in the Starleague, he thought there might be more to it. Kozachuk earned a degree in psychology, then enrolled in a graduate program at UCF. As part of his coursework, in 2014 he tracked down five hundred high school students who had just completed a three-month esports season and surveyed them about their experiences. The results revealed that when instructors were hands-on and the teams were structured, the students' grades tended to be higher, the kids were more likely to say they identified with their school, and less toxicity was present when they played. "The negative effect of playing a lot of video games went away," said Kozachuk, "and you had all of these incredible benefits." He published the peer-reviewed research and began presenting it at academic conferences and distributing it to educators.

Kozachuk knew he wanted to pursue the high school esports space further. But he recognized that creating an organization that could scale would take just more than his research—it would require building relationships and cutting through bureaucracy.

Two years later, he was living in Orlando doing consulting work on collegiate esports when Jackson Dahl, a member of 100 Thieves' founding team, connected him with Delane. Almost immediately, Delane recognized Kozachuk as someone who could be valuable and offered him a job. Kozachuk saw the partnership with the NFHS and understood it to mean the company already had made significant progress toward the vision he'd hoped to realize someday. He accepted the offer, bought a ticket to Los Angeles, and moved across the country to start working for PlayVS.

As is often the case with startups, early roles at the company didn't come with strict job descriptions. Delane hired people if he liked them and they knew about esports, then assigned them to handle issues as they arose. Kozachuk would write marketing copy alongside Yalda one day, then spend time on the phone with publishers the next. The exception, at least in the earliest days, was the team in South Africa. Loubser and his two engineers, Graham and Justin, had strict marching orders: build PlayVS's software. Making things even more challenging was the nine-hour time difference between California and South Africa. From a small coworking space in Johannesburg, the trio would code by day while the Santa Monica team slept; then, around their dinner time, the folks in the States would come online, and Loubser's team would have to attend meetings and brainstorming sessions via video chat until the wee hours. Delane preferred to be hands-on with the development side, which sometimes led to conflict.

"You would shift a pixel here, add one more pixel there," recalled Loubser. "You would do that quite painstakingly, and then three days later, the design would change, because Delane would have a different idea, or he had spoken to somebody else." The process began to wear on the engineers. "I remember at like 3:00 a.m., Graham and I just saying, 'Okay, we're halting.

We're going for pizza now.' We'd find the one twenty-four-hour pizza place that was open and just sit there, too tired to talk or anything. We would just be there, and fight with Delane in between, about small little things that don't actually matter, but they mattered to Delane."

The hours were long, the pay was paltry, and the equity the employees had received had no value even on paper. Still, Loubser reminded his engineers that the payoff could be huge if things worked out. "We had been involved with other small startups before," he recounted, "but there was something different about this one. It had a lot of potential. So, I spent a lot of time motivating them: 'This is worth it. Hang in there. This is going to be something big.'"

NOT LONG AFTER the NFHS deal was finalized, the Science partners offered Delane $500,000 in seed money. Delane knew the funding would be a boon to PlayVS's growth, but he balked at the idea of surrendering the large chunk of equity that the firm required in exchange. While driving with Marcus Carey one day, Delane spoke with the partners on the phone and told them about his hang-up.

"He was pretty hesitant about doing it, and pretty vocal with them about his challenges with it," recalled Carey. "They really had to sell him on it." When Delane hung up, he and Carey talked it through. "I was sitting there saying stuff to him like, 'Yes, what they want is a lot, but there's still something for you there, and they could really lift you up.' He was already leaning in that direction. I think he was just negotiating, expressing his displeasure."

Delane decided to take the deal. At the time, it made Science the second largest shareholder in the company after himself. Years later, as the company grew in size and value, Delane would think about how much equity Science held compared to how much money it had invested and wonder whether it was worth it. He usually ended up in the same place. "Without Science, I don't get this off the ground. I'll admit to that," he said. "It's just a matter of how expensive that was. Truthfully, I always sort of reflect on that old-age saying: Would you rather own a percentage of something, or 100 percent of nothing? So, I'm okay with that." When the money hit PlayVS's bank account, one of the first things he did was pay his employees the wages he owed them for the previous several months of work.

Before Delane could begin pitching VC firms for PlayVS's first true funding round, its Series A, the company would need a pricing model, which was necessary to show potential investors how the startup would actually earn revenue. Delane, Rosenthal, and Science's Tom Dare huddled together to discuss. They wanted to charge less than $20 per month per student, but felt they could charge more than Netflix given the many hours of engagement the platform would provide. Using that extremely unscientific formula, they settled on $16 per head. But creating a monthly subscription model, they realized, would leave more opportunities for teams to drop out midseason, which would be a negative for both the other participants and PlayVS. They decided on an upfront cost of $64 for the four-month season, with each school year being divided into fall and spring seasons.

Pham reached out to his network of VCs to kickstart the search for potential investors. He soon had more than a dozen firms willing to meet with Delane, most of them in the Bay Area. The duo scheduled all their meetings over the span of two days, a Thursday and Friday in April. The idea was that pitching late in the week would keep PlayVS fresh on the investors' minds and increase the likelihood that Delane would get invited to the weekly meetings, typically held each Monday, in which each firm's partners held their final votes on potential investments. Over the course of those two days, Pham and Delane bounced between the offices of renowned firms like Andreessen Horowitz, NEA, and Sequoia Capital, holding a handful of video meetings with firms in other locations in between. Sitting in the conference room in Sequoia's headquarters, Delane studied the wall plastered with the logos of some of the firm's more lucrative investments: Apple, Google, PayPal, LinkedIn, Instagram, Oracle, Cisco, You-Tube. He asked the person seated across the table how many of the companies on the wall had Black founders.

"None, I believe," the person told him. "You could be the first."

Delane, who had made a habit of asking the question of potential investors, noted the unsatisfactory answer.

After the successful visit to NEA, during which Rick Yang and Jon Sakoda offered to lead the round, Delane did, in fact, get invited back to the firm's partner meeting the following week. There he pitched the concept of high school esports to a dozen investors in the room and another ten watching via video. "An idea like this is not obvious," Sakoda said later. "It's new; it's different; in some ways it's controversial. And in that meeting, he took a roomful of healthcare investors, enterprise software investors, and people of all different backgrounds—maybe none of whom have ever played a recent video game—and convinced them to build a high school esports league."

NEA soon presented Delane and Pham with a term sheet stating the firm would lead the round and invest $10 million into PlayVS. Several NEA partners, Sakoda included, separately made offers to invest in the company with their own money—a level of commitment that made the firm look like an increasingly attractive option.

Delane had once read a blog post by a VC about leveraging the media to drum up hype while fundraising. With that in mind, he decided he would retain a public relations firm—a fact he hid from the Science folks until it was done, suspecting they might advise against burning up some of his precious capital before he even had a product. He selected ASTRSK, a New York City outfit that had tech clients like Weebly and Managed by Q. Armed with the groundbreaking and still-unannounced NFHS deal, the agency was able to land Delane interviews with a number of publications in the days leading up to April 19, when the NFHS would officially announce the partnership at its board of directors meeting in Indianapolis. That morning, articles about PlayVS graced the pages of the *Wall Street Journal* and the websites of ESPN, *Variety,* Business Insider, and TechCrunch, each of them highlighting the startup's deal with the NFHS and revealing that esports would become an official high school sport that fall. The hype train was in motion. None of the stories mentioned the little-known detail that the company making this happen had only two employees and three contractors.

There was no time to pop any bubbly. Delane hopped on a plane back to San Francisco to try to capitalize on the newfound momentum. "Just imagine, for the past two weeks, investors have been hearing about this thing, and they've been getting excited about it," Delane said later. "Then suddenly we're the hottest startup in the news. It sped up the process. Everyone wanted to invest. And, oh man, it was an insane time."

The next week, Delane's schedule was booked with investor meetings from 8:00 a.m. till 10:00 p.m. each day. Suzy Ryoo's Cross Culture Ventures and Matt Mazzeo's Coatue Management were interested. The investment arm of the San Francisco 49ers reached out. Delane got a call from Anthony Saleh, a partner at the VC firm WndrCo and manager for the rapper Nas. PlayVS suddenly had interest not only from players in the tech space, but across the wider worlds of sports and culture.

One investor who wanted in on the action was a venture capitalist whom Delane had gotten to know at SXSW several years earlier. The VC had become interested in the wagering platform Delane was about to build and agreed to invest several hundred thousand dollars in the startup. The two stayed in touch after the company fizzled out. When Delane decided to move to LA and join Science, he gave the investor the option to take the rest of his money back or transfer his shares into the new venture. The VC liked the high school esports idea. He told Delane to let it ride.

Now, as Delane sought out investors for the Series A, the VC wanted to up the ante. He told Delane he wanted to invest at least $500,000 to $750,000 into the business. When Delane didn't immediately take him up on the offer, the investor followed up via text:

You don't think we will be below the numbers we have been talking about, do you? If something changed, let me know.

Delane wrote back:

So, unsure until we decide on the lead investor. This is when I can let you know.

After a few days with no news, the VC started growing impatient, texting Delane to ask if there was a chance there wouldn't be room for his firm in the round at all. Delane told him again that PlayVS was still sorting through its offers and figuring things out. The investor became more aggressive, sending Delane dozens of texts over the course of several weeks and telling him he felt disrespected. He accused Delane of being dishonest about his role in the decision-making process and keeping him from gaining access to the Science partners, writing in another text:

I actually get it now. Science is running the company and you're just along for the ride. I feel bad for you, man. It's a tough hit to the ego. I'll be praying for you. Sounds like you need it.

Delane stopped responding. Shortly after, the investor sent emails to the firms he knew were considering investing in PlayVS's round. In them, he disparaged Delane and advised them not to give him money. One firm soon reached back out to Delane with a new set of terms that would grant it oversight of his decision-making. Delane promptly removed the firm from the round.

Yang and Sakoda remained undeterred through it all, honoring their verbal agreement to lead the round. "They stuck by me," said Delane. "But that almost blew up the round, right in the middle of it."

Delane decided he would take NEA's offer. Under the terms, NEA and Science would have one board seat apiece and Delane would have two. The first round would total $15.5 million—$10 million from NEA and an additional $2 million from Science on top of its original $500,000. That left $3 million to split among remaining investors, a crop that included Cross Culture, Coatue, the 49ers, the NBA's Baron Davis, the NFL's Russell Okung, Dollar Shave Club's Michael Dubin, plus Saleh at WndrCo and his client, Nas. Through Saleh's connections, soon LeBron James was interested in investing, as were Drake and a handful of other well-known hip-hop artists. By the time PlayVS received a firm commitment from any of them, though, the $15.5 million was already all accounted for. Delane, Science, and NEA briefly debated removing a few firms to make room for the superstar investors, but it just didn't feel right. And so it came to be that, one year after arriving in Los Angeles, Delane was turning down money from Drake and LeBron James.

PlayVS announced the round in early June. At $15.5 million, it was the third-largest Series A ever by a startup with a Black founder, trailing only two real estate companies (Compass, cofounded by Robert Reffkin, and Cadre, cofounded by Ryan Williams)—which meant it was the largest ever for a consumer company. When the news broke, one of the first people to reach out to Delane on Twitter was Tristan Walker, the founder of the grooming firm Walker & Company. Walker, himself one of the disproportionately small number of Black entrepreneurs to wrangle a newsworthy amount of venture capital, over the previous five years had grown his brand from an idea to a formidable company with a presence in Target. He sent Delane a long message congratulating him and advising him on the pressures that came with being in his position.

There's a classic moment in music history circa 2002, chronicled in the documentary *Fade to Black*, when an up-and-coming Kanye West gets the opportunity to present his songs to Jay-Z, already long established as one of the powerhouses in the industry. Sitting in a recording studio, he starts playing one of the tracks. Jay bobs his head while he listens, pulls off his hat, falls back in his chair and utters, "My God!" Kanye, seeing this, can't help but break into a wide grin. In his reply to Walker, Delane told him he now knew how Kanye must have felt in that moment.

"I care very deeply that there are more people who look like me succeeding," Walker said later, reflecting on his message to Delane. "I care very deeply that I'm not the only one. It's important that we look out for each other. I told him that I was proud of him and I told him some things to watch out for. It's a burden, and there are a lot of things that come with bearing that burden. His success begets other people's success, and that's a lot of pressure."

A year later, Delane received an email with the subject line *Apology*. The sender was the investor who had tried to sabotage PlayVS's Series A. In it, he explained he had been going through a difficult time and apologized to Delane for hurting him. Delane never responded to the message.

"I was like, 'Man, fuck this guy,'" he said later. "I'm a kid from the hood trying to do the best I can, trying to make it out and build something that hopefully impacts generations of people. You're a grown man who tried to leverage your privilege to lie about me and ruin my career. I struggle to find forgiveness for somebody like that. So I didn't. I just kept moving."

A few days after the Series A was announced, Delane returned to Detroit to spend the weekend with his family. He made plans to visit his grandmother for a Friday evening supper. That afternoon, he got lunch with some friends at a restaurant downtown. As they chatted, their conversation was interrupted by a visitor with a message: Dan Gilbert was in his office across the street; he'd heard the news and wanted to meet with Delane. *Oh shit*, thought Delane, who had only encountered Detroit's most powerful businessperson a handful of times. When lunch ended, he walked across the street to One Campus Martius, took the elevator upstairs and walked into Gilbert's office. The congratulatory phase didn't last long.

"I just have one question," Gilbert asked with playful brashness. "Why the hell did you leave Detroit and go do this somewhere else?"

"I met with Jake a year ago and he told me that I should leave!" Delane blurted, speaking of his last-ditch meeting with Jake Cohen.

Gilbert looked at one of his partners sitting in the room and shook his head. "Can you believe this?" As Delane made moves to leave, Gilbert stopped him. "Don't go anywhere," he boomed, and demanded that Delane wait in a conference room down the hall. He did so. Some minutes later, a few members of Gilbert's team entered.

"You're going to Cleveland," one of them said. That evening was Game Four of the NBA Finals, with the Golden State Warriors looking to win their third title in four years against Gilbert's Cavaliers.

Delane was baffled. He wasn't dressed for the occasion, and he had those plans to see his grandmother. "What? I can't go to Cleveland," he said. "I don't even have a car in Detroit. What are you talking about?"

The staffers could hardly stifle their laughter. "Dan's plane." A few moments later, Gilbert's security team was escorting Delane into an underground garage that, despite living his whole life in Detroit and working for one of Gilbert's companies, Delane had never known existed. Two black SUVs awaited. Gilbert's family and staff took their assigned seats. Delane found an empty space.

Wow, he thought. *So this is how billionaires move.*

Soon the vehicles rolled up to Coleman A. Young Airport, where the travelers were divvied up between the two private jets sitting on the runway. ("We all could have probably piled into one," Delane recalled, "but there were two fucking planes!") Delane boarded along with Gilbert's two sons. Gilbert got on, checked on his children, and took his seat. Once the flight was in the air, he unbuckled and sat down across from Delane.

"So," Gilbert asked him, "what the hell happened?" Delane rehashed the story of how he visited the DVP office when he was conflicted about leaving Detroit, and how Cohen had advised him to take the opportunity and move to Los Angeles.

"Don't worry about it," Gilbert assured him. When the twenty-minute flight landed in Cleveland, the group took another set of cars to Quicken Loans Arena and visited Gilbert's ownership suite for some quick eats. Gilbert made it a point afterward to have a conversation with Cohen within the bowels of the arena.

Down at floor level, Gilbert, Delane, and a handful of others settled into their seats in the first row. Sitting in a folding chair a few feet from the hardwood, Delane watched Steph Curry drop thirty-seven points, Kevin Durant record a triple-double, and the Warriors finish a four-game sweep of the Cavs. When the game ended, Delane boarded the plane back to Detroit. Gilbert's seat remained empty—he had stayed back to talk with LeBron James to try to convince him to re-sign with the franchise in the off-season. He ended up being unsuccessful; that night would turn out to be LeBron's last game as a Cavalier. But Delane didn't know any of this at the time. He was on a private passenger plane back to Detroit, still dressed in the clothes he was supposed to wear to his grandmother's. The whirlwind trip was over, but to Delane, the night felt like a beginning. Like he had truly arrived.

8

LIFTOFF

CHARLENE HAMM WAS sitting at home in Los Angeles one day scrolling through Twitter when she spotted something that made her pause.

Personal News: I will be joining the @PlayVS team as a designer in Santa Monica after I graduate, read the tweet, followed by a second one asking for leads on apartments.

The author was Parker Henderson, who, she learned after a few more clicks, was a high schooler in Northern California. *What esports company is hiring kids fresh out of high school?* she thought. *And they're paying enough that he can move out of his parents' house and live in LA?* The twenty-four-year-old Hamm clicked PlayVS's handle and found there was only one tweet—a link to an ESPN story announcing the existence of the company. She sent the account a direct message:

Hi, do you need any help building your social media presence?

She received a reply almost immediately. *Our CEO would love to talk with you*, it read, and provided his email address.

That was how Charlene Hamm found herself entering a Zoom chat with Delane a few days later. He hadn't asked for a resume or cover letter, only an interview via video chat. The meeting began, and there was Delane, sitting in front of a cinder-block wall that appeared to be in a windowless basement.

Oh no, Hamm thought to herself. *This is just this guy's passion project, and he's going to want me to work for free.*

Still, a little interviewing experience couldn't hurt. She stuck around and discussed her love of gaming with Delane. At the time, she was running social media for OpTic, an esports organization that competed in *Call of Duty* and *Counter-Strike*. Before that, she'd worked at GameStop and organized esports events on weekends while taking classes at a community college. Then she'd gotten an offer to manage a professional *League of Legends* team. She excitedly accepted. "I blew everything up on my way out," Hamm remembered. "I dropped out of school, quit both jobs, and moved into a house with a bunch of pro gamers. So, definitely a jarring experience for my mother." Like Delane once did for ProoFy's squad, Hamm served as a manager to the players, making their travel arrangements and, well, reminding them to eat. Unlike Delane, she loved it. The team earned decent money and eventually got acquired. Hamm hadn't left the gaming space since.

Now, as the interview wound down, Delane asked about her pay requirements.

Oh, this is the end of the conversation, she thought. *This is when I tell him he has to pay me, and he's just gonna peace out.*

"Something that's competitive with my current salary," she said.

"Okay," Delane said. "We can add 25 percent to that, and it comes with benefits."

"Cool," replied Hamm. "I'll put in my two weeks today."

Two weeks and a day later, Hamm began her job with PlayVS in the Science office. She spent her first few weeks studying pro esports teams and companies like Twitch and Discord to see what kind of identities they created for themselves on social media and how they engaged with users. She assembled a deck outlining PlayVS's social media plan—the tone, the types of content—and presented it to Delane. "Thanks," he said, "but there's nothing to post online yet, since we don't have a product." He admitted he'd hired her without having a specific job in mind—he simply recognized passion when he saw it and figured he'd have a need for her eventually. Hamm reluctantly accepted the explanation and returned to glorified busy work until that need arose.

Passion would be the primary requirement for any hire in PlayVS's early days. Hamm's first day of work coincided with that of another new employee with a love of all things esports: Laz Alberto, who had become so intertwined with the company in recent months that he and Delane decided he should come on full-time. Alberto's role as vice president placed him at the forefront of PlayVS's relationships with publishers—critical since, without publishers letting the company use their games, PlayVS had nothing. In the startup's first few months, Delane and Alberto cast a wide net, trying to nurture connections with the companies behind some of the world's most popular multiplayer titles: Riot Games (*League of Legends*), Epic Games (*Fortnite*), Activision Blizzard (*Overwatch*), Take-Two Interactive (*NBA 2K*), EA Sports (*Madden, FIFA, NHL*), Psyonix (*Rocket League*), Hi-Rez (*Smite*), and Nintendo (*Super Smash Bros., Mario Kart*), to name a few. They turned the bulk of their attention to Epic and Riot early on, given the massive popularity of *Fortnite* and *League of Legends*. Delane and Alberto flew out that spring to visit Epic Games's headquarters in North Carolina. The talks went well—so well that at one point Epic floated the possibility of announcing a partnership at the Electronic Entertainment Expo in June. "It felt almost too good to be true, to be honest," recalled Delane.

It was. While the company liked the idea of a formal presence in the high school space, it concluded that it didn't yet have the internal infrastructure to manage such a partnership. Epic decided to put the talks on hold.

Riot Games, on the other hand, had been entrenched in the education world for years. Back in 2014, the company had noticed that college students were organizing their own *League of Legends* competitions, so it held a series of online qualifiers, flew the top teams out to California for a tournament, and awarded the winners $100,000 in scholarship money. Later that year, Kurt Melcher, the associate athletic director at Robert Morris University Illinois, called up the folks at Riot Games to inform them he was planning to launch the first ever collegiate esports program—a varsity sport for which the competing students would receive scholarships for up to half their tuition. Nobody at Riot seemed to have any idea what he was talking about. *Is this guy asking us for money?* He wasn't, and soon enough it all made sense. The university began recruiting dozens of highly skilled *League* players to build its program, and Riot, in turn, created an internal task force to focus specifically on collegiate competitions. As the number of varsity programs slowly grew in the US—universities like UC Irvine and Ohio's Miami University came online next—Riot started thinking about the next logical step: high schools. But the publisher tread carefully.

"We're a game company," said Michael Sherman, one of the Rioters on the initial college team. "Even in college, there were always the questions of, *Is this a space we can understand? Is this a space that we would be welcomed into?* That's why we were so shocked with how college went, because we didn't think administrators would ever think of us as a complementary part of the university experience." Riot started to consider taking an approach modeled after the way high schools built robotics programs, with less focus on the competitive aspect and more on learning. Ultimately, the company decided not to pursue it. "It was early," said Sherman. "We didn't feel like we had enough of a brand in the rest of the academic space to want to then go play a role in a space with minors."

Delane and Alberto held several discussions with Riot about a potential partnership. The publisher soon assigned Sherman and another staffer on the college side, Matt Birris, as the points of contact for PlayVS. That summer, Delane, Alberto, and James Kozachuk headed to the Riot headquarters in Los Angeles, a sprawling newly built campus complete with a cafe, arcade, and outdoor basketball court. Inside, the group sat down across from Sherman and Birris and excitedly talked about the NFHS deal. They presented PlayVS as a turnkey solution to tapping into the high school market: just lend us your intellectual property and we'll grow your customer base for you.

The pitch fell flat. Sherman and Birris didn't share PlayVS's vision—they wanted to make sure Riot had a seat at the table, that it would have input into how high school *League of Legends* operated. Delane simmered as the meeting wore on. "You're sitting there talking to a company that's made $20 billion over the course of its lifetime," he said later. "They didn't really understand the value that we brought to the table."

When the meeting ended, the dejected trio headed outside to their car. "Man, fuck this," Delane grunted. "We're never going to work with these guys."

He was growing disheartened. PlayVS had nearly $16 million in capital and a deal with the NFHS, but no product, no states on board, and no partnerships with publishers. "I was raising all this money and building this company off of this idea that I could get this done," Delane recalled, "and we were struggling. As an entrepreneur and as a leader, I felt like an imposter." The company was in serious jeopardy of failing to launch the first season. A PlayVS platform with no publisher integrations would be like Spotify with no music—completely useless.

Delane called Birris's cell phone one night sporting a new tone. "Listen," he said. "We respect your approach. We want to find the best way to work with you." They held a heart-to-heart, agreeing to hit the reset button on their relationship and try again. Riot drafted up a document outlining the kinds of decisions with which it wanted to be involved—details like the format of the matches and the length and structure of the season. Plus, if high school esports was going to be attracting first-time players, there were some factors the publisher feared could turn them off if not handled properly, such as having fewer champions to choose from than their classmates who had been playing for a while, or simply getting their asses kicked by more experienced opponents.

The two sides reviewed the document during a several-hour meeting at Riot's headquarters. Shortly after, Delane and Alberto met Birris at a cafe next to the Science office. Delane knew that Riot, like practically all publishers, had been losing market share to Epic, which had seen *Fortnite*'s base rocket to 125 million users in the year since its launch. *League of Legends*'s monthly active user count, meanwhile, had climbed from 67 million in 2014 to 90 million in 2015, then edged up to 100 million the next year before Riot stopped releasing data, which was soon followed by reports that its growth had plateaued. What PlayVS was offering initially would likely total only a few thousand new players at most. But if the company could deliver what it was promising, that number would grow rapidly, and each of those high schoolers had the potential to become a dedicated *League* player. (Both *Fortnite* and *League* are free to play, but players can pay for cosmetic in-game goods or to bypass tedious early levels.) During the conversation, Delane casually mentioned that Epic had verbally agreed to partner with PlayVS and that the startup shouldn't be too far off from rolling out *Fortnite*. He and Alberto left the meeting feeling good about where things stood.

Not long after, Riot Games reached out and told PlayVS that it was coming on board. The deal was official. PlayVS finally had at least one game to launch with in its first season—and it was *League of Legends*, one of the most popular titles on the planet.

AS DELANE MADE more hires and PlayVS approached double-digit employees, Science relocated the startup to a larger space on the third floor with its own dedicated conference room. Delane bought his staff new monitors, and the team set up their new workstations in an area next to a virtual sticker startup and around the corner from a prayer app maker. At Delane's request, Yalda's seat remained next to his.

"Man," Delane said one day while the two shot the shit, "no matter how big this company gets, we'll always sit next to each other."

Hell no, thought Yalda, who was starting to get tired of the constant collaboration while he was trying to get work done, though outwardly he agreed with his boss.

One day, Yalda couldn't take it anymore. While Delane was out of the office, he unplugged his own computer and moved it to a desk on the other side of the room. Delane tried to woo him back, unsuccessfully. The two would have heated discussions on everything from design decisions to the direction of the company as a whole. Delane, still harping on the lessons he learned from his last startup, was focused on hiring on the business development side, while Yalda wanted more developers to help build the product. The other staffers would watch while disagreements between the old friends escalated into wrestling matches. Yalda, trained in martial arts, proved a worthy adversary, so Delane started resorting to sneak attacks. Yalda eventually placed a mirror on top of his monitor so he could see him approaching from behind.

"It kind of lightened the mood for people, though we always joked about how we weren't going to be able to do this once we had an HR department," recalled Yalda. "I grew up with brothers and cousins. It wasn't like I was getting bullied or anything. There was always love and respect. I think he just needed to get the energy out."

Delane chatted during the summer with an employee at Quarterly, a gift-box subscription startup being incubated by Science. Alinn Louv, the company's marketing director, had watched PlayVS's growth from the very beginning, when Delane, fresh off a flight from Detroit, came into the office and pitched his business. She had a front-row seat as he and his team secured the NFHS partnership and their first round of funding. Now, with Quarterly's growth stagnating, cash dwindling, and the writing quite legibly on the wall, she spoke with Delane about the possibility of coming to work for him. She became employee number eleven at PlayVS in July 2018, a few weeks before Quarterly shut down.

Not long after, an Arkansas educator named Adrian Risley reached out to Delane. Risley was a gaming enthusiast who grew up in a backwoods town hosting local area network, or LAN, parties, which generally entailed lugging desktop computers to a friend's basement, connecting them to the internet, and competing against one another online. He went on to land a job as chief technology officer of a nearby charter school. When students found out he played *League of Legends* at home, they prodded him to create an after-school club where they could hang out and compete in the game together under his supervision. In the school lounge one day, Risley talked with the school's athletic director about how esports would be the next big thing in high schools. She was skeptical, so he scoured the web for evidence to help his case. That's when he came across an article about

PlayVS and its deal with the NFHS. As he read more about the venture-backed startup and its founder, Risley realized he didn't just want to bring sanctioned esports to his school. He wanted to go work for the company—1,500 miles away in a state he'd never even visited. "It was 100 percent the answer to what I'd envisioned," Risley said later. "I absolutely knew it was going to work." He talked with his wife, Melanie, who worked in the same school district. They agreed he would apply for a job and see what happened.

One video interview with Delane later, the Risleys broke the news to their families that they were taking their one-year-old son and moving to California. They sold their house and a car, left their pensions behind, and a month after Adrian got his offer, the family was road-tripping across the country to settle down in Los Angeles.

While Delane beefed up PlayVS's roster in anticipation of the launch, Yalda and the engineers spent the summer building the software. The goal was to make the process of forming an esports team a plug and play solution for the schools; fewer chances for them to screw something up meant a higher likelihood that the season would be a success. Thus, the platform had to control all the minutiae of an athletic season: roster management, tracking wins and losses, compiling statistics, making a schedule—things that for any other interscholastic sport would be handled by a combination of coaches, officials, referees, and administrators. The developers built separate portals for students and coaches to log in to, access their team info, and view their upcoming opponents. When it came to scheduling, they created algorithms that would measure each team's skill level and generate fair matchups in an effort to minimize the number of blowouts.

But for any of that to matter, PlayVS needed something it still didn't have: students to play the games. As Labor Day approached and kids across the country returned to class, not a single state had committed to adopting esports for the upcoming season. Delane and Alberto had spent much of the summer meeting with associations that had shown interest, visiting many of the NFHS section meetings where decision-makers gathered. One of the states that had always seemed closest to coming on board was Connecticut, where more than a dozen high schools had esports teams that predated PlayVS by several years.

Back in 2016, Clint Kennedy, the director of tech and innovation for the New London public school system, had overheard two students goofing off in the school computer lab and approached them to ask if they could keep it quiet, only to have them tell him they thought the game they were playing, *League of Legends*, could make for a good addition to the tech curriculum. "I called their bluff," recalled Kennedy, "and said, 'Then I'd love to know more. So why don't you please be the teacher and show me how to play this game.'"

They did. And as Kennedy watched the boys strategize before the match, communicate throughout it, and improvise when things went awry, he realized he was witnessing them employ many of the soft skills his district had been trying to emphasize. Later that week, he made an announcement over the school's PA system: "Anyone looking to join an esports club should meet in the computer lab next Monday."

Eighty students showed up. Kennedy brought on a few interns and grew the single club into a statewide league, and Connecticut partnered with the Electronic Gaming Federation to help organize the competitions. So when PlayVS arrived on the scene with its NFHS deal in hand, signing up was the logical next step. Just after the school year began, the Connecticut Interscholastic Athletic Conference, the state's governing body for high school athletics, agreed to officially adopt esports. So began a domino effect. Four more states—Massachusetts, Rhode Island, Kentucky, and Georgia—soon followed, and others began more seriously considering it. Around the same time, PlayVS was able to finalize a deal with another publisher, Hi-Rez, to let students play *Smite*—a game similar in style to *League of Legends* though far less popular. But as Delane and the team looked at the amount of work still to be done before the season began, they decided the best course of action was to hold a controlled launch. PlayVS would concentrate its efforts for the first season solely on *League* and the five states that had thus far signed up. In turn, the startup dubbed the first season "Season Zero" to brand it more as a beta test than the real thing, a form of hedging in case things went off the rails.

Each new state that registered got handed off to Louv, who was tasked with briefing the administrators and providing them with emails they could blast out to their schools advertising the launch of NFHS-sanctioned esports. With Yalda busy working on the website and software, Louv was left to create the promotional messages on her own. "They looked very amateur," remembered Louv, "like someone who doesn't know how to use Photoshop put it together, which was exactly what had happened."

Still, the emails generated interest, and teachers and school administrators were soon reaching out to PlayVS. They had questions, like how exactly they were supposed to form their team or why this supposed "esports" league wasn't offering any sports games. (Many educators, it turned out, were under the impression that "esports" referred solely to titles like *Madden* or *FIFA*, so the startup was left to educate them on why *League of Legends* would hone many of the same skills as a sports game.) Delane made Louv the leader of a newly formed community team, which included Hamm, Risley, Kozachuk, and several others. Suddenly Louv, one of the startup's newest employees, found herself managing a unit in which some staffers were older, most had been there longer, and almost all knew more about esports than she did. But she grew into the role, so much so that Delane designated her to be his proxy in the office on days when he was gone. "It was rough," Louv admitted later. "I was constantly talking to Delane, telling him, 'I cannot believe that you're not here right now.'"

But the system worked. The community team chatted with the coaches at every newly onboarded school, ensuring they had the appropriate equipment and an up-to-date operating system. Risley, fresh out of his school district tech role, was often entrusted with walking the teachers through any technological issues, helping them upgrade their software as needed, download *League*, create accounts for the students, and communicate any requests to their schools' IT departments. The PlayVS team quickly realized there was no cookie-cutter solution to bringing the schools on board. Each was unique when it came to technology, administrative involvement, students' needs, and even billing, as some schools didn't have credit cards and thus needed to pay their students' fees by mail. "We had not planned for that at all," said Louv. "That was very novel for a lot of us who had been so ingrained in web-based tech startups—like, 'Wait, you want to mail us a check?'" Other schools would call the startup to complain they hadn't been receiving its onboarding emails, only to realize that all external messages were blocked by their IT department and the PlayVS domain needed to be explicitly approved.

For many of the coaches, consumed by class and after-school activities for much of the day, the most convenient time to chat was before homeroom. Every Season Zero school was located in the Eastern Time Zone, which meant those calls had to take place around 4:00 or 5:00 a.m. Pacific. The unwritten rule at PlayVS became that the first person to the office each morning would grab a community jug of coffee and box of doughnuts. During their brief breaks from work, employees would go downstairs and hop on a Bird electric scooter—the company had recently launched its pilot in Santa Monica—and zoom down to Sidecar Doughnuts, then ride back with the sugary treats in tow. As the season approached and requests from coaches became more urgent, the members of the community team gave out their personal email addresses and cell phone numbers so they could be reached at any time.

"The cell phone number thing was interesting," recalled Charlene Hamm. "I would get calls on Saturdays and early in the morning, waking me up at five o'clock. It was just one of those things—it was a startup and we were all invested in its success, so if a coach picks up the phone and calls us, we're going to pick up the phone and answer it. It wasn't a policy; it was just the culture. And I'm extremely glad that it's no longer the culture, because it was terrible."

When she wasn't fielding predawn phone calls, Hamm was building a guide for coaches—it covered everything from the best ways to assemble a *League* roster to how to sign up for Discord's chat feature—and writing the first season's official rulebook based on input from both PlayVS and Riot. Each week would have one competition day with two matches held back to back; all players on a team were required to be in the same location with a coach present, and the squads needed to be accessible to one another during the match. In the final weeks before launch, communication with the schools became an all-hands situation. Even the engineers—typically the furthest thing from an outward-facing role—were hopping on the phone with teachers at all hours of the day to make sure they'd be ready to go when the first matches began.

Launch day arrived for the sleep-deprived team. The staff, which had waited until the last possible moment to finalize the first week's matches in case any schools wanted to sign up at the eleventh hour, scrambled to set them just minutes before game time. Teams at ninety-seven schools across the five states had signed up for the first season—a drop in the bucket compared to Delane's nationwide ambitions, but a starting point.

Four p.m. on the East Coast hit: match time. With it came an ominous sound. *Ping. Ping. Ping. Ping.* Dozens of emails from coaches flooded into PlayVS's inbox. In almost every case, the coach in question was reporting that a handful of their students weren't able to activate the Champion Unlock feature, leaving them with only fifteen characters to choose from instead of the full 140-plus. Panicked, Louv picked up the phone and called Riot Games, secured batches of new codes, and sent them out to the coaches one by one. (The problem would continue for weeks until PlayVS discovered the source: the spreadsheet in which the codes were stored was automatically dropping the digit at the front of any number that began with a zero.) Other schools found out the hard way that their IT directors had failed to unblock the *League of Legends* domain in their web browser, leaving them clambering to get technical help while the matches were supposed to be getting underway.

But, finally, they did. Kids booted up *League of Legends* on PlayVS's platform and started to compete in America's first-ever officially sanctioned high school esports matches.

Late at night in Johannesburg, the engineers sat in their quiet coworking space, the only three people in the office, observing the matches across several monitors. They ran flawlessly; not a single one dropped.

"We were almost in tears," remembered Loubser. "It suddenly felt real. It's a small thing compared to somebody who launches a space shuttle, but I know what they felt like seeing the rocket go up and not crash."

• • •

DELANE WALKED INTO the restaurant of a swanky Midtown Manhattan hotel just after 9:00 a.m. wearing a black hoodie and black baseball cap, his eyes slightly bloodshot from a late night playing video games. He sat down at a table and a server in a freshly pressed white shirt handed him a menu. On it were items like smoked salmon flatbreads and $14 açaí bowls—which Delane didn't know because he didn't bother looking at it. When the waiter returned, he politely yet firmly asked for scrambled eggs and bacon. The man abided, though he could barely hide his surprise.

It was a few weeks after PlayVS's first season launched. The previous evening, Delane had met with representatives from Take-Two, the publisher of *NBA 2K*, a title he desperately wanted to be able to offer on his platform. After this breakfast with a reporter, Delane would be on his way across town to meet with a group of New York City investors. He wasn't going back to his room to change first—this was his VC meeting getup. Delane years earlier had decided to stop catering to the fashion tastes of the white and powerful. For the first few years after he'd entered the professional world, he'd switched his wardrobe to button-downs and Chelsea boots, concerned with what people might think otherwise. He created a squeaky-clean persona on Twitter, declining to follow his friends from back in Detroit and withholding from posting about the rap and hip-hop music he loved.

"I was a friendly, acceptable Black man for this white community," Delane said. "As I got older, I realized that it made me so unhappy. So I started to be who I am, follow who I want to follow, talk to who I want to talk to." He switched his wardrobe back to the clothes he liked. Sometimes he heard about it from those with whom he did business. "People have told me, 'Don't wear your hat to the back,' like they can control my appearance," he said. "I can't be proud of who I am, be proud of our culture? I can't wear my hat to the back when that's authentic to me? What if polo shirts are offensive to me? I'm not telling anyone not to wear polo shirts."

Delane noticed the looks when he showed up to events with educators or meetings with potential partners wearing a hoodie and basketball sneakers. Though he was happier to be expressing something closer to his true self, the nuances of the choice weighed on him. "This is a very relationship-driven business, and we've got a goal to get into every school in every state, and eventually different countries," he said, munching his eggs and bacon. "That's going to take some sacrifice on my part. I don't want to sacrifice who I am, but I do oftentimes battle with it—like, do I have to be more cautious of these things? Sometimes my pride and ego can get in the way of that, because it'll be like, 'Why should I have to do this when my white counterparts don't?' They don't have to worry about this level of scrutiny. But then, I've got an employee who literally sold his house. He quit his job that he had for ten years, his wife quit her job, and they moved across the country with a baby to work for me. I've got other employees who left family, left friends, left comfortable environments to come and be lonely in LA and focus only on work. I've got a responsibility to them. I've got to do what's in the best interest of them. So it will probably always be a struggle for me. It's a crazy world that we live in."

The concept of pattern-matching has existed for just about as long as venture capital. It's a process by which investors study past successful investments and try to replicate them by seeking out companies with similar characteristics—factors like industry, target customer demographic, and the age, education, and personality type of the founder. In today's tech world, that leads to a disproportionate number of investments using a tried and true formula: young, male, Ivy League- or Stanford-educated, and white. In 2018, the year PlayVS secured its Series A, only 1 percent of venture capital went to Black founders. Given the overwhelming percentage of VCs that are white, and the fact that individuals' social groups tend to look like themselves, finding founders of color can take extra effort. Which was why, speaking with a prominent angel investor before a trip to Atlanta, Delane was so disappointed to learn the man had never visited the city, long considered a Black mecca. As his stature rose, Delane began using his platform on Instagram and Twitter to promote other Black entrepreneurs. He encouraged investors in his circle to give a look at those who had been too often passed over.

"I think this is the case for so many Black kids who grow up in similar impoverished circumstances as me," he said. "All you have to do is expose us to the game, teach us the rules, give us the boundaries of how we have to play, and we'll excel at it. We just need that chance."

Delane had spoken of becoming a billionaire since he was a child. At the time of PlayVS's launch, there were 607 billionaires in the United States. Only three of them were Black: Michael Jordan, Oprah Winfrey, and the investor Robert F. Smith. While entrepreneurs like Mark Zuckerberg, Jeff Bezos, Snapchat's Evan Spiegel, and Google's Larry Page and Sergey Brin became billionaires by the time they were thirty-five, the tech industry hadn't created a single Black billionaire. But Delane kept the goal in mind. When he was struggling, he would think about the way the game had been rigged against him since birth.

"I've had that chip on my shoulder my whole life," he said. "There's so few Black people who are given opportunities in tech. I'm trying to break the mold. So I'm not carrying just my chip, but a stack."

Jon Sakoda at NEA had noticed Delane's chip—or chips—for some time. The mindset seemed to give him an extra gear as he built his company and tried to take high school esports nationwide. "He wants to prove people wrong, because there are people that didn't think that he'd be able to do this," Sakoda said. "But it's not at anyone else's expense. It's not a zero-sum game. So that chip on his shoulder is being harnessed in a way that's incredibly positive."

That positivity revealed itself almost as soon as PlayVS's first season got underway. As matches began, coaches and parents from across the country began emailing Delane and his staff, describing how joining their school's esports team had already made an appreciable difference in their student or child's life. There was the girl who had tried and quit all the other sports she'd played, joined as the only freshman and only girl on her school's esports team, and liked it so much she was considering pursuing a career in it. The boy with no limbs who was able to participate on his first varsity team. Countless teachers who saw their introverted students finally breaking out, their unengaged youths now interested in school again. Delane and the community team started collecting the emails and reading them out loud to the entire staff at the all-hands meeting each Monday, a tradition the company would continue through the years.

One mother didn't think a letter was enough. The woman in Massachusetts wrote a note explaining that her son had never played sports and didn't have many friends. He'd joined his school's team, made a bunch of new companions, and turned out to be a damn good *League of Legends* player too. She asked if, the next time she was traveling to California for work, she could bring her son with her to meet the PlayVS employees. They told her she could. A few weeks later, the woman and her son showed up at the Science office. Delane was in a meeting at the time, and when he walked out, he and the woman ended up face-to-face.

"I stood there and put my hand out to shake," Delane recalled, "and she just busted out crying. I couldn't believe it. I hugged her and then I go and shake her son's hand. He's like shaking, kind of nervous. She was telling us how much this meant to her, how much this meant to her son, how excited and happy he was being on this team, having this experience.

"It was such a surreal moment for us. We sit in this room every day thinking, *How do we impact kids' lives positively? How do we build the best esports experience they can have at this level?* But it's not often that we get a chance to physically meet the people that are most affected by what we're doing. Having that moment, and sharing that moment with our team, was just so wild. It was one of the greatest things I've ever been a part of."

ASHLEY HODGE HAD a challenger.

It was one of the first days of esports practice at Colquitt County High School, a boxy structure that sits in an unincorporated part of southern Georgia, miles away from anything. The brash boy approached Hodge, who had recently been named the team's head coach, in the computer lab and asked whether she was actually any good at *League of Legends*.

"How about," she said to him, "you play me one-on-one and find out?"

The student agreed. He and Hodge sat down at two machines side by side. She didn't plan to make a big deal out of the showdown, but he called over his friends.

"Gather around," he hollered. "I'm about to beat the coach!"

Hodge and the boy chose their champions. They started the match. And Hodge absolutely obliterated him.

The boy walked away, his swagger noticeably absent. Hodge assumed—quite accurately, as it would turn out—that his team-mates wouldn't let him live the whooping down for months. She was satisfied.

"That's one of the true joys I get in life," she said later. "To watch the devastation come across the boys' faces in those moments."

He wasn't the first, and he wouldn't be the last. Other boys, some of whom had never played *League* in their lives, would routinely walk into the computer lab and proudly tell Hodge they'd be able to defeat her. She started referring to their boldness as "macho man syndrome." Invariably, she would tear them apart.

"I'd be like, 'Yeah, bro. That's why I'm coaching you. Because I play this game, and I play it well.'"

Soon, the boys mostly learned their lessons. When any of them pushed back against her instructions, she would ask if they wanted to challenge her.

"No, Mrs. Hodge," they'd reply.

"Well okay, then," she'd say, and thus would end the attempted insurrection.

What the boys didn't know was that Hodge had been selected to be the coach largely because she'd been a successful gamer all her life. Of course, they didn't know anything about the gaming abilities of her male assistant coach either, but they didn't make any assumptions about him.

Hodge had started playing online competitively as a teen. She would enter in-person *Call of Duty* tournaments with cash prizes, often showing up only to be asked whom she was there to watch. "No, man," she'd say with her Georgia drawl. "I'm here to compete."

She would then proceed to sweep the floor with the males in the room. Playing in tournaments, where the competition sat physically next to you, was fun, especially when you got to beat them. Playing online was more of a minefield. Competing in *Call of Duty* with her headset on, Hodge would shout out some instructions—"Let's check behind the building!"—and the direct messages from her male counterparts would stream in, mocking her twang or cracking immature sexual jokes.

Gamergate made things worse. Entire books could be dedicated to the ordeal—and several have been—but the essential details are that the episode began in 2014 when a young man wrote a blog post about his ex-girlfriend, video game developer Zoë Quinn, and in it implied she had slept with a reporter at the gaming website Kotaku in exchange for a positive review of her game—never mind that no such positive review actually existed. An angry online mob formed around the idea of "ethics in video game journalism." The movement soon morphed into a hotbed of misogyny, a backlash to what those gamers viewed as an unacceptable years-long feminization of the video game industry. While it's unclear how many of the men and boys tweeting and commenting actually grasped the nuances of the supposed cause for which they were fighting, what was clear was that they used it as an excuse to unload on women in gaming. Quinn received thousands of threats, as did Brianna Wu, a developer who came to her defense in part by mocking male gamers for "fighting an apocalyptic future where women are 8 percent of programmers and not 3 percent." Both women were doxxed—having their home addresses posted online—and Wu fled her house after receiving death threats, rape threats, and photos of mutilated dogs. The FBI identified four suspects but didn't press any charges.

The incident energized the darkest corners of the gaming world. Suddenly, online trolls felt empowered, like their male toxicity had justification. "Things got way worse after Gamergate," recounted Hodge. "People would pile on, and everyone else would just let it happen." During gameplay, guys would ask if she wanted to blow them, then make gagging sounds through their microphones. Others would make comments about raping her. Hodge ended most gaming sessions upset. She stopped wearing her headset to play *Call of Duty*—an integral aspect of competing, but no longer worth it.

The abuse waned over the years, and Hodge would go on to marry one of the good guys, a fellow video game enthusiast whom she met in college, and get a job teaching English at Colquitt. It wasn't long after that she was called upon to lead the esports team. More than four hundred students showed up to the first meeting. Many were turned away because of the GPA requirements, left trying to get their grades up so they could join, but 130 did end up on Hodge's Season Zero roster. She created an A-team of her best players, then let the rest of the students form their own units and shifted them around as needed. They came from a wide range of academic ability levels, some in honors courses and some in remedial ones. Many were shy, socially awkward, and lacking friends. The kids remained mostly quiet for the first few practices, only speaking as necessary during gameplay. But as weeks passed, the relationships grew into friendships. Hodge would spot the members of the team, previously from different social castes, mingling in the hallway or eating together at lunch.

"Honestly, when we first started, I was jealous," she said. "Why couldn't this have been a thing when I was in high school? It would have made school so much easier for me. Maybe I wouldn't have been bullied nearly as much. But I'm happy that I was given this opportunity. I don't want my kids to have to go through all of the nonsense that I went through."

Hodge noticed one girl barely speaking during her *League of Legends* practices. The girl had a knack for the game, though, and wanted to improve. Hodge told the girl that if she wanted to log on after school, Hodge could teach her a thing or two. The one-on-one sessions helped the student up her game. Soon she was breaking out of her shell, acting as a leader during matches. She went on to become the captain of her team. Another boy, a senior, was a habitual class-cutter on the verge of flunking out. He joined the esports club, made some friends, and started actually showing up to school, even dropping in on Hodge's extra help sessions despite the fact that she wasn't his English teacher. He salvaged his grades, graduated, and secured an esports scholarship at a local college.

"A lot of these students' stories," said Hodge, "still make me cry when I think about them."

Two of Colquitt's *League* teams climbed into the state's top-ten rankings during the season, landing the esports club on the cover of the local paper multiple times. By the following year, when the coach of the school's state championship–winning football program was fired due to improper behavior, the esports team was getting a more raucous ovation than the football team at Friday afternoon pep rallies.

But most of the students' parents weren't concerned with how good the team was or wasn't. When the coaches held a cookout and awards ceremony for the players after the season, a group of parents approached to thank them. "We're a Title I school, which means this is a high poverty area," Hodge said later. "A lot of those parents are working multiple jobs. Now they knew that their kid had a safe place to go until they got home. They were just grateful for that and for the friends the kids have made."

While hundreds of teams up and down the East Coast were having their own unique esports experiences, Laz Alberto was essentially living on the road, crisscrossing the country by plane to meet with state athletic associations. He spent thirty consecutive days that fall without landing back home in Los

Angeles, traveling from bustling Nashville to the mountains of South Dakota and Utah to spread the gospel of high school esports.

The Season Zero state championships in January would send him on tour once again. PlayVS had decided to help the states run their title matches, thanks in part to the input of Charlene Hamm, who knew from her past experience organizing live competitions that things could go haywire if there weren't people there who knew exactly what they were doing—and in some cases, even if there were. The startup hired a small Philadelphia-based esports company to handle event production, including livestreaming, emceeing, and having a duo of shoutcasters (the esports word for broadcasters) perform commentary during the matches. The slate would consist of five championships in five states over the course of nine days.

With nearby Connecticut, Rhode Island, and Massachusetts already on board, PlayVS was pushing hard to get New York, home to nearly a million high school students, to officially adopt esports. The governing body there had been heavily considering it, as esports clubs had sprung up all over the state, many of them using companies like HSEL to run their matches. In the weeks leading up to the Connecticut state championship, a group of executives from New York expressed interest in checking out one of the championships in person to PlayVS. Alberto tried to convince them to come to Massachusetts, which would be holding its matches in the Gillette Stadium complex, but the group opted for Connecticut; the event was in Meriden, just over two hours' drive from Albany. The PlayVS team arranged for a bus to pick them up in the state capital and drive them out.

The same week as the first esports championships, an unwelcome visitor made its way into the eastern United States: the polar vortex, a mass of frigid air that occasionally escapes the North Pole and pushes its way down south. Alberto arrived on his plane from Southern California, stepped out of the airport in Albany, and was smacked in the face by single-digit temperatures and a subzero wind chill. He and the New York administrators rode to Maloney High School, which had recently renovated its one-thousand-person-capacity auditorium. The championship would be a best-of-three series between undefeated Manchester High and Woodstock Academy, which had lost only one match all year—to Manchester. Pride, bragging rights, and the first esports trophy ever to be awarded in the US were on the line. On the auditorium's stage, two rows of computers sat parallel to the audience, a black curtain dividing them so the teams couldn't see each other. Each monitor was outfitted with a camera to live-stream the players' faces on Twitch.

As the school day ended, it became clear that some combination of frigid temperatures and a lack of communication about the event to Maloney's student body and the neighboring districts had warded off any would-be spectators. The theater's chairs remained empty, save for twenty athletics executives from New York. While Alberto helped prepare for the match, he detected a distressed look on the faces of some of the hired production crew. He went backstage to find out what was going on.

The answer wasn't pretty. On the drive up from Brooklyn, the Arctic temperatures inside the van had frozen the team's equipment. Nothing—not the cameras, not the microphones—was turning on.

Alberto ran from backstage to the seating area to let his guests know there would be a slight delay. When he returned, he found out that the frost in the equipment had started thawing out, and the resulting condensation had made the problem even worse.

No audience. No equipment. This was very bad.

Back in Santa Monica, Hamm sent Alberto yet another in a series of increasingly panicked texts. It was match time, and he had gone dark.

What is going on over there??

Still no reply.

Backstage, the crew tested the equipment again and again, only to be disappointed. "I'm running around and trying to keep everyone calm," Alberto recalled, "talking to the teams and coaches, saying, 'Don't worry! Just a little longer,' then composing myself and coming back into the audience to tell the executives it was going to be fine, then going backstage and freaking out all over again. It was incredibly stressful. And this went on for at least an hour, maybe two."

Mercifully, the crew got the equipment running—kind of. The event could be played and the shoutcasters could shout, but the streaming equipment was completely fried. Finally, the games got underway; Alberto's heart rate returned to normal. In front of an audience of twenty, Woodstock Academy pulled off an upset and took down the undefeated team from Manchester in two straight matches. Afterward they high-fived, gave interviews to a couple of local newspaper reporters, and accepted their trophy in front of flashbulbs.

"It wasn't until they were standing there holding that state association trophy," remembered Woodstock's coach Thomas Young, "the same one they see in the case at school for soccer or basketball, that it set in: This is a big deal. You just won. This is not something that has been done before. You're the first-ever state champions."

As he left Maloney High, Alberto couldn't believe his misfortune, that an esports event—an indoor gaming competition!—

could be so derailed by the weather. He went to dinner with the New York folks and attempted to smooth things over, explaining that this wasn't exactly the best representation of what PlayVS envisioned for its championships. They were plenty polite about it, but somehow it felt like damage had been done.

"The Connecticut state championship," Alberto said later, "set the tone in a very alarming way."

Hamm flew out and met Alberto in Massachusetts the following day, and the pair drove to Foxborough for the next event. Hamm listened to the story from the day before, the two of them sharing a laugh about it but praying to the gaming gods that things would go better the second time around.

They did. The lure of an event on Patriot Place next to Gillette Stadium—the work of a well-connected state executive—had drawn packed buses from schools all over the state. The students filled a theater and watched two schools duke it out, for many of the kids their first time visiting the hallowed grounds where Tom Brady played. Observing the *League* matches from the audience, the Mahar Regional kids were in their element. Justin and Isaiah volunteered to run a fifty-fifty raffle and chatted casually with a rep from Riot Games, the maker of their beloved game. It didn't matter that their team wasn't playing.

For a day, Kyle Magoffin thought to himself, *my boys are on top of the world.*

IN THE GYMNASIUM of Collins High School in the Kentucky town of Shelbyville, Seth Reinhart stood wearing his only suit, waiting for his guests to arrive. Reinhart had grown up obsessed with video games, at one point ranking as one of the top *World of Warcraft* players in North America. His knowledge of computers landed him a job as the IT director at his local high school.

Reinhart was on his way to troubleshoot a classroom machine one day when a teacher stopped him in the hallway.

"I know you're a gamer," he said. "Did you see that the KHSAA"—Kentucky's governing athletic body—"approved of esports?"

"Dude, you're pulling my leg," said Reinhart. "There's no way that's a thing."

The colleague brought up the press release on his phone and handed it over. Reinhart had seen enough. He marched down the hall to the athletic director's office, introduced himself, and gave a breathless pitch as to why Collins High needed to create an esports team, throwing in the fact that the *League of Legends* world championship that year had garnered more viewers than the Super Bowl.

"E-what?" came the reply.

But a few days later, Reinhart found himself pitching the school principal using a deck he'd cobbled together on his laptop. He presented his first slide, which focused on the idea of getting more kids involved in after-school activities. The principal stopped him short.

"I don't need to hear anymore," he said. "I'm mad that we're late to the game. If this is going to get more kids involved, shame on us for not having it already."

That was how Reinhart—the kid who failed to take school seriously and, much to his mother's chagrin, played video games isolated in his room for hours on end—became the esports coach at Collins High. "If you would have told me a few years ago that I would have a job even interacting with students," he said later, "I would have laughed at you. If you'd told me that job would involve gaming, I would have walked out of the room."

The school decided to keep the roster small for the first season, treating it as something of a trial run. Reinhart recruited a group of four friends who played *League*. But he still needed a fifth. That's when he learned that a quiet student named Connor had heard about the team and was sending Instagram messages to his classmates trying to find out who was in charge. Connor had moved into town a few years earlier. He didn't have many friends. Reinhart figured he would give him a shot. He invited him down to a practice, where the teammates slotted him in as their fifth player for the day.

He proceeded to almost single-handedly destroy the opponent. *Oh*, thought Reinhart, *we've found our guy*.

Collins's squad was formidable, routinely dominating on match days. Word spread throughout the school. Connor, practically anonymous a few months earlier, started wearing his jersey on game days and getting fist bumps from students in the hall—"That's Connor; he's the best player on the esports team." The team made it weeks into the season before it lost its first match. "It was a ragtag group of players and myself," recalled Reinhart, "and we were building something and really, really pouring our hearts and souls into it. Sometimes it felt like a Disney movie." Later, when the high school decided to make an announcement inviting students to come out to join the team, Reinhart arrived at work the next morning to find a line of students waiting outside his office, armed with questions about the games the team would be playing and what kind of GPA they needed to reach to be eligible. "It was like opening the floodgates," said Reinhart. "This is something I tell people when I'm talking through why they need a program. It's no longer a question of 'if'—it's inevitable. It's not, 'Build it and they will come.' It's, 'They're already here, and now we need to catch up, put guardrails around it, and steer it in a positive direction.'"

As his team pushed its way into the Kentucky playoffs with only a single regular-season loss, Reinhart convinced the school's administration to host the state championship in its gym. The hope, of course, was that it would be a home-field match for Collins, but the team went on to lose in heartbreaking fashion in the semifinals. Still, Reinhart was pumped to be at the center of the esports universe for a day. Outside, Alberto and Hamm pulled up in an Uber and moseyed across the school grounds, not having the slightest clue where they were supposed to go. They set the state championship trophy onto the football field turf and snapped a few photos to post on Twitter. A security guard traversed the lawn to confront them.

"What are you guys doing?" he asked the two fresh-faced professionals. "Are you supposed to be in class?"

Inside the gym, Reinhart's walkie-talkie crackled. His guests had arrived.

After a successful event that crowned another inaugural champion, Alberto and Hamm prepared to order a ride back to the airport in Louisville. "Not gonna happen," Reinhart told them. "You're in the middle of nowhere." He offered to give them a ride, then changed out of his suit and into a windbreaker sporting the logo of the gaming company 100 Thieves.

This guy is pretty into this, thought Alberto and Hamm.

Meanwhile, the temperature outside was plummeting below freezing as the polar vortex forced its way farther south. Alberto and Hamm got to the airport and boarded their plane to Atlanta for the final championship. After they sat on the runway for what felt like way too long, an announcement came over the PA system: the aircraft's landing equipment had frozen. Back in the terminal, the pair learned there were no more flights to Georgia that night. The only option was to book a roundabout connecting flight to Chicago, where temperatures were even lower.

While they waited to board their new plane, Hamm called up Alinn Louv back in Santa Monica to update her. "I'm just so angry," she said.

"About what?" asked Louv.

"Nothing's going right," she complained, still thawing out, "and I'm tired . . . and I'm cold, Alinn!"

Louv laughed. "Let me know when you get to Georgia."

Alberto and Hamm made it to Atlanta and concluded their championship marathon at a freshly built gaming cafe in an exposed-brick loft. After nine days of video games, chaos, cancellations, and relentless frozen temperatures, they hopped on a plane toward the welcoming blue skies and yellow sun of California.

In the Science office, when the last championship wound down, Delane gathered his staff by the water cooler. Never one to dwell on victories, he delivered a short speech about how far they'd all come and how far they still had to go.

Privately, though, Delane felt some sense of accomplishment. Throughout the season, PlayVS had gotten dozens of emails directly from students, and the topic they touched on most wasn't getting to play video games in school. It was finding people with whom they enjoyed spending time. "I can certainly relate to kids who don't feel like they're part of the school community," Delane said later. "I grew up independent of my family for a large part of my life. Even in my own family, I felt like an outcast. So that aspect, of building community and bridging that gap for people who feel like they don't have community but desire it—it's personal for me. I keep that in mind when we think about the work that we're doing."

After the season, Mahar Regional's co-principal took the team's first varsity letter, mounted it in a shadowbox, and shipped it to PlayVS. Delane displayed it in the office for all to see, a tangible reminder of the effects of the work they were doing. A successful first season that, hopefully, would be the first of many.

Delane (left) and DaeLon, circa 1997.
Courtesy of Olivia Thompson

Delane, Terri, and DaeLon.
Courtesy of Olivia Thompson

Delane with a four-monitor setup in the early PlayVS days. *Photograph by Sean Yalda*

Laz Alberto and Delane in Scottsdale the morning after securing their deal with the NFHS. *Photograph by Laz Alberto*

The makeshift PlayVS office in a Science conference room. *Photograph by Laz Alberto*

Laz Alberto, Delane, Sean Yalda, and D'Andre Ealy in Austin for SXSW 2019. *Photograph by Marcus Carey*

(ABOVE) Kyle Magoffin instructs a student on Mahar Regional High School's esports team. (RIGHT) Delane posts up against Peter Pham in Austin. *Courtesy of PlayVS/Marcus Carey*

Cherry Creek (Colorado) High School students compete in a *League of Legends* match. *Courtesy of PlayVS*

The early PlayVS team. Clockwise from top left: Delane Parnell, James Kozachuk, Adrian Risley, Zachary Carter, Alinn Louv, Heather Shelton, Will Smidlein, Laz Alberto, Spencer Thurston, Charlene Hamm, and Sean Yalda. *Courtesy of Laz Alberto*

9

THE MAKING OF

A HUSTLER

FOR THE YOUNG men on Burgess, life more or less revolved around basketball. The next road, Chapel Street, had a small park with a court where they could play. But the city seemed to have forgotten it existed. The park's grass was often ankle-high, and the cracked cement playing surface housed a single netless rim. The court itself was shaped like a half-circle drawn by a drunk person, and it was far too small—taking a three-pointer required stepping off the pavement and onto the uneven terrain. Occasionally, someone in the neighborhood would create an alternative by installing a hoop on a small dead end off Burgess. The makeshift court was packed after school and on weekends. Each Sunday, neighbors came down to play games of three-on-three or four-on-four. The winners stayed on and the losers went to the back of the line, which made the matches extra competitive. This would last until the hoop was broken by a forceful dunk, or until the police came and confiscated it, and then it was back to the park.

When Terri got internet for the house, Delane—always plugged into the latest music—would download the newest hits on LimeWire, load them onto a flash drive, and give it to a friend's uncle who deejayed at local clubs in exchange for some cash. Delane and DaeLon started a lawn-mowing business when they were young. Delane's job was to secure customers while DaeLon performed the physical labor. The innocent operation earned them a few bucks, but it was chump change compared to what kids in the neighborhood made dealing drugs. Dope was the easiest and most reliable way to make money. Plus, being part of the game at least meant that you were part of something.

"In the hood, it's easy to fall into all of this stuff that you're not supposed to," Delane would say later. "You just want to be a part of that community. The last thing you want is to be an outsider. Being an outsider is how you get fucked with."

Surviving the streets meant proving you wouldn't be pushed around. Once, while Delane and his friends played on the dead-end court, a young kid kept riding his bike through their pickup game. Fed up, one of the guys tossed the basketball into his path. The kid rode off, came back a few minutes later, reached into his pants, and stuck the barrel of a gun into the guy's stomach.

"Play with me if you want," he said.

"Whoa!" the other guys yelled. "Chill out! Chill out!"

The boy held the gun there for a moment before deciding he'd made his point. He tucked it back into his waistband and rode off.

Living on Burgess, Delane's mother Terri had become close with the Bibbs family down the block. One of their sons, Keith, was four years older than Delane. Keith wasn't much of a basketball player; he would come down to the court and take a few jumpers but step aside when the games began. If he was passing by and saw Delane on the court, though, he would stick around and watch him play. Keith took a liking to the kid. He watched out for him. He would refer to Delane as "my little homie"—something that people in the neighborhood took notice of, including some of the other guys Keith's age with status on the streets. If Delane did or said something that could have pissed off the wrong person, Keith would defuse it before it caught up with him, and Delane often didn't find out about it until after the incident was over. Keith was in the game, but he never pressured Delane to do things he didn't want to. It was quite the opposite:

If guys from the neighborhood were planning to rob someone or get into other trouble, Keith would pull him aside. "You sit back," he'd say. "This ain't you."

Keith, for his part, was involved in his share of extracurricular activities, but he always looked out for Delane.

"You're gonna make it out of here," Keith would tell him. "I'm gonna make sure of it."

"He kept me out of trouble," Delane recalled. "Whatever I needed, he made sure I was good. He made sure nobody messed with me. He made sure people respected me, and even if they didn't respect me, he made sure they showed me respect."

When Delane was about eleven, his Aunt Libby had purchased and moved into her own house in Southfield while taking classes toward her MBA. She had begun subscribing to business magazines like *Forbes* and *Inc.*, which sat in stacks on the dining room table where she did her work. She noticed that Delane would leaf through them when he came over.

"You had this determined, business-minded kid who was trying to decide what he was going to do next," she recalled. "He had the type of personality where he was willing to try things and fail. He would read these stories about companies with young founders, and it seemed appealing and attainable. It seemed like he was thinking, 'Hey, I can do this, too.'" Libby started buying Delane copies of the magazines. She and Terri would ask him questions about them, making sure he read certain articles. Delane's interest in business and entrepreneurship grew.

The young men from Burgess and Chapel hung out with each other, but if it came down to it, they had loyalty to their own streets. One afternoon Delane and some friends played basketball at the park against some guys from Chapel. The Chapel team's ringleader was deeply embedded in the local gang, which made him practically royalty. The day's matchup had been heated.

Tensions were high. The guy fouled Delane hard, and the two started arguing. People like that knew they were untouchable—they could keep yapping and nobody would do anything about it. Delane was usually smart enough to back down. But he was also extremely competitive. On this day, his anger grew, and he kept shouting back. Soon, a circle formed around the two young men. As things escalated, another one of the Chapel guys stepped into the middle of the pack and sucker-punched Delane square in the side of the face. Delane stumbled back, then lurched forward to take a swing. Keith jumped in and wrapped both arms around him.

"No, no, no," he yelled, keeping Delane restrained while he wrestled him away and out of the crowd. "You don't want to do that. That shit will end up really bad."

Delane cooled off, and Keith talked to him as he walked him home. "We can't go to war with each other," Keith told him. "It doesn't make sense. Especially over a basketball game."

The punch was the only injury that day. It could have been far worse. Not long after, an equally petty argument at the local high school would result in a sixteen-year-old teen being shot dead and three others hurt.

"People kill each other, unfortunately, over things like stepping on each other's shoes," Delane recalled about the neighborhood. "There's no value associated with your life, so what's this other person's life worth? So, people kill each other over stupid senseless things."

Terri knew she needed to get her sons off the streets. When they were fourteen and thirteen, she secured DaeLon a job at a butcher and Delane a job at a Sprint Nextel store owned by her friend, Sam, located in a strip mall on Telegraph Road in neighboring Southfield. On school days, Delane would sneak onto the afternoon bus with a friend who lived in an apartment complex near the store, get off at the closest stop, and walk the last half mile. Just around the corner from the strip mall were attractive houses with lush gardens and large front lawns. It was only three miles from Burgess, but it felt like a different world.

"I was in a store with hundreds of thousands of dollars of merchandise," remembered Delane, "and I was safe. No robberies, no break-ins, no guns. It was just great. It was great to have freedom, it was great because I was learning, it was great because I was making money."

Delane took on any menial task Sam assigned him. He held a sign on the sidewalk next to the main road directing people to the little shop in the strip mall. He swept and mopped the floors, took inventory, and cleaned the bathroom. All the while, he observed Sam hawking Blackberries and flip phones, customers walking away pleased, the register racking up hundreds of dollars with each transaction. It took only a few months before Sam invited him to try his hand at sales. He sent him out onto the floor without any formal training. Delane spent the first few weeks figuring out what worked. If a tactic failed with one customer, he tried a different approach with the next one. If it succeeded, he filed it away for next time. He learned what features to emphasize based on the questions a customer was asking and how to vary his level of aggressiveness to match their dispositions. Still not old enough to work legally, he got paid in cash. He would get home and shove most of the bills into a shoebox he kept under his bed, money he eventually began thinking of as a college fund. The rest he carried around in wads in his pocket. During football practice, instead of storing the money in his gym bag, he stuffed it into his uniform pants to keep it from getting stolen.

Back home on Burgess, if you wanted to buy something, the primary option was a sketchy gas station on Chapel and Eight

Mile where customers on their way in or out frequently got held up. "There was always someone outside of that gas station," remembered Libby. "I wonder if there's someone outside right now, trying to sell something. A CD, a shirt, some drugs, something." Now, working in Southfield, Delane had the freedom to safely buy himself clothes, records, gadgets, and anything else he wanted with the money he'd earned. He soon opened his first bank account and watched with great interest as his balance grew following each deposit.

Delane's older cousin, Juan, paid close attention to his younger relative's work ethic and encouraged him to keep working hard and making money. "That's the person that believed in me more than anybody," Delane said later. "My cousin Juan is my heart." Delane often spent weekends at Juan's, sleeping in the spare bedroom his cousin kept for him.

All the while, Delane watched people in his neighborhood fall victim to drugs and violence. "You were always on edge," he recalled. "Any moment, something bad could happen. Anything could trigger anybody. In the blink of an eye, your life could be different. When I was able to go to work, I was out of the hood for six to eight hours a day. It was an escape." Delane helped a friend from a nearby neighborhood get a job at the cell phone store. The kid proved to be lazy, complaining, and sometimes refusing to perform simple tasks. "I fired him quick," said Delane. "I wasn't letting anybody mess up my money."

Around that time, Ashley, a girl on the football team's cheerleading squad, caught Delane's eye. It turned out that their families knew each other, though the two teens had never met. Delane would treat her to the ice cream truck that parked next to the park where they practiced and try to impress her by buying it with his wads of cash. The two became a couple, an on-and-off relationship—mostly on—that would last through high school and beyond. Delane spent some of his limited down time at Ashley's house with her and her family. Soon enough, he stopped playing football so he could dedicate even more time to work. He would stay until nine at night and complete his homework during breaks. He picked up weekend shifts and was soon working more than forty hours a week while just fourteen.

Getting Delane to and from the store when the school bus wasn't an option became a community affair. Sometimes Terri would pick him up. Other times Delane would hitch a ride with a neighbor or his Aunt Courtney.

Some days, it was Keith's turn to serve as chauffeur. He would come get Delane driving Terri's black Oldsmobile, which she would lend him for the errand. One night, Keith and Delane were on their way back from Southfield when a police cruiser pulled them over. The two cops had them step out of the car, then pushed them up against it. They pulled out anything inside the vehicle that wasn't glued down and tossed it on the ground. When they didn't find any contraband, they sent the young men on their way. It wasn't the last time it would happen.

"They would search your car without a warrant or any probable cause," Delane recounted, "not clean the mess they made, and then let us go after holding us for thirty minutes. They'd handcuff you, slam your faces and bodies against the car, sit you on the curb while they berated you, all sorts of crazy nonsense. Unfortunately, that stuff's pretty normal in Black communities."

Before Delane entered high school, he and Terri moved out of the house on Burgess and into a new one she rented on a main thoroughfare in Southfield. This allowed her to send Delane to Southfield High instead of Henry Ford High, a school that had endured the effects of Detroit's decline as much as any. A recent examination found that more than 80 percent of students were eligible for government-subsidized lunches. Just one in every twenty tested as proficient in reading; one in thirty was proficient in math. The school had begun equipping its entrances with metal detectors, an action that only stopped some of the violence. Southfield High wasn't exactly Hogwarts, but Terri knew it was measurably better and safer than the alternative. An arts and sciences school, it offered a culinary track and courses such as radio and robotics. Delane opted to take electives like public speaking, theater, and writing—subjects that honed skills he thought might be useful in the real world. In classes he wasn't interested in, like science, he did the minimum to get by. He steered clear of AP courses, thinking they'd be too time-consuming. Some of his teachers hassled him about it, but he didn't care; outside of school hours, he was focused on making money. Sometimes he paid classmates to do his homework for him. It was a simple equation: if he could pay someone $25 to do the work and make $50 at the cell phone store in that same time frame, he'd come out ahead.

During his freshman year, Delane quickly became friends with Gene Donald, a boy in his grade who lived three houses away and rode the bus with him. He made a fast impression on Gene with his ability to make people laugh. Gene took mostly advanced classes, so he and Delane didn't much overlap throughout high school, but Delane would come by his classroom during his off period to torture the science teacher, Mr. Peters, an easily ruffled man who operated a store out of his closet from which he would sell snacks and school supplies to students. ("See," Gene recalled with a laugh years later, "even the teachers were hustling!") The duo would tease Mr. Peters by locking him out of the closet and hiding the key. At one point, Gene started selling similar goods in his class, angering the teacher for cutting into his profits. Gene and Delane grew to be best friends, troublemakers in class who stayed clean outside of it. They took a radio class together in which they created a show called *Whoop, There It Is* that broadcast on a local station, and classmates would call in during free periods to chat. In class, Delane would come up with complex jokes to roast his peers, often sending his classmates into fits of laughter. The roasts revealed Delane to be a master of quick thinking and improvisation, but they also spoke to something bigger that Gene noticed about his friend from a young age: he viewed everything as a competition.

"I don't care if we're playing one-on-one basketball," Gene said years later. "I don't care if we're seeing who can make the most threes the fastest, playing Rock Paper Scissors, Monopoly. We can literally just be walking to the car, and he'll be like, 'I'll bet you I'll beat you to the car.' His competitive spirit, he's like Kobe Bryant. He wants to win at the highest level, all of the time."

Delane and Gene were part of a large clique with busy social lives. The group would go to the football or basketball team's games after school, then hang out at someone's house afterward. "He missed a lot of important stuff," remembered Gene, "and there was never a complaint. He had money, so he could have called out of work, taken a weekend off, but he never did. I was with him all the time, and I've never seen him take an off day."

After Terri and Delane spent a little more than a year in the home, Terri's parents moved out of the house on Burgess and into a house in Southfield. Terri and Delane moved back to Burgess, but she listed her new address as her parents' house so her sons could keep attending Southfield High. Delane started picking up new hustles in addition to working at the cell phone store. Gene worked at The Athlete's Foot, and when hot new sneakers were coming out, Delane gave him money to buy a few pairs ahead of time so they could resell them to kids at school. All the while, he was working toward something.

"He wanted his independence, his own money," said Libby. "And he saw opportunity. He had been exposed to drugs, to all different worlds, but he said, 'I don't have to go that route. I still have other options. That's not the future that I'm looking for.'"

THE SOUNDS OF Gucci Mane's new mixtape *The Movie* drifted from the stereo resting on the tiny front porch of the house on Burgess. DaeLon sat in a rocking chair, Delane, Keith, and another friend on plastic chairs on the concrete slab that measured just a few feet wide by a few feet long. Some days, the boys would hang out and play Monopoly or Spades in the shed their grandfather had built in the backyard. More often, ever since Delane's aunt had added electrical wiring, they went in there to play video games. The shed now had everything a bunch of teenage boys would need: chairs, folding table, lamp, TV, PlayStation 3, and a space heater for when the weather turned. That summer, the one after Delane's sophomore year of high school, the boys played video games like *Madden* or *Call of Duty* late into most nights. The winner stayed on; the loser had to surrender their controller.

On this day, though, the boys took in the last days of summer warmth out front and chatted with a kid from the neighborhood walking by. They were caught off guard when the gunshots ripped through the afternoon air. On the lawn, the teen ducked behind one of the oak trees. Up on the porch, DaeLon leaped feet-first over the bannister, hit the ground, and dashed around the side of the house. Delane ripped the front door open and ran inside, crouching low as he scurried toward the back.

When the boys reached the backyard and realized they hadn't been hit, they breathlessly rehashed what they'd just lived through, their adrenaline still pumping. In the front yard, they found bullet holes in the siding and in the oak tree, which had probably saved the boy's life. It was clear the drive-by had been an attempt on him. Now safe, the friends headed back to the shed to play video games for the rest of the evening. They didn't see the other boy for a few weeks after that, but they heard from others that he was fine. The situation had been resolved.

Delane and DaeLon soon patched the house with a piece of plywood. Around that time, while Delane spent his days bouncing from school to the cell phone store and back again, day after day, a thought began to crystallize in his mind. This neighborhood was his home. There was no denying that. But he believed he could accomplish more than what it could offer him. Delane set a clear goal for himself. He would work his ass off. He would continue earning as much money as possible. He would save as much of it as he could. And he would get out of this destitute section of Detroit, tap into his potential, and make the most of his life.

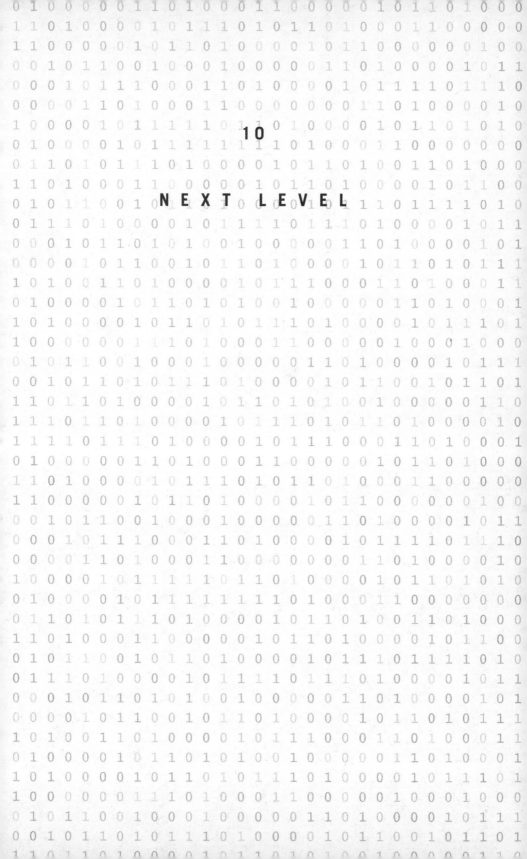

10

NEXT LEVEL

DELANE'S CAR CRUISED slowly past the perfectly manicured hedges, blooming flowerbeds, and extravagant mansions of Los Angeles's Holmby Hills. Walls, fences, and towering landscaping concealed most of the homes, but it was an open secret that some of America's richest people lived in this enclave. Here was the legendary music producer Jimmy Iovine's house. There was the one Ellen DeGeneres recently sold to Napster's Sean Parker for $55 million. Around the corner stood the Playboy Mansion and Michael Jackson's old estate. Delane eased his car to a stop in front of a black iron gate guarding a property that seemed to stretch on forever. From the street, all he could see were leafy, ten-foot-tall shrubs punctuated by equidistant white columns, followed by a second row of taller bushes, just in case the first layer didn't provide quite enough privacy from gawkers. He rolled down his window.

"It's Delane Parnell," he said.

"Who?" crackled the voice on the other end. The guard eventually located his name on the list. A click, and the gates slowly swung open. Delane rolled his car up the stone driveway and through the wall of hedges. Once he was inside the fortress, a spectacular white mansion appeared in front of him, the largest house he'd ever seen.

Soon a house manager materialized next to Delane's car. Delane rolled down his window. The man directed him down the driveway that ran the length of the mansion. "Park between the Bentley and the Maybach," he instructed, gesturing toward the two several-hundred-thousand-dollar vehicles a single car length apart.

"What?" asked Delane.

"Park between the Bentley and the Maybach, and don't hit them."

With the manager watching closely, Delane maneuvered his car between the two cars, practically in slow motion. It was the most nerve-wracking parking job of his life. He finished and the man led him into the mansion, then handed him off to the home's head butler, who stood wearing a tailored suit and a pair of black Yeezys. The second man escorted Delane through the gourmet kitchen, where a team of chefs prepared that evening's dinner, and onto a spectacular patio in the backyard. A single pad of paper and pen sat on the table.

"Mr. Combs likes to sit in this chair, so you should sit over here," the butler announced before leaving.

Alone, Delane stared out at the enormous backyard, where a basketball court and massive in-ground pool sat enveloped in an impeccable green lawn. *So this is where he lives*. The butler soon returned. Change of plans. Combs wanted to meet inside. Now Delane was escorted into the house again, through one living room and to an even grander one. He stood surrounded by expensive furniture, framed photos, and priceless music memorabilia, trying to process it all.

From around the corner, footsteps. Delane felt his heartbeat quicken.

Suddenly, there he was. Sean "Diddy" Combs smiled, flashing his brilliant white teeth. For one of the first times in his life, Delane was speechless. He tried to say something, then staggered a few steps forward. A few words finally fell out.

"Come on, man," he sputtered, then went in for a bear hug. Combs embraced him back. *Holy shit. This is really happening.*

Combs and Delane took their seats on the couch. Delane, though still just twenty-six, wasn't one to be impressed by status or celebrity. This feeling went deeper: genuine admiration. Like Delane, Combs had started with almost nothing. He too had lost his father to gun violence before ever getting to know him. Then he had made it, and made it big—hip-hop artist, fashion mogul, entrepreneur, multimillionaire. To Delane, Combs was much more than just a celebrity. He was an idol.

Throughout the conversation, Delane occasionally paused to absorb the moment, still trying to shake the disbelief.

"Come on, man."

The two men talked about life, music, Diddy's work. Eventually, they got to talking about PlayVS, which was just a few months removed from announcing its first funding round. Combs had learned about Delane and the company soon after the raise and asked a mutual acquaintance, the talent manager Guy Oseary, to set up a meeting. Now, Combs listened to the young founder, impressed.

"I want to be part of your journey," he told Delane.

He meant it. He wanted to invest in PlayVS. As the conversation ended, Combs gave Delane his phone number and told him they should do this again soon. Delane figured it was merely something polite that famous people say. But a few days later, Delane got another call. Combs wanted to meet up for lunch. As Delane soon learned, he wanted to put $1 million of his own money into PlayVS.

Delane at the time was in the midst of raising capital for the startup's next round, its Series B. A few weeks earlier, he had reached out to his investors seeking an introduction to Overtime, a New York startup that created online content focused on high school sports. It seemed like a natural connection for PlayVS to make. One of the investors introduced him to Tim Katt, a venture capitalist who had a stake in Overtime. Katt also helped run an accelerator that was hosting an event for sports startups in a few weeks. The affair would be held at Dodger Stadium—the Dodgers were partners in the accelerator—and the folks from Overtime were going to be there. Katt presented Delane with a quid pro quo: come to the event and give a presentation about PlayVS, and I can introduce you to Overtime. *The hoops I have to jump through to meet these people!* thought Delane, though he agreed to it.

Delane pulled into the mostly empty parking lot at Dodger Stadium one afternoon not long after. He marched up to the appropriate suite, took a seat at a high table at the back of the room, pulled his laptop out of his backpack, and put the finishing touches on a slide deck. When his turn came to speak, he delivered to the collection of investors, corporate executives, and entrepreneurs a presentation about PlayVS and the esports season that was about to get underway. He finished, and the group erupted in applause.

Afterward, Delane ventured outside and plopped down in one of the chairs overlooking the field. He had never been a baseball fan, but it was hard not to be mesmerized by the immaculate empty stadium, its vast expanse of lush grass and brown dirt glowing under the midday sun. Suddenly, a pair of men sat down beside him—Tucker Kain and Cole Van Nice, the managing partners of Elysian Park Ventures, the Dodgers' investing arm. They wanted to know whether Delane was looking to raise more money. Since the Series A was announced four months prior, Delane had gotten some inquiries, but he hadn't yet been seriously considering another funding round. But conversations with Kain and Van Nice gained momentum over the next few weeks. If the Dodgers were going to invest, they told him, they wanted to invest a sizable amount—at least $10 million. Delane was open to it, but with a pair of stipulations. One, if they were going to invest that much, they needed to lead the round; and two, the group couldn't have a board seat, since Delane didn't want to mess with the board structure it had just created in the previous round. The Dodgers agreed.

The two groups soon decided that the Series B would be capped at $30.5 million and PlayVS would be valued at $150 million. The startup was in the midst of preparing to launch its first season, so Delane made a rule for the round: anyone who wanted to invest would have to come to him. "I was busy," Delane said later, "so if you wanted to talk about it, you could come to the PlayVS office."

Many did. The venture arms of Adidas and Samsung invested. NEA, Crosscut, Coatue, and WndrCo all got involved a second time. Science put in an additional $8 million. Soon, the round was full, with the Dodgers getting to contribute their desired $10 million.

But the most meaningful $1 million in the Series B came from Combs. Delane now had financial backing from one of the people he idolized most. In the months that followed, Combs would often have Delane to his house for dinner or just to hang out, and the two would grow to be friends. They'd go to star-studded events together, Delane traveling in a small entourage with some of Combs's children. "He welcomed me into his family, as if I'm family," said Delane. "What else can you really ask for? He bet on me. He bet on me, by the way, in a space that he really doesn't even understand, so he really just bet on me as a person. I'll always have love for him for that."

For Delane, building the relationship wasn't about the money—PlayVS, at that point, could have gotten investments that size from any number of VC firms. It was about having a relationship with someone who had inspired him, having the support of someone he'd always looked up to. The money, that $1 million, was tangible proof that the man from the pictures above his desk, from the photos on his wall at home, believed in him.

CHARLENE HAMM GRIPPED the sledgehammer with both hands, swung it back gently, whipped it forward, and bashed it into the wall of Science's office. It was January 2019, and PlayVS had reached sixteen employees with plans to hire more fast. In the span of several months, the company had outgrown its section of the second floor, moved to a larger area upstairs, and exceeded the limitations of that space as well. The next region to conquer was a million-dollar movie theater right in the heart of Science's office. It was used often by a media upstart that Science was incubating, but PlayVS's need was pressing, so the partners decided it was time for it to come down. They contracted Laz Alberto's father to raze the theater and turn the area into workstations. On demolition day, his crew gave each employee the chance to take a swing and smash through a designated piece of drywall, a symbolic gesture as the startup expanded beyond its previous confines.

Delane had given himself one year to see how things went in Los Angeles. In that time frame, he'd founded a company, earned a deal with the NFHS, and secured millions in funding. He wasn't going anywhere. PlayVS was his life. He was rising early each morning, plugging away at the office all day, and continuing to work from the living room, where he'd arranged his desk into an exact replica of his space in the Science office, until 1:00 or 2:00 in the morning. There were no weekends off. He sought fast expansion, both due to his own personal ambitions as well as those of his investors. All of this left little time for Ashley. Back in Michigan, Delane had always been working a lot. But there Ashley had her friends and her family. Now she was halfway across the country, stuck working by night and sleeping by day in a city where she didn't know anyone. Over time, a realization dawned on her. This wasn't temporary. And it wasn't working. She'd decided her only option was to pack her belongings and move back home to Detroit.

Delane had once told Sean Yalda he needed to be willing to sacrifice everything to be a cofounder in this company. Now Delane was understanding what that really meant. PlayVS, for all the opportunities it had created for him, had also cost him a relationship that had spanned more than a decade with a person he had loved. Like the employees who had come from across the country to work for PlayVS, Delane too was now alone in Los Angeles.

The first season of official high school esports, by just about any measure, had been a success. Students had fun. The technology had mostly worked. As the first season wound down, the startup sent a survey to its coaches to find out, among other things, what went right and what went wrong. One of the more eye-opening realizations was a statistic: 42 percent of the players had never before participated in an after-school sport or activity. Not lacrosse. Not Mathletes. Not the school paper. Nothing. For 42 percent of those kids, this was the first time they weren't simply walking out the door when each school day ended. Even so, would-be coaches across the country were telling PlayVS that the biggest obstacle to starting their programs was getting it approved by the school's administration. In some schools, this meant asking the principal or athletic director. In others, it required getting through several layers of bureaucracy and pitching to the district superintendent. More red tape, of course, meant slower growth for PlayVS. Alinn Louv and the community team began reaching out to coaches to ask them to send along the presentation they'd used to get esports approved.

Using those materials, they assembled a manual of talking points on the benefits of esports that teachers could deliver to their administrators—the teamwork, the communication, and of course, the 42 percent figure.

That spring, the second season of esports would give students the option of playing three different games, thanks to a pair of new deals with publishers: *League of Legends*, *Smite*, and *Rocket League*. It would also feature five more states—Alabama, Arkansas, Hawaii, Mississippi, and New Mexico—bringing the total to ten. Just before the season began, Delane was finally able to turn some of his attention back to hiring new staffers. He called up his old friend D'Andre Ealy, who, now two years into his stint living in California, was working as a product manager at Disney, and convinced him to come take on a similar role at PlayVS. He brought on Melanie Risley, the wife of Adrian, and now the couple that had moved from Arkansas on a whim were both working for PlayVS. Soon, Clint Kennedy, the educator who had helped establish an esports league in Connecticut, reached out asking about job openings, and Delane hired him as the startup's first remote employee. Kennedy took on the role of director of education, a job that entailed speaking often with the NFHS and various state associations and flying around the country to preach about the benefits of esports within schools—things he'd seen firsthand even before PlayVS existed. Delane had realized that those with experience at the intersection of esports and education could be invaluable assets to the PlayVS team. As such, he also agreed to hire Seth Reinhart, who had stayed in touch with Laz Alberto and Charlene Hamm since hosting the state championship in Kentucky. Reinhart dreaded telling his principal he was leaving—in the midst of the esports season, nonetheless. But when he did, he received a surprising response: the principal wanted him to go.

"You leaving to take an esports job in California," the principal told Reinhart, "shows the kids on your team that there are opportunities for them beyond their small blue-collar town."

A few weeks later, Reinhart's team held a dinner to say goodbye. The students presented him with a card they'd all signed, then picked him up and hoisted him on their shoulders. "I keep the video on my phone, of them carrying me around like some emperor," said Reinhart, who had evolved from his school's IT guy to its esports coach to an employee at a venture-backed gaming startup in the span of six months. "It's super corny. I was like, 'Really, guys? I don't think you have to go this hard.' But it meant a lot."

As CEO, Delane had always overseen PlayVS's finances and hiring process. He wanted to bring on a chief financial officer to get some of the more mundane responsibilities off his plate. The Science team brought him several candidates, all with impressive resumes, but he didn't vibe with any of them. Finally, they introduced him to Gabi Loeb, a University of Michigan graduate who was recruited to MySpace's financial department in its waning days and had since served as the CFO of several startups.

"Delane and I talked a lot over the course of a few weeks," recalled Loeb, "and now that I know him so well, I realize it must have driven him crazy how often we spoke. We finally went for this hour-and-a-half-long walk in Santa Monica, talking about the vision and the idea that he wanted to bring in someone at a senior operational level who had helped grow companies before. One of my big complaints to anybody who would ever listen to me, which was not very many people, was that startups always bring on some version of finance way too late—it's usually a messy cleanup process rather than a forward-looking, growth-oriented job. So having the ability to make my own mess, instead of cleaning someone else's mess up, was really intriguing."

Not long after their long walk, Delane decided to hire Loeb.

Even with $46 million in the bank, Delane had always been cautious about spending, largely because being frugal had been ingrained in him since he was old enough to know what money was. "As a board member and as an investor," said NEA's Rick Yang, "you're always nervous when a company is able to raise a good amount of money. Companies will generally spend to the amount of money they've been able to raise, instead of spending the right amount. But raising the money didn't change Delane's sense of really being thoughtful around spending in the business. He stayed laser focused on making sure that he was running a tight ship."

Sometimes, that was to a fault. Sean Yalda would ask about hiring outside illustrators to help with design for a few hundred dollars and be met with pushback. Delane wanted copywriting for the website and marketing materials done in-house, even though the startup had no trained copywriters on staff. So entrusting another person with the company's finances was difficult for Delane at first. But over time, he loosened his grip on the startup's wallet. Loeb hired a recruiting firm and put an actual hiring process into place. The company began offering salaries that could compete with other venture-backed LA startups. Loeb brought the fun and scrappy startup a sense of maturity, serving as an HR department and overseeing facilities.

"Having Delane deal with offer letters and payroll and things like that was just a total waste of his time," said Loeb. "It was my job to make sure that the engine could actually run, so that he could drive."

Delane had been speaking throughout the winter with Neel Palrecha, the vice president of engineering at the online real estate company Snapdocs. Delane was growing frustrated with PlayVS's software. It was mostly functional, but accessing data was difficult—finding out, for example, how many matches were going on at a given time was a complicated process. Sometimes the team would discover that the performance stats being provided to players and coaches at the end of each match were flat-out wrong. Delane wanted to bring on someone who could lead the team of engineers in Los Angeles—in person and without a nine-hour time difference to complicate things—and help revamp its software. After NEA introduced Delane to Palrecha, who had previously held high-level technical roles at Apple and the meditation app Headspace, the two started discussing the possibility of his coming on as the vice president of engineering. Soon after the second season began, Delane formally offered him a job. Palrecha began the role in March.

In building the PlayVS platform, Loubser and his team in South Africa had used what would most aptly be described as a custom solution, as opposed to the best practices that had become commonly accepted in the tech world. While this allowed the team to scale rapidly, it also meant newly hired engineers had difficulty learning how the system operated. When Palrecha arrived, he found the software's back end in disarray. "All the engineers on the team were essentially fighting fires," he recalled. "That's it. There was no product being built."

Palrecha wanted to do a total overhaul of the platform. Delane was on board, and it was agreed that this would be done once the spring season was over. Delane, recognizing the talent he'd gotten in Palrecha, began poaching his former colleagues from Headspace. Through the first six months of 2019, the startup doubled its headcount to thirty employees, with many of the new hires on the product and engineering teams. Headspace's head of growth, Robert Lamvik, had previously been identified as a top target by the recruiting firm Delane hired, but he refused to even take a call from the agency. Once Palrecha joined, Lamvik's tune changed, and he soon agreed to abandon Headspace for PlayVS. "Probably ten to fifteen people joined the company afterward just because Neel did," said Delane, "people that we can't get if he doesn't join. The talent level of the company just shot up. He ended up raising the bar of the talent one hundred times over."

Loubser didn't know what to make of Palrecha's hiring. The company's first person on payroll, he had owned the title of chief technology officer since his first day. Now here came this hotshot engineer from Apple and Headspace who reported directly to Delane. "One of the early things Neel was unhappy about was being VP of engineering," recounted Loubser. "He wanted my CTO title and sort of said so." Delane's solution was to drop the CTO position entirely, switching Loubser's title to chief architect. Loubser and Palrecha were side by side in the company hierarchy, but the entire engineering team in LA—which now outnumbered that in South Africa—was reporting to Palrecha. As the engineering staff in Los Angeles grew, Loubser and his team began to feel even more distanced than usual from the rest of the company. Pinning down the folks in California for calls or video meetings became difficult.

"We were growing suspicious of where this was all going, what the motives were," recalled Loubser. "We became treated a bit more like just normal engineers, as opposed to the senior people that built this thing."

The four members of the Johannesburg team—Loubser, Graham, Justin, and another junior engineer they'd brought on board—decided to fly to the States and spend several months in Santa Monica. There they could get to know the rest of the employees better and help with the platform rebuild Palrecha was leading. They got their work visas approved, bought flights, and made housing accommodations near the Science office. A week ahead of their departure, just before an all-hands meeting,

Loubser received a message on Slack from Delane: Palrecha was being named CTO. Loubser would now be reporting to him.

That was the last straw. Loubser and the engineers gathered at a coffee shop in Johannesburg and debated whether they should deal with the new state of politics and stick it out. Impossible to ignore was the issue of their company stock: They all owned shares of PlayVS that fully vested after four years. They'd each been with PlayVS for less than two. Walking away would mean leaving more than half their equity on the table—potentially worth millions someday should PlayVS ever go public or get acquired. But the money, they decided, wasn't worth sticking around for. They composed an email explaining their decision and offering to ensure a smooth transition. Before they received a reply, they discovered they'd been cut off from accessing PlayVS's back-end software, email, and Slack channels.

"Boom!" recounted Loubser. "That was it."

They were out.

"From a financial perspective," said Loubser, "it was a very stupid thing to do. But I think there's something more to life than that."

With the South Africa team out of the picture, Palrecha and the engineers in Los Angeles continued on with the software overhaul. Throughout the summer, they rebuilt PlayVS's product from the ground up, rewriting nearly every line of code. The objectives were to create a platform that operated efficiently, was easily scalable, and produced robust data that the company could analyze to easily track its progress against its goals. To help lead the charge on the latter, Palrecha recruited his former Headspace colleague Ryan Le, a young sports fan and statistics nerd who, naturally, was mildly obsessed with the movie *Moneyball*. At his first company-wide meeting, Le introduced himself to his new peers and told them to think of him as Jonah Hill's character in the film, the number-crunching nerd who helps his team operate efficiently.

Le early on asked his coworkers what issues were taking up too much of their time. "Communication with the schools," they told him, "is a massive time suck." If a match day ended and a game's results didn't appear in the PlayVS system, they had to figure out what went wrong. Was it a software glitch on the company's end? A no-show by one of the teams? Then one of them needed to consult a spreadsheet to locate the appropriate contact, send an email asking what happened, and figure out how to fix it—all under a time constraint, since the following week's matchups were determined by the current week's standings.

Le created a system that would automatically send an email to the appropriate people at each school if something went awry; then, after they responded, the software would create a ticket that would be placed in a queue and ultimately handled by a member of PlayVS's customer experience team. To make the process even easier, Neel Palrecha and a handful of engineers created a feature that let coaches reschedule matches on their own at a mutually agreeable time. "It was all about reducing the redundancy of manual things and helping people save time so that they can go ahead and work on more important things," said Le. "If this thing is going to scale to twenty thousand NFHS schools, we're really going to have to be efficient."

Another early Le project was perhaps even more critical: revamping the process—to the extent that one even existed—for reaching out to potential new schools. The system had mostly been ad hoc before, with members of the community team fielding inbound requests from potential coaches and chatting with them as needed. Le began building a model that analyzed the sizes, demographics, and geographic locations of the schools PlayVS had already signed up. It would then apply that analysis to all the high schools in the country and produce a list of the five hundred or so schools that should become the community team's priority based on the projected size of their team and the predicted likelihood they'd sign up. Employees used customer relationship management software to mark when a school's contact had last been emailed, called, or texted, and the model could determine which schools were due for a follow-up. Outreach was becoming a science.

DELANE AND PALRECHA found themselves in the conference room of a San Francisco office, sitting across from Dick Costolo, the former CEO of Twitter. With PlayVS increasing its headcount and expanding, Delane had been thinking about raising money yet again. Costolo had recently cofounded the venture firm 01 Advisors with former Twitter COO Adam Bain, who joined the group at the table. Costolo, with his balding head and thick-framed glasses, was known in the tech world for his long-windedness and quick manner of speaking. Sitting in the meeting room, he put those traits on full display, firing questions about esports and PlayVS at Delane, who would start answering before Costolo could finish. Then Delane would rip through his answer, and Costolo would interject with another question. It was like a world class ping-pong match. "I just started laughing," remembered Costolo. "I said, 'You're the only person I've ever met who speaks faster than I do.' Now I understand what people have been telling me for the last twenty years."

Costolo and Bain agreed after the meeting that they should invest in the startup. As he prepared to fundraise, Delane didn't want to expand the size of his board or surrender one of his own seats—so he asked Rick Yang and NEA, which already held one, if the firm would be interested in leading the Series C. They agreed to, and it was soon decided the round would be capped around $40 million dollars. Delane found a few more investors, including Michael Ovitz, cofounder of the talent and sports agency Creative Artists Agency, and soon had $30 million in commitments. He connected with Roger Lee, a partner at Battery Ventures and an OG of the Silicon Valley venture capital world. Battery had been investing in esports companies for the past several years and had purchased several teams in the US, China, and South Korea. The firm for a while had been looking for an amateur- or scholastic-focused esports startup in which it could invest.

"This is a product that lends itself to a winner-take-most or winner-take-all outcome," said Lee. "It would be really awkward if two schools in the same district were using different platforms and they couldn't actually communicate with one another. PlayVS had a lot of the early momentum. They had the most schools. The had the NFHS relationship. They had, at the time, fifteen or twenty states that had already signed up. The dominoes were all falling in their direction. They were clearly going to be the winner in this space."

Lee wanted to invest, but he would only agree to do so if the firm could go in big—the $10 million available in the Series C wasn't going to cut it. Delane agreed to push the size of the round to $50 million, further diluting his own shares and those of other shareholders to get Lee and Battery on board. The round was finalized in the summer of 2019. PlayVS had raised $96 million in the span of less than fourteen months and was now valued at nearly $300 million.

In Rick Yang at NEA and the folks at Science, Delane always had a reliable group to turn to for business advice. But Costolo and Lee gave him two more mentors—each with decades of startup experience—who weren't on PlayVS's board. As a rule, Costolo didn't take board seats with the startups he invested in, since he believed founders wouldn't be as forthcoming with him if he did. That proved useful to Delane, who, as a solo founder, didn't have an equal at the company with whom he could talk through issues. (Bryan Smiley, whom Delane had given the honorary title of cofounder, wasn't involved in the company's operations.) Costolo became Delane's go-to, the first call he would make when he had a question or when something went wrong. Sometimes, the advice Delane sought was about how to present things to his board, as he did when the company fell short of its growth targets. But the main goal was to help Delane avoid needing to have those conversations at all. Costolo ingrained in the young CEO the concept of objectives and key results, or OKRs—essentially a fancy Silicon Valley term for goals. Each objective was broken down into a handful of metrics that could be used to measure it, and progress was closely monitored. That way, if PlayVS, say, wasn't on track to hit its goal for the number of new schools onboarded by October, it wouldn't come as a surprise days before the deadline—there would be milestones to hit in the previous July, August, and September. Costolo taught Delane to ask employees to provide weekly ratings of how confident they were that they'd be able to achieve their longer-term key results. If the confidence rating changed from the previous week, the staffer would provide comment as to why, cluing Delane in to what needed to change.

Under Costolo's mentorship, Delane began to address one of the leadership issues he'd found most challenging: delegating. Delane had long struggled to divorce himself from the business's day-to-day tasks, fearing the loss of control that came with it. Costolo hammered home the idea that he had to trust the people he'd hired to execute. Perhaps even more challenging to implement, he taught Delane to let them decide on their own the best ways to achieve those things.

"If you just tell people what to do," said Costolo, "then when it doesn't work, they just come back to you and go, 'Now what do you want to do?' You've paid all this money to hire this person, and it's still your problem. If, instead, you let them own the problem and say, 'Hey, here's the metric you own; figure out however you want to achieve it,' then when the first try doesn't work, believe me, they're going to try four more things before they come and ask you for help."

Delane ate up the advice. "Dick's training me to be a great CEO," he said later. "Getting him on board was like getting a book of all the answers."

While Costolo guided Delane largely on issues of management and leadership, Lee encouraged Delane to scale the company quickly. And while PlayVS's most-involved investors had been there from the early days and shared a common vision with Delane around high school esports, Lee often urged him to think bigger.

"It was a tough few months, to be honest, when Roger joined the cap table, because that was new behavior from him compared to my other investors," recalled Delane. "He pushes me very hard on everything. Sometimes, it can be pretty frustrating, because I have a really supportive cast of investors who also challenge me. But they don't push me as hard as he does, and not as frequently as he does."

Lee believed that, to grow as quickly as possible, PlayVS should pivot from its scholastic product and focus on amateur esports in general, perhaps using an AAU-style model by which coaches could form their own teams and compete against one another. Delane resisted, believing the education infrastructure was critical to the company's growth and its larger objectives. But the conversations led him to think about expanding PlayVS's market.

Heading into the fall 2019 season, the startup had nearly twenty state associations on board with high school esports, having recently added Alaska, Arizona, California, Colorado, Texas, Virginia, and Washington, DC. Many others were still dragging their feet. Most frustrating to Delane was the reason some of the states provided: sanctioning esports would amount to declaring it a sport, a designation they disagreed with. In a way, the directors had a point. Esports does not require significant strength or endurance. At the same time, it's hard to argue esports is any less physically intense than fishing or billiards, which have been broadcast on ESPN for decades, or archery, which is featured at the Olympics. Some state administrators refused to even refer to esports by name, opting instead for "e-gaming" or "e-activities." Having the conversations drove Delane mad.

"If I were an executive director," he said later, "I'd be introducing programs that help me reach and engage as many kids as possible. Going back and forth on the semantics is a complete waste of time, and it deprives millions of kids who just want to be a part of their school community. Sometimes these conversations can be frustrating because we've already proven the benefits of esports, the educational and career upside. So adopting esports should be an easy 'yes' for every executive director or state association board. To even debate about it baffles me."

After his discussions with Lee, Delane decided on a solution. PlayVS would create a new nationwide product that operated outside the parameters of the company's partnership with the NFHS. He named the original NFHS-sanctioned offering "Varsity"; the new product would be called "Club" and wouldn't operate under the NFHS umbrella. Schools anywhere in the country could compete using the Club product, whether their state's athletic association had approved of esports or not. States would be grouped into leagues based on their time zones, so students from Fargo down to San Antonio could play for a Central Region championship and trophy—not awarded by the state association, but by PlayVS. For its third season, PlayVS would finally operate high school esports in all fifty states and the District of Columbia.

THE VILLAGE OF Nome, Alaska, sits on the coast of the Seward Peninsula that juts out into the Bering Sea, a mere half-hour flight to the Russian mainland, if one was so inclined. Snow remains on the ground eight months of the year. Homes and establishments are powered by generator. There are no roads in or out—the only access is by plane or boat.

Aaron Blankenship was fresh out of college when he saw a job listing to teach social studies at Nome's only high school. He'd been raised in suburban Ohio, where he mostly kept to himself as a kid. He didn't participate in organized sports. He played the flute in band, poorly. His GPA was lackluster, so much so that he received rejection letters from eight of the nine colleges to which he applied. He stayed local and studied education. While an undergrad, he got into long-distance training and ran his first marathon. He got hooked. Sometime during all that running and thinking, he realized he needed to get the hell out of Ohio. That's when he started fantasizing about Alaska.

"I've heard that people who move to Alaska are either running from something or searching for something," said Blankenship. "I was searching."

The journey from Cleveland to Nome required three separate flights, the last of which was aboard a small bush plane from Anchorage. Blankenship started his job at Nome-Beltz Middle High School, in his first year helping students fundraise nearly $100,000 to take a field trip to Washington, DC. A couple years in, when the school's principal learned that esports had been

approved in the state for the upcoming fall, Blankenship enthusi-
astically put up his hand. Video games had been his outlet as kid,
the place where he made his friends. "I really didn't care about
school," he said. "I was just kind of biding my time, waiting to
get back home so I could play more video games." His titles of
choice were massively multiplayer online games, or MMOs—
games like *World of Warcraft* that are played by thousands of players at once, all traversing the same digital world. Within their
chat functions, Blankenship conversed with people from all over
the world, engaging with them about gaming, politics, and life.

To play sports in Nome, high school teams have to raise
money—$7,000, $8,000, or more—to cover flights to weekend
competitions in other villages across the state. Together, the
athletes climb into small prop planes, just as frigid on board as
the air outside, and spend the weekend away for their basketball
game or volleyball match. Esports offered a way for students
to participate in a sport that didn't require travel. Nome-Beltz
gave Blankenship a $2,000 budget in the first season, half of
which he spent on a long-term investment: mini-computers
that would support *Rocket League* and *League of Legends*. A few
days after the boys and girls held their first practice, parents,
teachers, and other students started showing up in the computer lab to watch them. There weren't many other forms of
entertainment in the village, population 3,900, so residents
tended to rally around the high school's teams. Match days
would be standing room only, twenty spectators crammed in
to watch the kids battle students from other Alaskan towns.
The Nome team held its own. It even beat some schools on the
state's road system, teams from places like Fairbanks or Anchorage that tended to dominate their smaller foes in other sports.
"When we started to win these games, people were losing their
minds," recalled Blankenship.

It wasn't long before other students in the school started giving the kids grief. Whether out of jealousy or simply teenage spite, they railed on the players, telling them what they were doing wasn't a sport. One day, the coach gathered his students together.

"I'm serious about this team," he told them. "Are you guys all serious about this team?"

"Yeah!" they replied.

"Good," he told them. "We work hard. We compete. If that's not a sport to someone, who really cares?"

That was the end of that. Blankenship stopped listening to the haters, and it seemed his players did too. "Call it whatever you want," he said later, "but it's equal to any other sport. I try not to focus on the word because it doesn't mean anything to me. It's not really worth arguing."

In the Science office, the employee tasked with acquainting Blankenship with the PlayVS platform was Seth Reinhart. In addition to his home state of Kentucky and a random smattering of regions out east, Reinhart was responsible for onboarding schools up the entire West Coast. He soon learned what those who had been on PlayVS's community team for longer already knew: there was no one-size-fits-all method for preparing teams for their first seasons. Reinhart was dealing with schools in tiny fishing villages in Alaska, private academies in California with state-of-the-art equipment, and schools in Washington, DC that ran on government servers and required every necessary web domain to be carefully whitelisted. But despite their wide-ranging socioeconomic makeups and technical capabilities, Reinhart soon realized the schools all had a common denominator: someone like Aaron Blankenship.

"There's always that one person who is really, really passionate about this," said Reinhart. "That coach or prospective coach who's super excited to build their program and impact their students in a positive way."

Down in the town of Van Buren in northwestern Arkansas, that person was Wes Yandell. When Yandell, a technician at the local high school, heard that esports was coming to the state, he approached the principal and asked for permission to form a team. The school had limited room in its budget, so Yandell, who also taught soccer and basketball through the Boys & Girls Clubs, offered to coach without pay. Naturally, the principal took him up on it. After the team's first full year, two of its seniors earned scholarships to play competitively at nearby colleges. But the most fulfilling experience was with a student who a few years earlier had been diagnosed with multiple sclerosis. The boy's mind was as sharp as ever, but his body failed him, and he moved about in a wheelchair. He joined the team and turned out to be a prodigious *Smite* player. The staff that assisted him each day detected an unmistakable change in his mood—he had something to look forward to, something that got his adrenaline flowing. He even started to think about a career in gaming, perhaps as a shoutcaster or, following in Yandell's footsteps, a coach.

"I do this because of kids like him," said Yandell. "It sucks that this happened to him. I can't tell you how many tears have been cried over that kid. I will fight every day for kids like him to have an opportunity to play competitively."

At many schools across the country, esports programs weren't just about playing the games. Students at Honolulu's 'Iolani School took on ancillary roles like managing the club's social media channels and casting for viewers on Twitch. Gabe Yanagihara, a computer science teacher, and Chris Butler, the school's surf coach, led the team and gave the students autonomy, letting them set up livestreams and chat with local businesses about sponsorships. Many of the students participated in other activities and sometimes had to miss their esports practices or matches, like the star of the boys' soccer team who was also a solid *League of Legends* player. For other students, the esports team was their first-ever school activity. After joining, one girl, a freshman boarding student from abroad, decided to try out for the cheerleading squad. She made it. Another boy, a quiet senior, joined the esports team, made some friends, and suddenly had the courage to audition for the school musical. He landed a part and participated in his first show during his last semester of high school. "We had no idea he could sing," recalled Butler. "These kids have gained confidence. They feel validated now that the school is supporting something they love."

Butler and Yanagihara knew their team would be under extra scrutiny given the many stigmas of gaming, so they decided to set a higher standard than other sports, requiring students to maintain a minimum 3.0 GPA. They also figured that demanding good grades would help increase the likelihood the kids could earn a few of the growing number of scholarships that colleges were offering to high school gamers. "Most of these students aren't going to be pro players," said Yanagihara, "so we want them to at least get an education out of it."

PlayVS, meanwhile, was hitting its stride. By the start of the 2019–2020 school year, with the doors thrown wide open and schools everywhere able to come on board, the startup had received inbound interest from at least one teacher or student from more than 13,000 high schools. The team for some time had been contemplating how the company could more effectively leverage coaches to spread the word about high school esports. For starters, the engineers built a feature within the PlayVS interface that allowed coaches to refer teachers from other high schools with just a few clicks. Another plan, concocted by Alinn Louv, entailed turning PlayVS's most dedicated coaches into brand ambassadors. The company would choose a handful of so-called "Super Coaches" in every state. Each would receive ten free student passes per season, priority support for any technical issues, and goodies like sweatshirts, jerseys, and gaming equipment for their teams. In exchange, the coaches would be responsible for recruiting a certain number of new coaches each season. PlayVS announced the program toward the end of the year, invited coaches to apply, then handpicked the Super Coaches based on several factors, including how long they'd been coaching and how involved they were in the esports community both locally and online. Kyle Magoffin in Massachusetts was selected as one. So was Ashley Hodge in Georgia. The system helped PlayVS grow even faster. By the end of the third season, the waitlists in some states were hundreds of schools long. The community team rushed to onboard new schools as quickly as it could.

PlayVS soon reached a big milestone: its own office. In January, the startup's forty employees loaded their belongings into moving trucks, traveled a few miles down the road to West Los Angeles, and resettled into a two-story building that was all their own. The space featured a kitchen on each floor and a second-story balcony wrapped around an atrium in which the team could hold its all-hands meetings—or play video games. The company had developed a work hard/play hard culture that carried over into the new office. Employees would often challenge one another in *Madden* or *Super Smash Bros.* after work, and a crowd would gather to watch their coworkers play and trash-talk each other. Ryan Le and some colleagues organized an *NBA 2K* season in which staffers played each other head to head, tallied the standings, then held a playoff tournament to crown a champion. In the first season, one of the company's engineers had defeated Delane in the championship, much to Delane's dismay and everyone else's delight. In the second season, Delane was able to beat Robert Lamvik. "He walks the walk," Lamvik said later. "He's the CEO of a gaming company, and then he beats us all at video games."

Delane didn't necessarily set out to build a culture at PlayVS. The company wasn't inclined to hold weekly happy hours, and the office didn't feature Silicon Valley perks like beer taps and rock climbing walls. But Delane set the tone through his natural curiosity and sociableness.

"He goes out of his way to make sure you're engaged, you're having fun, and you're interacting, whether you're the newest employee or someone on the C-suite," said Lamvik. "He knows everyone's name, and he can tell you a fun story about every single person at the company."

Delane pointed to someone else as the lifeblood of the company's culture: Sean Yalda. "When people talk about PlayVS having a great culture and being an amazing place to work, I think it has little to do with me," said Delane. "The dedication and drive come from me, but the other things come from Sean. Sean is our culture—an amazing spirit, amazing person. Those sorts of souls are rare in life."

Yalda's friendly, laid-back attitude made his colleagues trust him. On a few occasions, with peers weighing job offers or feeling like the work was becoming too much to bear, he talked them through it over lunch or in the parking lot. If employees were struggling but afraid to bring their issues to Delane, they would often confide in Yalda—the person at the company who had known him the longest—and he would offer to help facilitate a casual meeting. "I don't gossip or talk to anybody about anybody else," said Yalda. "My brain doesn't even really work that way. I almost immediately forget people's issues until I'm in front of them again. I think people find security in that."

Through all the long, intense days, employees stuck around. Surely, owning a fraction of 1 percent of a company with the potential to sell for hundreds of millions of dollars someday was an incentive, but offers came, and practically nobody took them. By the time the startup surpassed sixty employees, only two staffers outside of the South Africa team had left on their own accord. PlayVS wasn't just doing big things as a company. It was a place where people wanted to work.

SITTING IN FRONT of his laptop in his dorm at Virginia Tech, Joe Jacko tore his way through the worlds of *League of Legends* each day after class. His stellar play earned him a ranking of Master, a tier reserved for the top 0.1 percent of players worldwide. Jacko decided to join the university's esports club, the Virginia Esports Association at Virginia Tech, which at the time was about sixty students strong. The team had some good players, but it was mostly about having fun and making friends. Jacko saw no reason why the organization couldn't accomplish these ends while also being competitive, so he decided to do some recruiting. Mild-mannered by nature, he would bring a hype man to crash freshman orientations. "Hey, who likes *League of Legends*?!" the friend would shout, and once students wandered over, Jacko would inquire about their skill level.

He found two freshmen with Diamond rankings—the top 1 to 2 percent—and asked them to join the organization. That year, Virginia Tech's *League* team qualified for the playoffs in the South Conference—a collection of sixty-five universities that included schools like Duke, Clemson, the University of Virginia, and the University of Texas—for the very first time. The club soon grew to two hundred students. The next season, Jacko recruited some competitive gamers who were transferring to Virginia Tech, and the team made a run all the way to the semifinals. He graduated and quickly landed a job on the other side of the country, coaching the University of Southern California's fledgling *League* team.

Around the same time, at the nearby Westridge School, an all-girls school in the hills of Pasadena, a sophomore named Jadyn found out that esports were coming to California high schools. She and her friends often got together to play computer games like *Minecraft* and *Dungeons and Dragons* at each other's homes. Now there was a chance to play games at school. Some of the girls had dabbled in *Rocket League* before, so Jadyn presented the principal with the idea of forming a team. He was on board—but the school needed a coach. He reached out to USC's esports program, they referred Jacko, and the new college graduate picked up a second gig as Westridge's first esports instructor.

Jadyn and five of her friends formed two *Rocket League* teams. One was considered the Varsity team—each school was allowed one, per PlayVS's new rules—and one was a Club team. Most of the girls had ambitions of careers in some aspect of gaming. Jadyn, for her part, wanted to pursue narrative game design, a role that entailed weaving together gameplay and storyline. It was one of many potential career paths the industry offered outside of playing and coaching. There were software developers, audio engineers, writers who created the stories and dialogue, artists who created the worlds and characters, and animators who brought them all to life. As the video game industry grew by billions in revenue each year, more universities began offering courses of study around it. Jadyn's goal became to get into the game design program at USC, just a few miles away, which had consistently been rated as the best in the country for years. Jacko, as her coach, made it his goal to help her get there. By 2019, other top schools like NYU, Georgia Tech, Michigan State, and the Rochester Institute of Technology were all offering majors in gaming. Many more were dangling scholarships for students who were good enough to play on their esports teams.

Delane had long considered college the next target for PlayVS to pursue once it conquered the high school space. Toward the end of the year, he was in deep talks with Epic Games about a deal to bring *Fortnite* onto the startup's platform. The publisher that year had hired Nate Nanzer, an executive who spent years running a professional *Overwatch* league at Blizzard. The league featured a dozen independently owned *Overwatch* teams across the US, including a franchise in Boston owned by the Kraft family, owners of the New England Patriots, and a New York team that belonged to the Wilpons, who at the time owned the Mets. It held its first championship in 2018 at Brooklyn's Barclays Center, a two-day event that drew more than 22,000 fans. Some 10.8 million people tuned in to watch the matches on ABC, ESPN, and online streams, which would be a healthy number for a modern-day NBA playoff game. Nanzer, a powerful figure in the world of esports due to his role in forming the league, had been in discussions with Delane about a deal with PlayVS while at Blizzard. When he switched over to Epic, the two continued their conversations. By December, things had picked up serious momentum. But there was a major issue: if Epic was going to partner with PlayVS, it wanted the startup to host matches for it at both the high school and college levels.

This was far sooner than Delane had planned on tackling the world of college esports. But how could one possibly turn down Epic Games, the maker of the most popular game in the world? At PlayVS's fourth-quarter board meeting, Delane put forth the idea of expanding into the college space. "A lot of the people in the room were concerned," he recalled. "They were like, 'We should be focused on high school. I don't know if the college opportunity makes sense. Also, we don't have a really clear strategy about it.' I took that and I said, 'Okay, cool,' but I was going to continue to do it. That feedback didn't bother me."

Delane spent a weekend creating a deck highlighting the startup's vision, traction, and terms of a potential partnership. He sent it to Epic Games, and by early January, he had struck a deal with the publisher to launch the worldwide phenomenon known as *Fortnite* at both the high school and college levels.

This came as a surprise to the NFHS. *Fortnite*, it should be known, is a last-person-standing battle royale game in which characters build defensive forts, collect weapons, and try to kill one another. The animation is cartoonish and bright, and there's no blood or gore. But the protagonists use realistic weapons like rocket launchers, grenades, shotguns, assault rifles, and machine guns. PlayVS and the NFHS had agreed that the startup wouldn't introduce shooter games. That agreement, however, only applied to PlayVS's NFHS-sanctioned Varsity product; the startup was adding *Fortnite* as part of its Club product, which meant the game didn't fall under the purview of the organization or the state associations. Unfortunately for Delane, most of the online coverage of the announcement didn't make that distinction clear, including a TechCrunch piece with the unambiguous but false headline, "*Fortnite* Just Officially Became a High School and College Sport."

PlayVS suddenly found itself in a small crisis. Within days, the Kentucky High School Athletic Association commissioner emailed schools to tell them the state would be banning *Fortnite* from its after-school programs. "I want to personally assure you that we, along with the NFHS Network, are proactively taking steps to have this decision reversed," the commissioner wrote. "There is no place for shooter games in our schools." Not helping matters was that the announcement came just days before the two-year anniversary of a school shooting in the state in which two high school students were killed and more than a dozen were wounded.

A number of correlational and longitudinal studies in recent years have set out to find whether a connection exists between playing violent video games and committing real-world violence, such as school shootings. Almost all have found that exposure to those games doesn't meaningfully predict violence or crime. It is possible, of course, that youths with more aggressive personalities seek out violent video games, but a 2015 study found that playing the games did not increase aggressive behavior. And a Villanova University psychologist found that school shooters are actually less likely to play video games than the high school demographic as a whole. Perhaps fueling the American public's belief that there's a connection between games and violence are the frequent comments made by certain politicians. It's been a longstanding practice to cite video games as a scapegoat for school shootings rather than mental health or, say, guns. "We have to look at the internet," President Trump said after the Marjory Stoneman Douglas High massacre in Parkland, Florida, "because a lot of bad things are happening to young kids and young minds and their minds are being formed, and we have to do something about maybe what they're seeing and how they're seeing it. And also video games. I'm hearing more and more people say the level of violence on video games is really shaping young people's thoughts." Yet countries like Japan and South Korea, in which consumers spend more on video games per person than in the US, have next to no gun deaths annually.

Even when the "video games cause violence" argument isn't politically motivated, it still has little basis in reality. A report by the News Media, Public Education, and Public Policy Committee, a branch of the American Psychological Association, pointed out that so many youths engage with video games today, connecting violence with playing them would be like connecting violence with wearing sneakers or watching *Sesame Street* as a toddler. And while the amount of violent video games played by kids rose drastically throughout the nineties and aughts, youth violence dropped by 80 percent over the same time frame. Trying to draw a link between video games and violence, the report read, "may distract society from more substantive causes of violence such as poverty, lack of treatment options for mental health as well as crime victimization among the mentally ill, and educational and employment disparities."

For Delane, the NFHS's stance against shooter games came across as a bit hypocritical. The NFHS supported sports like riflery and archery, plus football, which had well-established negative health effects. But he understood the politics and optics involved. Part of the problem was that he hadn't given the NFHS a heads-up about the Epic deal, which had put the organization on the defensive when the news hit and educators started calling. After huddling internally, PlayVS decided to pause the rollout of *Fortnite* in high schools. It would revamp its messaging, drawing a more obvious distinction between its two products, then relaunch the game in the fall.

Meanwhile, the startup moved full speed ahead with the game at the college level. Epic paid PlayVS a fee, which allowed the company to offer *Fortnite* to students free of charge. It was a win-win—Epic got more players on its platform, and PlayVS earned revenue and raised the profile of its product.

Delane soon hired Aakash Ranavat, a former director at Activision and EA, to head up the company's college unit. Ranavat began in early January and was handed the aggressive mandate to get the college season off the ground at the end of February. In his first few weeks, he reached out to hundreds of colleges and universities, armed with PlayVS's progress at the high school level as evidence of what it could build in the education space. While the college esports space at that time was already bustling, it was fragmented, with universities often working directly with individual publishers that had created leagues around their own games or participating in competitions that weren't supported by publishers at all. PlayVS was bringing legitimacy to the market, offering a consolidated platform on which matches could be played across a variety of titles through partnerships with the publishers.

Ranavat's efforts were hugely successful. By late February, he'd gotten more than a hundred universities onto PlayVS's platform, including Arkansas, Arizona State, Auburn, Florida State, Johns Hopkins, Ohio State, Penn State, and Texas A&M. Most already had their own teams in place, but now PlayVS would be organizing their leagues and hosting their competitions. In a matter of weeks, the startup had muscled its way into a brand-new arena.

THE NUMBER OF mentors available to Delane grew along with his stature. Hanging with Sean Combs on the rooftop of the Waldorf Astoria in Los Angeles one day, Delane met Combs's friend Corey Jacobs. Combs and Jacobs had grown up together in the Bronx. Jacobs started dealing drugs in college. It eventually caught up with him. He was convicted on federal drug charges at the age of thirty and, for the nonviolent offenses, was sentenced to sixteen life sentences without the possibility of parole. Jacobs served his time in a violent federal prison in Louisiana among other inmates who were in for life. He eventually began petitioning for his release. His case got picked up by Brittany K. Barnett, a Texas attorney who had recently quit her cushy corporate job to do pro bono work for nonviolent offenders with severe sentences. Barnett was successful. In December 2016, after Jacobs had served nearly eighteen years, President Obama granted him clemency. After his release, Jacobs helped Barnett launch the Buried Alive

Project to help liberate others who had been locked up for life on similar charges. The project would go on to earn the releases of more than fifty people in its first three years.

Now living in Los Angeles, Jacobs had reconnected with his childhood friend. Combs made Jacobs his right-hand man, naming him his senior advisor at Combs Enterprises. When they met, Delane and Jacobs hit it off immediately. Jacobs was impressed by the kid—in rapid-fire succession, he could talk about his esports business, then recite lyrics to the latest hip-hop album, then talk about a YouTube star or an obscure piece of pop culture, then switch over to venture capital and back again. The two started hanging out on their own, talking about family, business, relationships, and how to manage them all.

"He has a good heart," Jacobs said later. "I learned my lessons from having so much of a good heart, being so loyal that it ended up being a detriment to me. It made me do things to please others and connect with people who didn't always have my best interests in mind. They were trying to see what they could get from me. I knew that he probably needed somebody that would give an unconditional type of relationship, someone that would appreciate him whatever happens."

Jacobs gave Delane advice, sometimes unsolicited. When Delane bought himself some jewelry, Jacobs didn't like it—he was worried Delane was making himself a target, and he told him as much. Delane respected Jacobs and all that he'd been through. When he was feeling anxious, he would call him just to talk. Over time, he came to call Jacobs one of his best friends.

"There's a lot of stress associated with the work I have in front of me that I don't think a lot of people recognize," said Delane. "He helps me manage and navigate that. Corey is an angel that I feel like God sent to me at the perfect time. That relationship is one of the biggest blessings I've gotten from this journey."

It wasn't lost on Delane just how absurd it was that he was hanging out with Combs and his inner circle. Still, he kept his head down and did his work. As a general life rule, he turned down most invitations, even when it was painful to do so. But when he did say yes, it was often surreal—like at a Grammys after-party, when he danced next to the rapper Meek Mill to one of Meek Mill's own songs. One afternoon, Delane sat in a photo shoot for a magazine in Los Angeles. As he prepared to have his picture taken, his phone rang. On the other line was a man who introduced himself as Jay Brown, cofounder of Jay-Z's entertainment company Roc Nation. Brown got right to the point: Jay-Z had read about him and wanted to meet with him.

Delane's instinct was to assume it was a prank call, but Jay-Z really wanted to connect with him. Over the next few months, Delane made occasional efforts to meet up with the legend. First Jay was traveling, then Delane was. The two never got on the same page. A few months later, Combs invited Delane to the Roc Nation Brunch, a highly exclusive event Jay-Z threw annually that gathered some of the biggest names in hip-hop and Hollywood. Combs told him to meet at his house. The morning of the event, Delane spent too much time getting a haircut and choosing his outfit, and he arrived at Combs's residence to discover that only a few members of Combs's security detail remained. He'd missed the group departure. Soon, though, the COO of Combs Enterprises pulled up, and he and Delane hopped in a car together and rode off to the mansion where the brunch was being held. (Having the address to the event put one in the upper echelon of guests—most were told to meet at another location and then shuttled there.) For Delane, being there was mind-blowing, pacing the grounds of a Southern California mansion surrounded by music royalty, and he even got to spend a few moments chatting with Combs and Jay-Z. Later that year, Combs threw himself a fiftieth birthday party and invited Delane. He showed up to the house in Holmby Hills and couldn't believe his eyes. Kanye West. Beyoncé. Kim Kardashian. Kobe Bryant. Dwyane Wade. Kevin Hart. It was like a fever dream. From across the room, he spotted Jay-Z chatting in a group with one of Combs's sons. He walked up and tapped him on the shoulder. He had more to say.

"I just wanted to say thank you for paving the road," Delane told him.

Jay seemed to know just what he meant. He placed his hand over his heart. "That's love," he replied, and shook Delane's hand. It had finally happened.

"Without Diddy, without Jay," Delane said later, "I'm not where I am today. I wouldn't have known it was possible. I certainly wouldn't have known that I could do it myself. Those guys gave me a lot of visibility into who I wanted to be and, ultimately, who I became."

Delane had gotten to meet the two people he'd idolized most, two people who had been giving him hope since he was a kid bouncing from one home to another. And he'd gotten to tell them, to their faces, how much they meant to him.

"Life is crazy," he said. "When I was a kid in Detroit, I never would have imagined this. So I'm extremely grateful to be here."

11

GUIDING LIGHT

IF THERE WAS one thing Delane had learned from all those nights playing Monopoly against family and friends, it was that amassing property early was an investment that would pay off in a big way later on. By the time Delane was sixteen, Sam had put him in charge of the cell phone store in Southfield, which was now a MetroPCS. Sam often wasn't around, since he owned several stores in the Detroit area and bounced between them from day to day. The Southfield shop had become one of the highest-grossing MetroPCS outfits in the state. Delane had gained a strong grasp on how the operations worked—he knew the vendors, the products, what it took to keep things running efficiently. He had enough money in the bank that he had started to think about buying a store of his own. The income, if all went well, would be far more lucrative than an hourly wage. Hoping his business's reputation would get him somewhere, Delane visited all the MetroPCS franchises within a ten-mile radius and asked the owners if he could buy in, offering to teach their employees the tactics his store used to help them increase their sales.

No one took him up on it. Soon, though, a former colleague who had left to work for the company's corporate office reached out to him. She knew of a couple guys in their twenties whose parents owned some commercial real estate and were thinking about opening up a franchise. The pair was looking for a partner in the mobile phone business—someone who knew the wholesalers and understood the market. Delane told the woman he was interested. She set up a meeting between him and the two young men, wisely declining to tell them how old Delane was until it was too late to bail. Delane met them and delivered his pitch. The two men agreed to partner with him; they pooled their money and launched a MetroPCS store. It quickly became profitable, and the group decided to open two more. Delane was now partial owner of three stores, yet didn't even have a driver's license; most days he had to ask his friend Gene Donald to ferry him to whichever store he needed to visit.

Delane's mother, Terri, had gotten married years earlier. Her husband owned an auto repair shop, which helped Delane connect with other shop owners in the area. Many had customers who came in looking to sell their cars but who weren't technologically savvy, so Delane would pay to have the vehicles fixed up, take flattering photos of them, and post classifieds on Craigslist. They would often sell for $1,000 or $2,000 more than the owner's asking price, and Delane would keep the margin. The hustling never stopped.

When he was seventeen, finally old enough to get an unrestricted license, Delane would often drive his mom's car to the cell phone stores, where he continued to work the floor and make sure things ran smoothly. He bought a portable basketball hoop on wheels with a fiberglass backboard and left it on the dead-end street off Burgess for anyone to play on. When he wasn't working or in school, Delane could often be found on the court, or shooting hoops with Gene in Southfield. They developed a friendly rivalry. (Years later, they both would claim to be the better Monopoly player and better basketball player.) "Playing basketball with him is like comedy," said Gene. "Delane is going to shoot, and he's going to be aggressive, and he's going to talk shit. You're going to argue with him. You'll get physical, you all might fight. It's the best. And then afterwards, it's just all love, you know what I'm saying?"

Still, most of the hanging out Gene and Delane did took place away from Burgess. Gene didn't spend much time in the neighborhood, often coming by just to pick up or drop off his friend. As an outsider, he tended to feel on edge in the area around Burgess.

The feeling was understandable. Over the years, tragedy would strike the neighborhood many times and almost strike it many more. One such incident came on a warm summer afternoon a few years after high school, when Delane played hoops with DaeLon, some cousins, and a few friends on a side street off Burgess. Their small pickup game grew in size, and soon there were dozens of people packed around the tiny makeshift court. Some, like Delane's young cousins, were there just to watch. Delane's team ran the table, staying on the court as they won game after game. Three in a row. Four. Five. On the sidewalk down the street, a couple of guys started talking shit to each other. No one paid them much mind. Then their voices grew louder, and the argument started to grow physical. Suddenly, gunshots rang out. Delane raced to his coupe, conveniently parked for an easy escape. Parents scooped up their kids and jumped into other cars. DaeLon, who had been parked around the block, sprinted the other way with a friend. When they couldn't make it, they hit the ground and crawled under a parked car.

Bang. Bang. Bang-bang. The two men were exchanging bullets, one set of shots ringing out twenty feet away. Delane called his brother and yelled into the phone.

"Where are you? I'll come grab you."

"I'm hiding under a car on Chapel," shouted DaeLon over the sound of gunfire. They remained cowering beneath the vehicle, waiting for the violence to end. Finally, the shots ceased. DaeLon and his friend wriggled out. The coast was clear; the guys were gone. Everyone agreed the day was over. The winning streak would stop at five today.

"It just happens," Delane said later. "It's normalized. The next day, we were back out there playing hoops."

Other days, not everyone was so fortunate. Over the years, the number of friends Delane had in the neighborhood continued to dwindle. Some were jailed, others were killed. One day, Delane and some friends were shooting hoops when they saw Keith Bibbs's brother rush out of his house and jump in his car. He seemed panicked.

"What's up?" they asked him.

Keith had been in an accident.

Delane and the rest of the friends piled into their cars and hurried to the hospital. Talking to their friends and Keith's brothers in the waiting room, they gathered some idea of what had happened. Keith had either lost control of the wheel or passed out, depending on whom you asked, and his car had plowed head-on into another vehicle. Everyone else was okay, but Keith was badly hurt.

Soon one of the doctors came out to deliver the news. He didn't make it. Delane was devastated. Just like that, Keith Bibbs, the person who had taken Delane under his wing all those years, watched over him and protected him by calling him his "little homie," was gone.

As sales grew at the MetroPCS stores, Delane and his partners decided to sell. They found some buyers and walked away with a healthy return. Delane didn't stay out of a job for long; he soon began working at the car rental, where he would help develop the company's new business model and rent to his classmates during prom season. During the second half of his senior year of high school, Delane started thinking about college applications. He had rooted for the University of Michigan's sports teams for as long as he could remember. He owned blue-and-maize hats, shirts, and sweaters emblazoned with the school's logo, and whenever he had a Saturday in the fall free from work, he watched Wolverines football. His high school GPA was good, even though he didn't stack his schedule with grade-inflating advanced classes. But while attending the school would fulfill a dream, he wanted to keep working, and getting to and from Ann Arbor would add ninety minutes of commuting time to each day. He decided to apply at the university's Dearborn campus, which would let him keep a full schedule at the car rental and put less of a dent into his savings.

Around this same time, Delane had begun thinking about startup ideas. He'd been becoming more seriously interested in tech and entrepreneurship, and the idea for the Plenty Discounts coupon platform had begun to percolate in his mind. One day, he sat playing video games on the couch in the gaming room of his cousin Juan's house alongside Juan and a friend, a deejay who went by Ubb. Delane told them about his business concept. Juan seemed impressed.

"You think he can pull this off?" Juan asked Ubb.

"Yeah, man," said Ubb. "DAP's smart."

Juan agreed with his buddy. "When it's time," he told Delane, "you let me know how much you need. I can help you get off the ground."

The Parnell family had a cluster of birthdays in late August and early September, including Delane's, his aunt's, and a few cousins', so Juan made sure the entire clan gathered every Labor Day weekend to celebrate. A few days before Delane started class, they went to Terri's mother's house in Southfield. They played cornhole and horseshoes in the backyard, sat around the table and played card games. Juan manned the grill as always, flipping burgers and cooking up dogs. The family was bigger now—some of the kids had kids of their own—so it was one of the few times each year when everyone could be together, having drinks and sharing laughs.

Delane began his courses at Dearborn a few days later. He'd decided to major in digital marketing as a way of gaining some expertise on this new world of online commerce that excited him so much. He figured after he graduated he could continue on to get his MBA. He arranged a schedule that allowed him to keep working at the rental agency full-time. Most days, he would finish up class and head straight to the shop.

One night in September, Terri burst into Delane's room in the middle of the night. Something terrible had happened.

Juan had been shot.

Delane dressed frantically. He and his mom raced to the car and drove to the hospital. Cousins and aunts and grandparents filed in, upset and bleary-eyed. They comforted each other in the waiting room. Soon the doctor came out and delivered the news. Juan's gunshot wounds were too much to overcome. He was gone.

Delane had known for a long time that Juan was involved in the drug trade. Juan was gregarious and affable, which made it easy to overlook. He had always made a good life for himself. But now the darker aspects of that life had tragically caught up with him. Without his cousin there, Delane fell into a depression.

"Delane was right in the midst of finding a new anchor in his life," recalled his Aunt Libby, "and it was ripped away."

When Delane returned to school, he found he was no longer all that interested in learning. Finding motivation at the car rental wasn't easy. He felt lost.

"I was depressed," he said later. "I didn't have my cousin there, who was always my guiding light. He kept me on track."

As Delane earned more, conversations with his mom seemed to steer more and more toward the topic of money. The house on Burgess began to feel crowded, even with just him, his mother, and his stepfather living in it. Delane, deeply protective of his personal space, would get annoyed when Terri's friends and their children came over. Sometimes there would be guests in the house, and he would leave to get away for a few hours, only to come back home and find them still there, their kids hanging out on his floor or in his bed.

One day, Delane went to Ashley's house and returned to find one of Terri's friends using his laptop. He confronted his mom about it in front of everyone. Terri took her friend's side. Delane was livid. He'd had enough. Fed up, he stormed over to the case where Terri kept her china, grabbed it with both hands and pushed it over. It hit the ground with a *crash*, smashing the cups and bowls into shards that splattered across the floor. Delane stuffed some clothes into a bag, rushed out of the house, and climbed into Juan's blue box truck, which he'd been driving in the weeks since Juan had died. He steered onto Eight Mile Road and drove with no destination in mind. As thoughts raced through his head, he found himself crossing over to the east side of town, toward Juan's house. Once he got there, he pulled the truck to the curb and looked at the home where he'd spent so much time with one of his closest family members. He thought about Juan and started to cry. He sat there for a few minutes, alone in the truck in the dark, missing his cousin.

Delane drove back across town to the house in Southfield where DaeLon lived with their grandmother and her husband. All the lights were out; it was too late to knock on the door. He shut the engine, pitched back his seat, and went to sleep. The next morning, DaeLon spotted the blue truck through the window and went out to find his brother sleeping inside. He woke him up and let him in. Delane showered and thought about his options. He wasn't going to go back home; he couldn't spend any length of time at his Aunt Libby's because he was deathly allergic to her cats. He had never been as close with his grandparents as his brother was, given that DaeLon had grown up with them. Plus, he got the feeling that his step-grandfather, Dave, didn't seem to particularly care for him. He asked if he could stay with them for a bit anyway. They agreed. But even though Delane was now living with his grandparents and brother, without Juan, he felt further from his family than ever.

"It was pretty traumatic, I think," said Delane. "I was pretty lonely back then."

Delane did well in his college courses, earning a 3.65 GPA. But he realized it wasn't the path he desired for himself. He wanted to be making money, not spending it. After one semester, he withdrew from the University of Michigan–Dearborn.

Delane spent the next year working at the car rental, continuing to learn more about the business and help it grow. Eventually, though, he started to think again about his Plenty Discounts idea. He had an itch that wouldn't go away. He needed to try to break into the tech world, to attempt to build something. Aside from Ashley, Juan had been the only person he had talked to at length about his idea. Juan had shown faith in Delane that he could get it done. There was no reason he shouldn't feel the same way himself.

"That was when I was like, 'I've got to change my life, because my cousin would have wanted me to, and I owe him that,'" said Delane. "As a kid, and still today, one of the things that drove me was wasted potential. I was around so many smart people, in my family and outside of my family, who were brilliant. But because they were in these circumstances, these environments where no one was pushing them, they didn't have someone in their life to motivate them to do better. They didn't have even the self-awareness to recognize that this isn't a good situation, and that they should tap into their talents. They ended up having all these dreams and all of the opportunity to go out and actually tackle these dreams, and they never did it. I never wanted to end up like that."

Losing Juan had caused Delane to hurt in a way he never had before. It spiraled him into a depression that lasted for more than a year, and it temporarily sapped him of the ambition that had always defined him. But, when he looked back on it years later, he recognized that it might have been the most pivotal event of his existence, the incident that led to the chain of events that determined the course of the rest of his life.

"Juan was one of the only people in my life that knew I wanted to build something in tech, and he believed in me," said Delane. "He didn't even know anything about it, but he believed in me. He was always pushing me to not fit in and to go against the grain, do what's in my heart, and always do the right thing. When he passed away, I was like 'I've got to get serious about something.' Tech was the thing that I had fallen in love with, and he believed that I could do it. Without that moment, I don't know if this happens. That moment is what pushed me in this direction."

12

ACHIEVEMENT

UNLOCKED

KYLE MAGOFFIN SAT on a stool in a microbrewery in Orange, Massachusetts, a cold beer resting on the bar in front of him. He'd been thinking a lot about Justin lately. His student only had a few months left in his senior year. If he maintained his grades and kept coming to school, he'd be able to graduate, something that had seemed like a long shot just a year and a half earlier. Still, Justin's home life wasn't pleasant. A few times, Justin, home alone in the trailer without a car or money, had texted Magoffin to tell him he was hungry, and the coach had brought him some food. Once, Justin sent a message while Magoffin and his wife were on vacation. The coach called up a shop in Orange and had a pizza delivered to the home. Still, despite the way the world tended to conspire against him, Justin seemed to be getting things together. He didn't know what came next, but he was thinking about community college. He might just have a future after all. Magoffin was hopeful.

Farther down the bar, two women chatted. Orange was a small town; everyone knew everyone. They congratulated Magoffin on the baby his wife was due to have in a few weeks. "How's the esports thing going?" asked the first woman, the mother of a girl in Magoffin's gym class.

"Going well," he replied. While they spoke for a moment, the second woman's face soured. It was clear she had something to add.

"Kids are obsessed with these games," she loudly pronounced. "I have a nephew who plays them all night."

Magoffin listened patiently. "But," he said, "we're giving them a space to do that constructively, with supervision."

The woman acted as if she hadn't heard, slightly shifting the subject of her annoyance to cell phones and tablets. "Kids are always on their phones," she said. "I've seen parents give their devices to their kids to keep them quiet. I don't like it one bit." When an awkward silence fell over the three patrons, the first woman looked toward Magoffin and spoke up again.

"I think it's a great thing, what you're doing."

It was the kind of conversation Magoffin, and just about all the newly minted esports coaches across the country, dealt with often. As the popularity of video games rose, so did the number of opinions on allowing kids to play them. Every parent or teacher who furrowed their brow at the mention of esports in school seemed to know someone whose kid stayed up playing until 3:00 a.m. or refused to do their homework until their match ended.

The concerns were legitimate. People do, in fact, get addicted to video games. In 2013, the American Psychiatric Association listed "Internet Gaming Disorder" as a condition worth studying further to determine if it was worth official inclusion in the next edition of its manual. The World Health Organization took the step of officially recognizing "gaming disorder" in 2019, defining it as gaming that continually takes priority over other interests, has negative consequences, and results in "marked distress or significant impairment in personal, family, social, educational, occupational, or other important areas of functioning." But that's not to say the condition is common. Various studies have found that anywhere from 0.6 to 6 percent of gamers could be considered addicted. Still, medical diagnosis or not, there are certainly plenty of kids who play games more than they should, or more than the adults in their lives would like. The debate raged on. Pushback came from politicians, school administrators, the media. When Colorado was on the brink of adopting esports, a former MLB pitcher who had since taken to coaching high school baseball wrote in the *Coloradoan* that the decision to include esports as an officially sanctioned sport was "an absolutely horrific, horrendous, ludicrous, terrible, and potentially damaging mistake." He continued: "The most discouraging and misleading thing about this is the notion that it's 'a different segment of the high school population' that will become engaged. That's not true. What this will actually do is take kids away from more productive and physically active activities and land them squarely on their couches, controller in hand."

As it played out in reality, kids across the country were finding ways of balancing their esports teams with their other sports and activities. Many others were participating in something for the first time. By 2020, as more schools came on board and more data became available, PlayVS found that 45 percent of the high school esports players in the country were participating in their first-ever extracurricular activity.

"The majority of these students are not on the basketball courts or softball fields. They're not playing in the band or part of the debate team," said Mark Koski at the NFHS. "So, this is another way for us to grab more students and put them within our educational walls after school and provide them a safe setting. . . . Any time we can get more students involved in after-school programs, it's a positive thing."

As Mahar Regional's team grew, though, it was clear there was still important work to be done. Through four seasons, the team still hadn't recruited a girl to its roster. Magoffin and his players, perhaps not surprisingly, hadn't found any volunteers to be the only girl on an all-boys team. At one point, the school spoke with the principal at the local elementary school about setting up an unofficial esports program to serve as a feeder into the middle and high schools, the idea being to get girls interested before they reached an age when social stigmas would be more likely to discourage them. The problem was far from exclusive to Mahar. Across the country, the number of girls playing esports was low, at many schools a single-digit percentage. Changing that was crucial—not only for the sake of giving girls the same chances as their male peers to make friends and spend more time in super-vised settings, but also to help nurture their interest in a field that was ripe with job opportunities. Increasing the urgency was a study that found that girls who played significant amounts of video games were three times as likely to pursue careers in STEM (science, technology, engineering, and math)—fields in which jobs tend to be relatively better-paying and future-proof. To help ame-liorate the issue, PlayVS in 2020 began charging all-girls schools half-price and providing discounts to schools fielding at least one all-girls team.

Bringing on female coaches, the company knew, was also important. In Colorado, the team at Cherry Creek High School won the state's first-ever *League of Legends* championship. The squad had two girls, a senior and a freshman, in its six-person starting rotation—a fact that was perhaps in part because it was coached by a woman, Alex Bak. PlayVS's community team began asking coaches to cover the topic of girls in esports, often during the "office hours" sessions that it hosted for coaches online as it tried to make its platform more inclusive.

For the startup and for the industry as a whole, there was still much work to be done. But there were also signs of progress. Down in Georgia, Ashley Hodge, the Colquitt County High coach who had spent years being mercilessly bullied while play-ing online, landed a new job at a high school thanks to her esports expertise. The new school, Dodge County High, wanted her to build and launch an esports program from the ground up, just like she'd already done for Colquitt. Right before she started the gig, she found out she'd been named to the five-person board of advisors for Riot Games's scholastic association, the governing body of its high school and college competitions. Now Hodge would have a say not only in how her own team would be built, but in how the games would be played across the country. Esports was growing. And women, if people like Hodge had anything to do with it, were going to be a big part of its future.

As PlayVS itself grew, it took efforts to ensure that under-represented voices were heard. At Delane's instruction, the company held a fifth "independent" board seat—an outside voice who could advise the company—that was always to be held by a woman. Among the startup's first sixty hires, more than half were women, people of color, or both—something that, statistically, should be true of any random population sample in America, but was far from reality for most of the tech world. Delane wanted to keep this momentum going.

The next step, he believed, was to hire a director of talent who could serve as a chief recruiter and oversee the company's growth. He decided early on that he wanted to hire a Black person for the role, both for the sake of being able to tap into the individual's network, and also to have them serve as the face of the company to job applicants. Delane several years earlier had met a man named Charles Kuykendoll at the Bay Area's AfroTech Confer-ence, and the two stayed in touch, mostly via a groupchat that several attendees had formed. Kuykendoll was well connected and had an impressive resume—he had worked as a recruiter for Facebook and was now serving in a similar role for Airbnb.

One day, Delane sent him a private text:

You're one of the best recruiters I know. Can you help me out?

Kuykendoll called up Delane. "Hey man," said Kuykendoll, "just tell me what you're looking for. I know everyone."

He was misunderstanding. Delane wanted him for the position. Kuykendoll was flattered, but it wasn't an option. Airbnb had paid to move his family from Northern California to Los Angeles when he began with the company just nine months earlier. He felt indebted.

"Nah," he told Delane. "Things are great here. I love Airbnb. I can't do it."

A few months later, Kuykendoll returned to the AfroTech Conference in Oakland. During one of the weekend's final sessions, he sat in the front row, watching Delane expertly handle an interview on stage. Dressed in a denim jacket over a gray hoodie and an all-black Detroit Tigers cap, Delane spoke about how he got PlayVS off the ground, what the startup had accomplished so far, and what he still hoped to achieve. He talked about how the company was building infrastructure for the 99.9 percent of gamers who were not pros, how students could now earn varsity letters alongside their basketball- and football-playing peers, and how colleges were offering esports scholarships to high schoolers. The audience ate it up. So did Kuykendoll.

"My jaw dropped," he recalled. "I only knew him as a friend. I had never seen him in that light before."

Not only was Delane inspiring, but the vision resonated. Kuykendoll had grown up on the West Side of Chicago. His parents couldn't afford to shell out the money for his college education, so they told him he'd have to join the Army, earn a scholarship, or pay his own way. He wasn't a star athlete; he was a talented singer, but not good enough to earn a free ticket. He ended up finding a nonprofit that helped cover his fees and taking out loans to pay for the rest. He knew how life-changing esports could have been for him.

A few days later, Kuykendoll called up Delane and told him he would come work for him.

"I'm a thirty-two-year-old guy, but I'm trusting my livelihood to somebody in their twenties," he said later. "That's not something that I took lightly."

On Kuykendoll's first day with PlayVS, Delane posted a photo on Instagram of the two of them on the balcony in the new office, the first floor stretched out beneath them, each of them grinning wide. "Rare to see a black CEO and Head of Talent at a high-profile startup," read Delane's caption. "Proud of what we're creating." It quickly became the most-liked post on Delane's account and garnered hundreds of comments of encouragement.

"HUGE for the culture. Your impact is going to be a legacy," read one, accompanied by an emoji of Black hands praying.

The same week Kuykendoll started, though, hanging over every conversation was the specter of a new virus that had been infecting pockets of people across America. By the following week, PlayVS decided to shut down its office due to COVID-19. Employees switched to remote work. All meetings became virtual. The usual chatter in the kitchen or gaming area was replaced by conversations on Slack. One by one, states across the country decided to send their students home. If PlayVS was going to try to salvage its spring season, it was going to have to adjust the way it handled its matches. The company's official rulebook had always stated that all matches needed to be held in-person, with all students in the same room as their coach. Clearly, this was no longer feasible. PlayVS quickly amended the rule to allow students to log on from home and play their matches remotely.

Not everyone was able to. The decision of whether to keep the esports season going varied from state to state, district to district, school to school—and sometimes team to team, depending on the technical capabilities each player had at home. At some schools, especially in rural areas, many students' houses didn't have internet. In Thorsby, a town of fewer than two thousand in central Alabama, Jay LeCroy's teams got sent home in late March. Practically none of the students had the combination of a capable computer and high-speed internet necessary for playing online.

"There's parts of this area where it's third world," said LeCroy, lamenting that he hadn't thought to take home some of the school's gaming computers and drop them off with his players when he had the chance. As it was, Chilton County High had a single team of three *Smite* players that was able to continue its season. "One of them has got his own computer, one's got a laptop, and one's got a friend," said LeCroy. "That's the only team I've got left right now."

Mahar Regional faced a similar issue. Without enough students able to play from home, Coach Magoffin had to call the season off. There would be no triumphant final stand for the Mahar Disruptors, no last hurrah in Justin's senior year. Trapped at home in the trailer without his esports team to distract him, Justin began to languish. He became depressed. He tried to keep up with his classes via Zoom, but his attendance fell, even though going to school now only required logging online. His grades slipped. Magoffin began to worry about his student. Justin was so close to completing the turnaround, and now, with only three months to go, it had been derailed.

Other schools were more fortunate. In Honolulu, the team at 'Iolani carried on. The students used Discord to communicate with one another about the matches, and each team had a designated captain who was responsible for making sure everybody logged on at the right time. Two boarding students on the varsity *League of Legends* team had flown back home, one to Singapore and one to South Korea, and they participated from abroad. The state of Hawaii hosted a full slate of esports playoffs and a championship remotely, making esports the only sport in the state that was able to hold its spring championship. The same was true in many other states—while baseball, softball, and lacrosse teams stashed away their equipment, esports players competed in officially sanctioned state championships from computers in their bedrooms and living rooms.

The show went on at the college level as well. Chaos initially reigned, with leagues canceling their matches as campuses figured out their plans for shutting down. But once students returned home, the vast majority were able to continue playing remotely. Throughout the summer, as COVID wiped out in-person activities, video game usage skyrocketed. Epic Games made a reported $400 million from *Fortnite* in April alone, its most lucrative month ever. Microsoft, maker of Xbox, during the spring revealed a 130 percent year-over-year increase in multiplayer engagement. Streaming viewership on Twitch rose by 50 percent. By year's end, the worldwide video game industry would grow to an estimated $180 billion in revenue—bigger than the global film and North American pro sports industries combined. PlayVS, of course, wasn't benefiting from any of this directly. People playing games at home, independent of their schools, had no bearing on the company's usership. But Delane was hopeful that the trend would help his company in the long-term. "People," he said, "are going to remember the time when video games were the only sporting competition left."

Some PlayVS employees were personally affected in the virus's early days. In March, Laz Alberto's parents and sister started experiencing symptoms. Soon, an aunt had to be hospitalized and intubated. All the while, Alberto was stuck forty miles away, unable to visit his loved ones and relegated to receiving updates via text and FaceTime. Everyone eventually recovered, including his aunt, who spent thirty days in a coma, but the experience was eye-opening for Alberto. Meanwhile, his younger brother, Evan, had been developing a career as a social media influencer, amassing millions of followers on Instagram and TikTok with his card tricks and illusions. Alberto in his spare time had been helping his sibling manage his social media profiles and work with sponsors. Evan had grown to be the most-followed magician on the platforms, and the job was earning him real income. Alberto wanted to dedicate himself full-time to helping his brother grow. The timing seemed right. Alberto's role at PlayVS had been diminishing as the company grew larger and took on more VPs and executives who handled its relationships with states and publishers. In May, he broke the news to Delane that he'd be leaving PlayVS. With the whole company working remotely, there would be no party, no farewell hugs. In lieu of that, Alberto tweeted a thread of his favorite memories at PlayVS: Earning the industry-shifting deal at the NFHS conference in Scottsdale. Holding meetings with the team in a dark conference room in the Science office while building the infrastructure for the first high school esports season. The Massachusetts state championship at Gillette Stadium during the subzero week of utter chaos. Alberto followed the photos with a note:

> *I couldn't be more grateful to @Delane and the whole @PlayVS team for the past 2 years. Endings are tough. But I know this company is just getting started, and I'm humbled I got to be a part of its beginnings.*

Delane responded with a tweet of his own:

PlayVS wouldn't be here today without you. I'm so grateful for all of the long hours and brainpower you put into my dream. I'll miss stealing stuff off your desk, but I'm glad you won't take more of my money in Madden 😂

Sitting in his parents' backyard not long after, Alberto reflected on his decision. "Family is super important to me. It's the most important thing to me," he said. "It definitely wasn't easy. It was hard to move on from that chapter of life. To be so involved with starting something in the beginning, to now not being there, it feels weird. But, ultimately, I think it was the right call for me."

Birds chirped in a tree nearby. He seemed at peace. There would be no more crisscrossing the country by plane, no more weeks and months away from home. After nearly three years of working with the startup, nearly two years as an employee, Alberto could turn his energy back to his family, the thing that had always been the paramount aspect of his life.

WHILE DELANE WAS working at the car rental and trying to break into a career in tech, Gene Donald was off in Kalamazoo taking classes at Western Michigan University. There he noticed that campus organizations and Greek houses all seemed to have T-shirts emblazoned with their logos and clever sayings. Gene, artistically talented and ever entrepreneurial, bought a vinyl cutter and taught himself how to use it to print designs onto T-shirts. He undercut the online shops the students had been using and launched a business that he operated out of his car. The cash rolled in—so much so that Gene dropped out of college and launched a storefront in the Detroit suburb of Oak Park called Fresh Baked Prints.

Gene and Delane stayed close through the years, two Detroit-area kids working on their own hustles. When Delane was first heading out to Los Angeles to begin working on the esports idea with Science, he called up his friend and told him about the opportunity. Gene did some perfunctory Googling about esports while Delane talked.

"I was like, 'I'm interested in that,'" recalled Gene. "'I don't really understand it. I don't see how you're going to make money off of gaming, when games are free. But whatever. If you think you can do something with it, here. Boom! Here's some bread.' That's the level of trust I have for him.'"

He told Delane to come by his house to pick up the money. When Delane pulled up, Gene handed him a brown paper bag filled with bills. "I said, 'Dude, I can't take this cash. Tell your mom I need it in a check,'" Delane remembered. "I was like, Gene thinks we're selling weed or something!"

Gene wrote a check for $5,000 and officially became the first investor in PlayVS. Later, after Delane had secured the NFHS partnership and was in the midst of raising the startup's first venture round, Gene and some friends rented a house with a pool for a week in Los Angeles. Delane came by to visit. There, he told Gene about the progress the company had made.

"Everything's looking really good," Delane told him. "If you've got some extra money or anything to invest, you should."

"I'm like, 'Shit, I don't even got no type of bread to make this make sense,'" Gene recalled. "'You've got $15 million! What do you want from me?' He was like, 'If you've got some extra money, and it wouldn't hurt, everything is going good. It would make sense to invest.' It was the way he said it. I got it. He always wanted to see his friends make money and win."

Gene wrote another check and, on Delane's advice, increased his stake in the rapidly growing startup. (Years later, Gene wouldn't reveal just how much stake he had in the company. "I don't want everyone to know how rich I am," he said with a laugh.)

As PlayVS grew and Delane was invited to speak at festivals and conferences like SXSW and AfroTech, he often asked Gene if he wanted to come watch. Gene didn't take him up on it until the *Forbes* Under 30 Summit in Boston in October 2018. Delane was about to be named to the list and was invited to give a talk. PlayVS had already launched to the world; it had announced its $15.5 million funding round and its partnership with the NFHS, and the first season of high school esports was about to get underway. Delane was the talk of the gaming world. He booked Gene a room in the classy hotel where he was staying. When he arrived, he told Gene to meet him in the lobby. Gene came down to find his friend surrounded by a group of people trying to introduce themselves to him. "People from everywhere, every state, every color," recalled Gene. "They're like, 'I'm so excited to meet you.' I'm just standing there next to him like, 'Are you serious?'"

Eventually, Delane slipped away, and the pair headed to the conference hall down the street where Delane's talk was taking place. After his interview, more attendees flocked to him, including executives from massive media and electronics firms. Gene finally caught Delane during a quiet moment.

"Bro," he said, "I did not know you were like this."

"Yeah, man," said Delane. "This is what I've been telling you."

Delane had invited a handful of other friends to come out to Boston for the conference. They watched him speak, and together the group headed to an after-party with other honorees and the *Forbes* staff. When Delane and his friends, all of whom were Black, reached the white security guard, the man asked to see their credentials. They pulled out their phones and brought up emails from *Forbes* indicating that Delane was a speaker at the event and the magazine had invited them. The guard refused. Eventually, several editors came out to tell the man that Delane was with them, and they could come in. Still, the guard declined to let them through, apparently not convinced that Delane and his friends were supposed to be there. "They had jewelry on, chains and stuff," recalled Delane. "They wouldn't let us in. I was the keynote speaker, and I was going to be the cover person for gaming, and the guy wouldn't let me into the party." Some of the *Forbes* staffers decided to leave the event and take Delane and his friends elsewhere.

Incidents like this were commonplace for Delane throughout his career in venture capital and tech. That changed little even as his profile rose. At SXSW the following spring, the same week Delane was to deliver a ballroom talk about the esports industry, he, Marcus Carey, and a small group of friends headed to a party organized by one of America's biggest tech companies. When they got to the entrance, Delane flashed the invitation on his phone. The woman checking credentials at the gate questioned its legitimacy. Delane explained who he was and why he'd been invited. The woman called over security; Delane and the group briefly pleaded their case before deciding to leave, annoyed and not wanting to escalate things any further.

"We were well dressed, we were respectful," he recalled. "Unfortunately, it's just a regular part of life. I try not to remember things like that and just give my attention to other stuff. It makes me sad. It breaks my heart." Over the years, Delane learned the most surefire way to ensure things went smoothly when he traveled to events. "I bring someone who is not Black," he said, "someone who works for me or works at an agency we work with, and they handle all of the communications. When I show up, I just get to come in. That's the only time we've been able to travel with almost no issue."

Delane was the CEO of a company that had raised nearly $100 million. He'd been covered in the most prominent business publications, spoken at some of the country's biggest tech conferences, appeared on countless "entrepreneurs to watch" lists. And he still often reverted to that familiar feeling of not belonging.

"I think the thing that people don't realize," he said, "is that in tech, no matter how much money you raise, how hot your company is, how much you've been dominating the market, it doesn't matter. People will always try to find ways to remind you that you're Black. And I think they try to conflate that with, like, being lesser. It's a wild thing, man."

Sometimes, people's biases directly affected the business's ability to grow. Most often, the acts were subtle, or disguisable as something else, like someone refusing to take a call if Delane was on it, or directing their questions toward his white colleagues in the room. But other times, Delane faced racism directly, usually from educators, septuagenarian white men who came out and said they wouldn't work with him because he was Black. After one such meeting, Delane left the Science conference room with tears in his eyes. He walked past Laz Alberto's desk. Alberto, as the son of two Cuban immigrants, had an idea of where Delane was coming from. He stopped Delane in his tracks. "No one can build this company but you," said Alberto. "Just remember that."

Growing in stature gave Delane the opportunity to bring other Black entrepreneurs along with him. When he got invited to a CEO conference in Hawaii, Delane looked at the guest list and saw that he was the only Black person on it. He sent a note back to the organizers with the names of half a dozen Black tech CEOs and said he would only come if they were invited too. The organizers declined. Delane told them he couldn't come. "They were kind of mad at me about that," he said. "But I'm no one's token Black guy. I'm not interested."

When Delane spoke at the AfroTech conference, the hood he wore up over his head was very much a conscious fashion choice. Thanks to entrepreneurs like Mark Zuckerberg, the hoodie had come to symbolize the new age in the business world, the relaxing of norms as a younger generation of founders built up the most powerful companies in the world. At least, that's what it meant for white people. For Black people, the hoodie meant something different, as Delane came to understand when Trayvon Martin was killed while walking home from a convenience store.

"That's actually one of the reasons why I dress the way I do, authentic to who I am," said Delane. "To show that Black people, Black men especially, we can wear our hoods and not be gangsters, not be what people try to portray us as."

Delane made it a habit to appear at events like AfroTech, where he could speak directly to Black people trying to break into the tech space and dispense some of the knowledge he'd gained during his climb. He helped organize meetings on the new audio app Clubhouse that listeners could tune in to and learn from him and people like investors Troy Carter, Suzy Ryoo, and Chris Lyons, as well as rappers like Meek Mill and Wiz Khalifa.

After one four-hour session, one attendee wrote on Instagram:

By far my fav room since I joined. @delane gave so much free game.

Following the death of George Floyd at the hands of Minneapolis police on May 25, 2020, it was clear to anyone who followed Delane on social media that something had changed in him. He had become more outspoken about social justice issues across his platforms during the previous months, but after Floyd was killed, he seemed to entirely stop holding back. The day after Floyd's death, Delane posted on Instagram a single white square with a Black fist in the center and the words:

> *I wish America loved us as much as they love our culture and money. Fuck them, I love us.*

In the following days and weeks, his Instagram story on several occasions featured images of Floyd and other Black Americans killed at the hands of white people, like Ahmaud Arbery, who was hunted down in Georgia by two white men in a pickup truck who believed he'd trespassed, and Breonna Taylor, who was shot to death in her apartment by Louisville police officers executing a no-knock warrant.

Delane wrote on Twitter:

> *For the few VCs who have black founders in your portfolio, you should be reaching out to show love and check on their welfare. Building a company is already stressful, even more so during COVID, but nothing compares to how we feel in moments like now with respect to George Floyd.*

Over the next few weeks, Delane used his social media accounts to publicize videos of police brutality and subtly, or sometimes directly, call out people in tech who he felt weren't doing enough for the Black community. It was a stark change from a few short years earlier, when he had tweeted "Black Excellence" with a Black fist emoji, then deleted it at the request of a state executive.

Those close to Delane noticed the shift. "I've seen him evolve in terms of using his platform to make a difference," said Hajj Flemings, his former business partner from the events back in Detroit. "The things that he talks about on social media, as they relate to racial injustice and trying to make sure that he's a voice for our community, he takes that extremely seriously. He also does it knowing that he's somewhat of a made man. So he's not worried about whether somebody likes him or not."

In the days after Floyd's death, Delane donated $15,000 apiece to Black Lives Matter and the Southern Poverty Law Center on behalf of PlayVS. The company announced publicly that it would match employee donations to any charitable organization that was meaningful to them and that it was making Juneteenth and Election Day company holidays.

On June 19, 2020, the anniversary of the day American slaves were finally freed more than two years after the Emancipation Proclamation, Delane and Kuykendoll hopped into one of Delane's vehicles and drove to Inglewood for a socially distanced celebration. They rode in a car parade that snaked through several predominantly Black LA neighborhoods. People danced and cheered on the sidewalks and in the streets.

"We wanted to say, 'Hey, we are all in this together,'" Kuykendoll said later. "It's not like George Floyd is some person that could not have been a Delane Parnell or a Charles Kuykendoll, because we have nice cars and have made lives for ourselves. No, that could have been us. That was the message that we wanted to give."

As conversations about social justice and equitable hiring practices rippled through corporate America, PlayVS was on its way to hiring its hundredth staff member. When the company reached that milestone in 2020, one-third of its employees identified as women, and half as Black, Asian, Hispanic/Latino, or multiple races.

"This is really where PlayVS is setting the standard," said Kuykendoll. "We are doing it. It can be done. And now there's no longer an excuse for it not to happen. Your C-suite needs to look a certain way, your VP level needs to be looking a certain way, and your director level. Attract, retain, promote. And if that's not something that you're focused on, you're going to get called out about it. People ain't playing games anymore." The company hadn't put hiring quotas in place—it happened organically. Having Delane at the top, Kuykendoll admitted, made his job of bringing in a wide range of talent much easier. "I've never experienced this at any other company that I've worked for," he said, "where people say, 'Hey, I didn't know about your company, but I saw a YouTube video of your CEO. I'm fully inspired by his story. That's why I wanted to reach out.' We haven't had to do anything structurally from a recruitment standpoint to make sure that diversity is happening. We're getting it organically, top-down."

With the protests and discussions about racial equality at a fever pitch, NEA asked Delane if he wanted to speak at a webinar hosted by BLCK VC, a nonprofit with the goal of increasing Black representation in venture capital. Wearing a gray T-shirt and large black headphones, Delane spoke through his camera to an online audience and offered advice on creating a more diverse tech world.

If you're a venture capitalist, he suggested, hire at least one Black partner, and let them bring in a Black analyst or principal. Dedicate some amount of money to investing in founders of color—even if it's small, it's a start. "If you're a non-Black founder," he continued, "be intentional and proactive about hiring Black talent. We might not have the traditional valued background, but we're passionate, we're talented, we will work hard. Give us a shot. Your probability of success is lower if you don't."

He advised hiring a Black recruiter, like he had done, who can help your company create a talented pipeline of people of color. And he concluded with some instruction that was less material, more inspirational. "If you're a Black founder, don't give up. I know it's tough. I know the journey's hard, but it's worth it. Keep going."

IN THE SPRING of 2020, Delane finally made a hire he'd been working on for months: a chief operating officer. He had long known he needed to bring on someone who could act like a deputy, handling many of the day-to-day business operations that had remained on his plate, but he'd had trouble finding the right fit. The candidate he chose was Chris Nakutis Taylor, who had held managerial roles and been among the first 250 employees at both Uber and Bird.

Delane's mentors had taught him that ensuring your subordinates' principles aligned with your own was the best way to ensure they could operate autonomously and make appropriate decisions along the way. On one of Taylor's first days with PlayVS, Delane presented him with a short slide deck that expounded on his vision for the company. It laid out that he wanted PlayVS to expand across high school, college, and the broader amateur level with the utmost focus on the player experience. It provided Delane's ideal head count at various stages of the company's growth. It described, in general terms, the steps the company would have to take to achieve Delane's goal of being one of the biggest, if not the biggest, esports companies in the world, the go-to platform for gamers on several continents. Delane also laid out his management style, as he'd begun doing for new hires who reported directly to him: he expected people to hit their goals; he wanted decisions to be based on data, not anecdotes; he valued overcommunication, but he liked messages to him to be short, for efficiency's sake—and if you needed a response, you should be sure to note that; and, if you were assigned to do something, and he had to check in with you about it, that was considered a failure on your part.

Giving up much of the daily business operations would have been unimaginable for Delane just a year earlier. But he'd been gradually letting go of more responsibilities, thanks in part to coaching from people like Dick Costolo. Costolo had instilled in Delane an important philosophy: the only decisions that a CEO should make are the ones that *only* a CEO can make. Over the past year, Delane had whittled down his direct reports to only a handful of executives and team leaders. He had stepped back from the hiring process unless it was an executive or VP, instead trusting the company's managers to choose the right people for the job. He was no longer involved in in-the-weeds operations or design decisions, and he only went to meetings when there was an express need for him to be present.

Robert Lamvik, the company's head of growth, had to depart the startup in the spring due to his wife's visa issues after a tenure of a little more than a year. "In my twelve to thirteen months there," said Lamvik, "Delane evolved so much as a human being and as a CEO. To go from being so hands-on to being hands-off and empowering the team—that's a dramatic, 180-degree shift as a leader."

The kinds of design decisions in which Delane still played a role involved things like the company's logo. Delane had wanted to change the emblem for some time. Though he had a soft spot for the pooch it was modeled after, he had never been in love with the symbol; it was unclear what kind of creature it was, and he wasn't a fan of the font that accompanied it. Many of the brands with which PlayVS's gamer audience interacted most often had widely recognizable characters for logos—Discord, a controller with a face; Twitch, a bot; Reddit, an alien; Snapchat, a ghost. Delane wanted an icon worthy of that lineup.

PlayVS hired a well-respected San Francisco design firm, and a few designers came down to visit the Santa Monica office on multiple occasions. One of them dozed off in several of the early meetings, which didn't exactly inspire confidence in the process for the folks at PlayVS. Then the firm delivered its first round of mockups, and they hadn't followed the company's most basic instruction—to create a character. The back-and-forth dragged on for four months before Delane decided the startup should cut its losses, settle up with the agency, and walk away.

Things went better with the second firm. After several sessions, it presented PlayVS with a handful of designs. Delane narrowed it down to two, then walked out of the meeting room and onto the office floor, where he gathered up Lamvik, Sean Yalda, D'Andre Ealy, Alinn Louv, and Ryan Le, all of whom he knew wouldn't be afraid to tell him their true opinions. Each person wrote down which of the two logos they liked best. The winner was an orange flame icon with a pair of eyes that looked vaguely like a gaming controller rotated to its side. Delane believed the symbol was fun enough for high schoolers, but not too childish for adults—plus, the fire emoji had a positive connotation in the online world. Internally, the new logo soon came to be known as "Fire Bob," an homage to Bob LeDuc, the employee who had spearheaded the process. This led to some confusion when unknowing staffers saw the phrase being used in the company's Slack chats and came to believe there was a company-wide movement to terminate their colleague. Soon, though, the misunderstanding was resolved, and the company launched its new flame logo in the spring.

After the *Fortnite* debacle, PlayVS had spent the first half of the year creating more distinction between its two products,

Varsity and Club, by reworking the messaging on its website and building two separate user platforms. As it was, NFHS-approved *League of Legends*, *Rocket League*, and *Smite* were offered on the Varsity platform, which meant students in the states where esports had been ratified earned varsity letters and competed for official state championships in those three games. Any other matches were lumped onto the Club product—so, *Fortnite* in all fifty states and DC, as well as *League of Legends*, *Rocket League*, and *Smite* in states that hadn't yet given esports the green light.

PlayVS and Activision Blizzard reached an agreement in the summer of 2020 that allowed the startup to add *Overwatch* to its offerings. Similar to *Fortnite*, *Overwatch* includes shooting and animated violence. As such, PlayVS slotted the game into its Club product. Delane believed the NFHS and states were in agreement that the Varsity/Club distinction was an acceptable solution. But as the year went on, some states began joining Kentucky in refusing to allow their schools to offer *Fortnite*, and then *Overwatch*, even as a Club offering. They believed there still wasn't a clear enough delineation between the two products. Even though PlayVS was giving them different labels, the Varsity and Club teams were playing in the same classroom—which gave the impression that the shooter games were officially sanctioned, regardless of what you called the product. Even if there wasn't an established connection between the games and real-world violence, state athletic associations were under political pressure, in some cases receiving flak from their governors or departments of education for allowing the games in school.

One summer night, Delane emailed some of the key players within the NFHS and state associations and asked if they could meet online the following week to work through the problems. They agreed. "I put together a deck," recalled Delane, "and basically outlined every single issue that we had been working through, everything people had voiced or we had voiced. I didn't let people get off the phone until we all came to alignment on every single issue."

What the parties agreed upon amounted to a compromise. PlayVS would have two offerings for high school–age kids: a "High School" product, which included *League of Legends* and *Rocket League*, and would be recognized by the NFHS and the twenty-plus state associations that had thus far approved of esports; and a "Youth" product, which would be player-led and have no association with particular schools—kids could organize themselves onto teams with other youths from anywhere in the state, and the matches generally would take place at home. "Over time," Delane reflected, "when you're building something new, the format has to change. It has to evolve. The way you market it has to evolve; the competition evolves. I think this is something that would have naturally happened anyway."

PlayVS revealed the new structure to its schools ahead of the fall 2020 season. In August, with kids across the country stuck at home, it organized a *League of Legends* tournament for high schoolers and a *Fortnite* tournament for college students, letting coaches and players form teams and participate in matches from home. The competitions were free, and the winning teams got prizes like laptops, headsets, watches, keyboards, and gaming chairs. The event helped raise the company's profile during a period when growth at the high school level had become more challenging. The pandemic had pinched the revenues schools received from their states, like in Massachusetts, where Mahar Regional had to trim its annual budget and let go of a handful of its staff—including Eric Dion, the co-principal who had once shipped the school's first varsity letter to the PlayVS office. Still, PlayVS began the fall season with more schools and students signed up than in the spring, marking a fifth straight season of positive growth since launch.

As PlayVS matured and the spotlight on it brightened, the company drew its share of naysayers online and elsewhere. Some complained the startup was getting undue credit in the press and the gaming space for "creating" high school esports, when in reality, organically formed teams had existed for years, and organizations like High School Esports League, NASEF, and High School Starleague had predated it. Others were alarmed by the idea of a private company playing such a substantial role in the implementation of a high school sport. The concern wasn't without merit. On the one hand, aspects of high school sports have been moneymaking machines for years: brands like Nike, Under Armour, Riddell, and Rawlings sell essential equipment and apparel; arena and stadium operators get paid to host games and matches; media companies like ESPN—and the NFHS Network—broadcast interscholastic competitions. But PlayVS was a venture-backed company with investors to answer to, and it controlled a high school sport—from the rules to the schedules to the recruitment of coaches and players—to an extent that no other business had before.

That control only seemed to grow over time. In 2020, PlayVS and Riot Games announced that their deal had become exclusive, meaning any high school that wanted to play competitive *League of Legends* would have to do so through PlayVS. As the startup grew and gained leverage, competitors in the space were increasingly boxed out. Through it all, Delane remained unapologetic about the company's trajectory. "Imagine if there was one basketball court," he said in an interview during TechCrunch's virtual Disrupt conference, "and every kid who ever wanted to play basketball, whether it's on behalf of their school, or pickup, or some sort of tournament, that's the court that they had to play on. That's what we're building." States and schools essentially were left to hope that PlayVS, which retained the power of having exclusive deals with the NFHS and publishers of some of the most popular games in the world, played fair and continued to scale with kids' best interests in mind.

It seemed to be. From a fiscal perspective, PlayVS was operating esports much in the way other interscholastic sports were run. State athletic associations earn income from sponsorships and playoff tournament ticket sales, money that can then be allocated toward employee salaries, officials' fees, and hosting expenses. In the case of esports, PlayVS paid the states directly each year. Then, the schools paid PlayVS per participant—so, if enough kids signed up, the company ended up in the black in that state. At $64 per student per season, esports was cheaper than just about any other sport. Students didn't need to travel. And in many cases, they were using equipment the school already had. To sell this point to high schools, PlayVS's community team collected budget data from athletic directors it worked with, then ran some math. It determined its own fee was far less than the average cost per student of other sports, like football ($800 per student), baseball ($1,150), basketball ($1,200), and cheerleading ($1,615)—figures the company then happily posted on its website. Even so, the startup began offering discounted rates for schools that couldn't afford the fees, lowering them to as little as $1 per student for Title I schools with high proportions of low-income families.

To further incentivize high schools to sign up, PlayVS at the start of the 2020–2021 school year announced it would reward $600,000 in scholarship money to winning high school teams and players, some of it contributed by Epic Games and Psyonix. (The former acquired the latter in 2019.) PlayVS's prize money aside, college scholarships were becoming a legitimate factor in high school esports. Hundreds of universities across the country were offering scholarships totaling tens of millions of dollars. PlayVS was working to bridge the connection between high school and college esports. Ahead of the school year, the startup inked deals with Psyonix and Riot Games to offer *Rocket League* and *League of Legends* at the college level, which gave high school players a straightforward path to continue gaming competitively.

Meanwhile, Aakash Ranavat, who was leading PlayVS's college initiative, and a new hire, an MIT business school grad named Dela Gbordzoe, cold-called universities throughout the year. By the fall, just nine months after it began building its college product, the startup had teams from nearly 380 colleges and universities on its platform.

Athletes in other sports had clear avenues toward becoming college athletes: Make contact with coaches at universities and have them watch you play. Platforms like Hudl let high school athletes upload videos of themselves for college coaches to see, and websites like 247 and Rivals.com served as online hubs for all things recruiting. Esports, still in its early days, offered little of that formal structure. In the fall, PlayVS launched a new feature that let players create personal gaming profiles that tracked their in-match stats across various titles. The company didn't initially unveil the feature's purpose: to serve as a recruiting tool for high school esports players. The newly hired Gbordzoe, who played basketball in high school and was lightly recruited by hoops coaches before walking onto Texas A&M's practice squad, recognized the potential impact the features could have for gamers. "When I went to high school, Hudl had just come out, and being able to put up my videos was an incredible treat," he said. "That's ultimately what we want this to be—the Hudl or the 247 of esports."

That fall, Delane determined that COO Chris Nakutis Taylor wasn't a fit at the company and decided to let him go. He had to take on all of Taylor's responsibilities, including business development; Gabi Loeb, the CFO, re-inherited people operations. Delane's workload once again piled sky-high—not anything he wasn't used to.

Just before the season, the company opened the doors to Canadian schools to sign up for its Youth platform, the company's first-ever international expansion. As the school year got underway in schools across two countries, traditional sports like soccer, volleyball, and football were forced to postpone or cancel their seasons due to the pandemic. But at many schools, gamers logged on from their homes or played in socially distanced computer labs. For high school esports, the show went on.

KYLE MAGOFFIN AND his team milled about in the computer lab at Mahar Regional, ready to begin practice. It had been a few months since the school celebrated its graduating seniors with an online ceremony. Now, Magoffin's esports squad was ready to begin the first practice of the school year. Many new faces, including the team's first girl, filled the room—gamers ready to begin their journeys as high school athletes. The vibe wasn't quite the same without Isaiah, who had graduated in June. But there was still a familiar face there: Justin. He was ready to play some video games.

Coach Magoffin was excited to see his former student. It had been four months since Justin defied the odds and graduated, taking part in a socially distanced car parade through the parking lot—complete with the local fire and police departments—as well as a ceremony streamed on YouTube, the name of each student flashing on the screen along with a senior photo. Justin had decided not to enroll in community college. For now, he was making money working at the Dunkin' Donuts down the street in the mornings, then as Mahar Regional's assistant esports coach in the afternoons, a role for which Magoffin had hired him and agreed to split his coaching stipend. The coach had convinced Mahar's principal to let him hold practices and matches at the school, even while students took classes from home. The players showed up in masks at 2:00 p.m. each day and played in the lab. Justin helped the students strategize before the matches—which now included *Overwatch*—then hovered behind them to offer guidance on in-game tactical operations.

"The amount of mental battles we have to go through while we're playing these games, it's mental chess, really," said Justin. "You need to react so fast. It's so important for people to learn these skills because they can help you outside in the real world. I think that is pretty impactful. I hope more schools get involved. This really is something that needs to be happening everywhere."

In the computer lab, Justin was motivating the other students to play better, and even let his coach know when he heard through the grapevine that a student's grades might be in danger of falling below the eligibility line. He was hoping to find a career in gaming. Magoffin had been in touch with some folks at esports organizations that he'd met through his coaching gig. For Justin, having a high school diploma and a couple of jobs, including one in a field he loved, was a good start. The impact the team had on him over the past two years wasn't lost on him.

"It's led me to be a better person," said Justin. "I was just sliding by. Now I've realized that I could find a career in this realm. Maybe I have a chance to make it somewhere in this world. That's what's really important to me right now."

Magoffin, meanwhile, continued pouring all his spare energy into esports. The coach who a few years earlier hadn't heard of *League of Legends* was leading a growing team. He was considering adding *Fortnite* for the next season, which, given its popularity, he knew would open the floodgates. But Magoffin was fine with being overwhelmed if it meant giving more students the chance to do what Justin had done.

"All the kids say they know they're not just loners anymore," he said. "They have five kids on a team that depend on them to be there for practice, to be there for matches, to not get in trouble. It's just like being on a traditional team, being on a football team, a basketball team—they have teammates that rely on them. All these kids know they have a job now that somebody else depends on them for."

The coach had found his calling. It didn't matter to Magoffin that his squad hadn't enjoyed the success of the football program he once helped lead. Mahar's esports team might not have won any trophies or hung any banners yet, and that was fine. There was something much more important at play.

JUST BEFORE HIS twenty-seventh birthday, Delane closed on his first house, a modern two-and-a-half-story home down the road from Venice Beach and a short drive from LAX, which would allow him to travel around the country with ease. After initially not paying himself a salary, he had started doing so on the advice of some of his mentors. Still, since he'd started PlayVS, he'd made more money outside the company, through various small investments that had proven fruitful. Delane and the music mogul Scooter Braun had together taken on advisory roles with Squad, a young social media app, in exchange for some equity. Six months later, the startup was acquired by Twitter, and they each walked away with cash. He was making good money—not life-changing money, but good money. He'd started driving even nicer cars. He would post photos on his Instagram story of his #KOTD (kicks of the day), always sure to sneak one of his nice watches into the image.

But many things hadn't changed. "As he's elevated, he's still the same person," said Hajj Flemings. "He hasn't lost that common touch. In his life now, he can have access to whoever and whatever he wants to. But Delane's focus is laser focus. There's zero distraction. I would never get jealous of him because I know how hard he works. Everybody wants to be successful, but everybody's not willing to put the work in."

As Bryan Smiley watched Delane hang out with some of the most famous people in Hollywood, he couldn't help but be astounded. "I've been in this business in LA more than fifteen years now," he said, "and he penetrated some of the most successful, famous circles of people, between entertainment and tech and finance, in as short a time as I've ever seen. As a Hollywood person, it even blew my mind. Circles that I had to still maneuver to get in, this kid just blew open the door." But Delane didn't let it go to his head. "He's still like that lovable nephew or cousin or brother that you grew up with," continued Smiley. "He has, yes, nicer cars now, and certainly hangs with interesting people. But he's still that normal dude I knew way back when."

Delane had long promised Smiley, one of the first people to believe in and invest in him, that he would take care of him, and that he would have the opportunity to exit PlayVS at some point in the future. "What Delane told me from the beginning was, 'I will always have your back. I will take care of you. Just follow my lead, and this is all going to be great for everybody,'" Smiley recalled. "I trusted him. He would send me all types of stock transfer and new things I had to sign for all the restructuring the company went through over the years. I looked at it, for sure, but I never gave it to my attorney. I had Delane explain to me what was happening, and I signed everything he gave me." When Smiley had the chance to sell his shares during PlayVS's Series

C round for a healthy multiple of what he'd initially invested, he took the opportunity and cashed out. "Everything he told me came to fruition," said Smiley. "I live a great life, and people often remark how well I've done in Hollywood. I tell them, 'Very little of this is from Hollywood. It's PlayVS.'"

Most of Delane's own wealth, meanwhile, existed only on paper. It was tied up in PlayVS until the company either went public—which Delane had no interest in doing—or was acquired. Still, Delane helped his family back in Detroit. He started paying the rent at the home where his mother and step-father lived. He flew his brother and some cousins out to Los Angeles for a week. Sometimes it didn't seem like enough. Many conversations with his family became about money.

"When you start getting press, and people start seeing these big figures, $100 million raised or whatever, it becomes more and more difficult," said Delane. "Peoples' expectations start to mount, because they're looking at it like, 'He's got access to money. Even if it's not his, he can figure it out.' I think with PlayVS, the expectations from people within my family have grown, and many of those relationships have deteriorated as a result. That's because the success, in their eyes, became quite measurable."

Delane seemed to serve the role of financial contingency plan to some of his closest relatives. He knew that if he lent money, he shouldn't expect to see it again, something his cousin Juan had taught him at a young age. Delane's rise from a poverty-stricken neighborhood to the top of a hot company created a tension the world didn't see when it watched him speak at conferences or talk about his startup on CNBC. He had to face pressures few CEOs had to face. "I can't even go back to Detroit without being cognizant of my environment," he said. "I can't even let people know I'm in the city. That's crazy."

Delane rarely paused to reflect on his own rise from the west side of Detroit to the head of a venture-backed tech company. But when he did, he was aware of a couple of things: one, that it was incredibly unlikely; and two, that it was the result of a combination of hard work and good fortune. While there were many along the way who dismissed him, there were others—the Bryan Smileys and Hajj Flemingses of the world, the Peter Phams, the Rick Yangs, and the Jon Sakodas—who believed in him before he had a track record, who invested time and money into him when they didn't have to or when others told them not to. Without them, his journey wouldn't have been possible. He was conflicted about what his ascension should mean to the outside world. He wanted to be a role model, someone all kids growing up in difficult circumstances could look up to, someone Black and brown children could look at and see a reflection of their own selves. Perhaps it would make them, too, want to build something. "Maybe it's in gaming, maybe it's in tech," he said, "but they'll know it's possible because of what I've been able to accomplish. Those are the people who I do this for."

At the same time, Delane didn't want to be held up as evidence that anything is possible to anyone, of proof that anything can be accomplished with hard work—that, he believed, was a gross oversimplification. In *The Vanishing Middle Class*, the MIT economist Peter Temin observes that escaping America's low-wage sector is a multidecade endeavor that almost always requires getting a college education—a catch-22, since families in the lower class by definition lack the resources to pay for a degree. The struggle is significantly harder for Black people given the systemic obstacles—mass incarceration, housing segregation, poorly funded schools—that disproportionately affect them.

Delane, of course, didn't need an economist to explain the long odds to him. He had lived it.

"I'm a unicorn," he said. "I'm the exception, not the standard. For every me, there's one hundred thousand, if not more, other people who should have gotten this opportunity but didn't. Someone seeing me doesn't know what went into me being who I am—the level of focus, the level of discipline, from a very young age. Do you know how many times I've wanted to go out and sit on the beach and hang out and party? Do you know how many of those nights I missed? Do you know how many moments and memories my friends have where I wasn't present, because I had work to do? I had to give up my whole childhood, and now much of my adulthood, to be here."

If luck is indeed preparation meeting opportunity, as the old adage says, then Delane is one of the luckiest people in the world. He spent much of his life trying to shift the odds back into his favor, putting himself in the best possible position to capitalize on that next opportunity or chance encounter.

One day long after PlayVS had launched, Peter Pham stood in line at the airport, looking through his phone for a particular email from Delane. As he scrolled through his inbox, he couldn't believe what popped up: a message from 2012. "Holy shit," said Pham. "I never saw this."

Hi. My name is Delane Parnell, and I'm a twenty-year-old entrepreneur . . .

Pham had always believed Delane had first entered his world on the dance floor that fateful day in Austin. But Delane had begun hustling his way toward him with a cold email five years earlier.

Delane's hard work, of course, didn't guarantee his success. All he could ever hope to do was leave himself in the best possible position to succeed. He did, and it took years, but it paid off. It takes someone as remarkable as Delane Parnell to overcome the odds being stacked so severely against you.

BEFORE THE SPRING 2021 season, PlayVS added *Madden NFL* and *FIFA* to its NFHS-sanctioned High School offering, meaning students could now earn varsity letters in football and soccer in video game form. The titles had always been highly requested from coaches—they were hugely popular; plus, convincing one's administrators to make a sanctioned sport out of virtual soccer was easier than doing so with a game that entailed casting spells and stealing dragons. The startup soon closed a deal with Nintendo to add titles like *Super Smash Bros.* and *Mario Kart*, and was still hammering out details with Take-Two regarding *NBA 2K*. More than twenty states had officially designated esports a high school sport, but there were still some big players to convince—including New York, which, two years after the Great Connecticut Championship Debacle of 2019, still hadn't signed up. But participation continued to rise. By the start of the season, nearly 9,000 high schools—43 percent of the NFHS-sanctioned schools in the US—had at least one esports teams competing through PlayVS, as well as more than 1,200 colleges.

One day a few months earlier, Delane had received an offer from a sports owner interested in buying PlayVS. He turned it down. He had no intention of selling any time soon—there was much work left to be done. Still, the company drew suitors. One afternoon around the same time, Delane drove one of his expensive new cars through Los Angeles while he chatted on speakerphone with the co-owner of an NFL franchise. He noticed a cop pull up next to him at a red light and speak into his radio. Soon, another squad car was driving behind Delane, boxing him in. His heartbeat quickened.

"I'm sure they were wondering, 'Who is this kid with jewelry on, driving this car?'" Delane said later. "You get so afraid to get pulled over, even when your paperwork and everything is straight and you know you've got no issue, because you just don't know where it can go."

Delane told the owner on the other line he needed to mute him for a moment to concentrate. The cops rode alongside his car for several minutes while Delane tried his best not to make any sudden movements. At a red light, he made a right turn out in front of cars coming from the left, not leaving enough room for either cruiser to follow him. He swung another right at the next intersection to make sure he'd lost them. He pulled into a 7-Eleven parking lot, unmuted his phone, and found that the owner had hung up. Delane called him back. He didn't bother elaborating on what had happened, not wanting to explain that he, a CEO speaking with one of the wealthiest businesspeople in the country while driving an expensive car he'd earned, felt it necessary to hide from the police in a convenience-store parking lot.

Near the end of 2020, Delane received interest from some investors at the famed Japanese firm SoftBank. He decided to raise an additional $10.5 million, money that would be considered an add-on to PlayVS's Series C round. He quickly pulled in a few new investors, including Brooklyn Nets owner Joseph Tsai and Glassdoor cofounder Robert Hohman. During the fundraiser, PlayVS garnered its highest valuation yet: $400 million. The new number meant the stock Delane owned was worth about $100 million. Delane wasn't in any rush to sell, but he knew it would be necessary someday. He had a family back in Detroit to think about—and a future. He hoped to eventually marry and have kids, and he wanted to ensure those children never had to live through what he had experienced. His wish was that one day, when he did sell PlayVS, its new owners would allow him to keep working there. The issues the company was working on were too important to walk away from. Delane didn't have a firm dollar amount in mind. But, he allowed, "I think it would be difficult to turn down a billion dollars. I think that's the number that every startup fantasizes about." It was a milestone that no Black founder had ever hit. Delane hoped he could be the first.

For PlayVS's first employees, the ragtag group of hustlers and gamers who got the little startup in Santa Monica off the ground, the valuation meant their fraction of 1 percent of the company could be worth millions someday. Delane was hopeful that some of those employees would go on to be founders too, that their financial security would help them make the leap to build the startups of tomorrow. One person he didn't expect this from was Sean Yalda. "One of the reasons I want PlayVS to be commercially successful," said Delane, "is because I want Sean to be able to provide for his family and move on to the next chapter of his life. I love him to death. I'd do anything for that guy."

Yalda had already started thinking about buying some farmland for his parents one day, perhaps something up in Northern California or Washington. He wanted to write and illustrate a children's book about sacrifice. He had dreams of a simpler life. The friendship between Yalda and Delane remained strong, two polar opposites who shared the common vision of building a successful gaming company for kids.

"Delane's got a good heart," said Yalda. "He takes care of his friends. He takes care of his family. I think his values and mine are different, but there's nothing wrong with that. His values are the kind of values you need if you want to get to the top."

Delane knew that his childhood goal of becoming a billionaire probably wouldn't be achieved through PlayVS—it would require well-placed investments, maybe founding and selling other companies without giving up equity. He often had light-bulb moments for other startup ideas. He thought about a gaming hardware company that, with a focus on sleek design and celebrity involvement, could be to gaming what Beats by Dre was to music. He contemplated a productivity app that would solve a problem he had at work, a concept he kept close to the vest, but he went so far as to create a mock-up of it to show to potential investors one day. Delane was full of ideas, and even the ones that didn't work out tended to be proven over time. As PlayVS took off, a number of wagering startups had begun to gain traction in the gaming space. One, Pllay, held money in escrow and used artificial intelligence to confirm a winner in games like *Madden* and *Call of Duty*. It launched with 50,000 users and soon earned a $3 million seed round. Delane hadn't been able to execute on the gambling idea. But he had been right about there being a market for it.

Whatever the future held, though, Delane's present was wholly focused on PlayVS. He was building a company that gave kids a place to play and feel like they belonged, a safe haven to spend time with friends. It was giving them something he wished he had when he was a kid.

"The way I think about my life," said Delane, "is that the trajectory of it isn't for me to build this big company at PlayVS and realize this wealth—whatever amount of wealth is attached to it—myself. I think about my life's purpose as building something that millions of kids desperately need and want. They want this product that we're building, this service, to play esports on behalf of their school so they can do things like put that on their college application, get a scholarship, meet friends, have purpose, be recognized for their passion, and just feel more connected to their communities. And, in addition to those kids, hundreds of people have dedicated their lives, their livelihoods, and careers

to this idea, and attached themselves to me in the process. I'll be
damned if I'll let them down."

DELANE CHECKED HIS phone one day to find that his mom had
texted him a photo. Terri had reconnected with a woman who
once knew Anthony Robinson, Delane's father. She'd asked the
woman if she had any photos of him. The woman didn't, she told
Terri, but she believed she still had the program from his funeral.
She dug it up and found that it had a photo of Robinson on the
cover. She snapped a photo and texted it to Terri, who then passed
it along to her son. Delane, at age twenty-seven, finally got to see
what his father looked like. It didn't make his life any easier. It
didn't change much of anything. But it allowed him to cover up
a small hole that had always existed.

While in Detroit one week, Delane called up his younger
cousin, Cydni, and invited her to lunch. He had always had a
soft spot for her—she was a hard worker and, as Juan's only
niece, she too had been close with him before he died. She was
about to enter her senior year of college, and she was getting
good grades. A few weeks into quarantine, her car had stopped
running, which made getting to and from class and work difficult. Delane took her out for lunch in Birmingham and the
two talked about family, life, and her future. When they left
the restaurant, Cydni found a surprise in the parking lot: a
brand-new Jeep with a giant red bow resting on the hood.
She burst into tears and hugged Delane. "It wasn't really even
something I thought a lot about," he said later. "I'm fortunate
enough to be able to be helpful, in that way, to my family. So,
I just figured, why not?"

Delane thought about Juan often as he grew his company.
When he would accomplish something, he would catch himself daydreaming about his cousin, wishing he could be there to

witness it. "Unfortunately, he hasn't been with me on this journey," said Delane. "But his early belief in me is something that drove me to take my career seriously and my life seriously. It's something I keep in my back pocket to push me forward on days when my optimism is low. Just knowing that I had someone who believed in me and my dreams before anybody else did. . . . His faith in me, his optimism around my career and my life, is something I'll always cherish."

Delane's ambition to build PlayVS into the biggest and best company it could be was unwavering. He wanted to muscle into all twenty-thousand-plus high schools in the country. He wanted to expand overseas to Europe and possibly Asia. He wanted to create a subscription service that operated year-round, one through which amateurs all over the world—not professionals, but casual, everyday gamers—would be able to log on and play on competitive teams that progressed through seasons, playoffs, and championships. He wanted to build the biggest gaming company in the world.

"I hope that it becomes entrenched into the fabric of competitive sports, and people for the next several decades, if not longer, are playing esports on PlayVS," he said. "I don't care if no one remembers me, as long as people remember PlayVS, and they care about the experiences that they have on PlayVS."

While recording a podcast with the venture capitalist Jason Calacanis, Delane said his goal was for the company to one day reach 100 million subscribers. Calacanis seemed taken aback. "You do realize that only five people have done that in the history of humanity?" He said. "Verizon . . ."

"Netflix, Spotify, Amazon," replied Delane. "It's all good."

Calacanis spat out the names of more companies as he tried to think of the fifth.

"And PlayVS," Delane interjected, then flashed a mischievous smile.

Later, Calacanis asked him how he ended up owning three cell phone stores by age seventeen. "Did you have a rich uncle?" he joked.

"I wish I did," Delane said. "Then I'd be a billionaire already."

It was something Delane firmly believed. He would gripe about it often during conversations with Aunt Libby, whom he continued to call a few times a week. "Out in LA, he's interacting with all of these individuals who have rich dads or trust funds or things like that," she said. "They have discretionary money to just play with an idea. He doesn't have that. I tell him that I think that makes him more invested. He had to work harder for it, so it gives a different perspective than being able to just start a new idea every day. You're invested in this because you know what you've put into it. Something wasn't just handed to you. You had to work for it."

Aunt Libby came and saw Delane speak at events when she could, got to watch him in business mode up on stage. He was still the same Delane she'd always known, but she couldn't help but be amazed. She sometimes reflected on how he possibly could have gotten to be where he was. It seemed almost impossible that the environment he was raised in could have produced the next great business mind, a potentially generational founder. Libby believed that, whether by nature or nurture, Delane had selected only the best qualities for himself. He'd ended up with her rationality. His mother's fire and entrepreneurial spirit. Juan's sociableness and warmth. "What makes this recipe," said Libby, "to create this best child? I believe that it takes a village."

Delane, for his part, still felt distant from much of his family, but he was trying. Even as he and his mother argued and struggled to overcome the distance that had been created when he was a child, Delane recognized an inarguable fact. When her sons were fourteen and thirteen, Terri had gotten them off the streets. She had secured DaeLon a job at a butcher and Delane a role at a cell phone store. Now, many years later, they had made it out, with DaeLon having worked as a restaurant chef and Delane a tech entrepreneur.

While Delane was back in Detroit one day, he and DaeLon went to visit the old house on Burgess. His mom had moved out years ago; it was vacant and had been boarded up. They stood by the porch where they used to spend time, the one they once sat on while bullets flew overhead. Delane stared at the house, which now seemed impossibly small.

"It used to look so big," said Delane.

"It *was* big," said DaeLon.

Around the corner, the city had repaved the basketball court at the park on Chapel Street. The grass had been cut to a reasonable length. There was a long way to go for the neighborhood, but there were signs of hope.

Delane loved his new life in Los Angeles. The city was home now. But Detroit still had a place in his heart. It was a life's goal of his to give back to it, to be a part of its revitalization. He and Bryan Smiley spoke about one day partnering on a real estate redevelopment project there. Delane had dreams of building a school in a low-income neighborhood that taught students STEM skills, like coding, that would help them get jobs one day.

With remote work remaining the norm throughout 2020, Delane sometimes spent a few weeks working from Detroit so he could be closer to his family. He would spend time hanging out with Gene Donald and Marcus Carey, who had recently moved back to the city to start a new travel company. They would get some friends together and shoot hoops at a park or play Monopoly on a collector's edition wood-and-gold set. Delane would stay at the Shinola, a beautiful, newly built boutique hotel in downtown. One day he gazed out the window at the room in the next building where, nearly a decade earlier, he had met with Josh Linkner, the investor at Detroit Venture Partners, and pitched him his idea for Plenty Discounts. Back then, Delane had recently lost his cousin Juan, and he was struggling. After that meeting, he'd been so disappointed that he had almost quit on the tech world for good. He reflected on what Linkner must have thought at the time, with the kind of refreshed outlook that only came with experience.

"Was I ready to take in a million dollars and go build something?" Delane contemplated. "No. I think as I've gotten more perspective, I've understood. It hurt, but I think maybe I needed to hear it."

That fall, Delane decided to look for a place to live in Detroit, a second home where he could spend a few weeks at a time. He bought a house not far from his mother's. It had a big backyard, and he planned to build a pool and a basketball court. None of his relatives had ever had a pool before. The idea of being able to sit around in the yard with his family—splashing, grilling, playing games, making memories—excited him. It was something he had longed for.

Recently, Delane decided to reach out to Jake Cohen at Detroit Venture Partners. It had been three years since he'd visited Cohen, hoping the investor would tell him to remain in Detroit, and had instead been advised to take the opportunity in Los Angeles. Delane hadn't forgotten it—in fact, he had sometimes used it as motivation. But he was willing to move past it. He emailed Cohen and asked if they could set up a meeting. He was going to be spending more time in Detroit, he told him, and was wondering if they could talk about a business relationship.

Cohen agreed to get lunch. The next time Delane flew to Detroit, the pair met at the Detroit Golf Club, a glamorous estate just off Seven Mile Road with a tennis court and a pool. It had been founded in the late 1800s and accepted its first Black member just six years before Delane was born. Sitting outside on the patio over lunch, Delane looked out at the golf course's perfectly manicured rolling green grass. It wasn't lost on him that he'd spent his whole life living just down the road from here yet had never been inside. Over their meals, Cohen and Delane talked about PlayVS and Delane's time in Detroit. They agreed on something: it would have been great if Delane could have built the company in Detroit. The two spoke for several hours and shared some laughs. Cohen explained that his telling Delane to leave had nothing to do with not believing in him. He simply thought the opportunity with Science in Santa Monica was too good to pass up. Delane was able to accept this. Now, Cohen told him, DVP was looking for help in making more investments in startups in Detroit. It wanted to find young new founders, a diverse group that could help turn the city into the hub they both believed it could be. The firm had been looking for a venture partner, someone deeply embedded in the tech space who could help guide its new investments. Delane agreed to take on the role. It would only require him to be in Detroit a few weeks of the year, but it could help him do some good for the city he loved.

Delane thought of it as a homecoming of sorts. He had only been gone three years, but it felt like a lifetime. Now he had the chance to help in the ways he'd always hoped to. He knew a wide array of founders who deserved opportunities, many of them people of color. He could help find the diamonds in the rough, the entrepreneurs who had been continually passed over. The underdogs whom others hadn't given a chance. The people who, perhaps at one point, were kids just trying to get by, hustling on their streets, staying out of trouble by working long hours and hiding away in their sheds.

Maybe one of them would be the next Delane Parnell, the next kid from Detroit with big dreams who wouldn't accept defeat, who beat the odds, who didn't let life's troubles prevent him from doing what he always believed he was meant to do.

ACKNOWLEDGMENTS

THIS IS MY first book. Its existence, like many aspects of my career, is largely the result of good fortune and the benevolence of others. It never would have come to be if Chris George hadn't reached out to me and guided me through a process that was new, exciting, and intimidating. My agent, Dan Conaway of Writers House, advocated for me and helped me find that one "yes." It came from the fine folks at HarperCollins Leadership, where Jeff James and Matt Baugher believed in this project, Tim Burgard shepherded all aspects of it, Matt Saganski provided great edits, and Leigh Grossman skillfully copyedited. Thanks to all of them and to the many other people who played roles in creating this book and getting it out into the world.

Ahead of the Game's many subjects were incredibly generous with their time. First and foremost is Delane Parnell—this book would have been impossible without his cooperation. In the midst of leading a fast-growth startup with investors and partners to answer to, he somehow found chunks of time for me. He allowed me to enter his world to a degree that must have been somewhat terrifying, and I'll be forever grateful for that. The employees of PlayVS were also endlessly accommodating, taking breaks from their high-pressure, deadline-driven jobs to stop and chat with me. The staff and administration of Mahar Regional School were far kinder than they needed to be about allowing a reporter to sit in on practices and competitions to witness this whole esports thing firsthand. Huge thanks to all of these people and everyone else who spoke with me.

Writing this book wouldn't have been feasible without the support of the people at *Inc.* magazine. Scott Omelianuk allowed me the time I needed to report and write. Christine Lagorio-Chafkin's badass reporting was what first drew me to *Inc.*, and I've since been lucky enough to receive advice from her that made this process way more manageable and less scary. Jon Fine also offered me helpful early guidance on book-writing, in addition to being a great editor of mine for many years. Other editors who have helped shape me into a better journalist include Lindsay Blakely, Kris Frieswick, Danielle Sacks, Maria Aspan, Laura Lorber, Graham Winfrey, Jim Ledbetter, Doug Cantor, Diana Ransom, Janice Lombardo, Marli Guzzetta, Bill Saporito, Leigh Buchanan, Jennifer Merritt, and Ty Wenger. Stephanie Meyers, thank you for your wit, grace, and wisdom—we miss all of it. And thanks to all my *Inc.* colleagues for the inspiring work they do every day. Their talent pushes me to be better.

A few days after I sat down to begin writing this book, the world became a crazy place. I want to thank, in print, all my friends who helped out my family as they fought COVID-19. Knowing there were people who cared about them—and who could bring Tylenol and a spare roll of toilet paper when I couldn't—made things a little bit easier. My thoughts are with everyone who lost someone during this time, as well as all the frontline workers. It would be feeble for me to try to summarize their work here, so I'll leave it at this: Thank you.

Since this book is largely about teachers, I'd be remiss if I didn't thank some of those who impacted me the most over the years. Susan Miller was the first person without a biological instinct to do so who told me I was capable of writing and encouraged me to pursue it. I'll never forget that. John Musmacker taught me that hard work and coachability can take you further than raw talent—lessons that extended far beyond the baseball field. Don Aucoin at Boston College pushed me to be a better writer and vouched for me along the way. At New York University, Meryl Gordon gave me an opportunity, and Mary Quigley spent two semesters teaching me what journalism is from the ground up. Gary Belsky provided me with my first break in this industry by telling a group of magazine editors that I was "not untalented." (He also gave me my second break, and my third.) Other great teachers include Jill Korwan, Pamela Hudson, Doug Delman, and Ben Benbasset, some of whom will be shocked not only to find their names here but to find out I was even paying attention.

Thanks also to Lisa Horton, Jamie Johnson, Maggie Squires, and Mikaela Akins for their contributions and for making my life easier.

Every day, I acknowledge how lucky I am to have my crazy family. My brother, Chris, served as my first audience on several sections of this book and provided critical feedback. He and my brother-in-law, Andrew, are two of the kindest people I know and make life fulfilling, fun, and hilarious. My parents, Tom and Jill, worked hard their entire lives so I could be in a position to succeed. I often think about how frightening it must be for a firefighter and a nurse—two of the most essential jobs in the world—to raise children who aspire to be a musician and a writer. They did it without ever letting us doubt ourselves, even when I gave them ample opportunities to do so. I wouldn't be here without their love and support. The great Barons of Buffalo have welcomed me with open arms and many pierogis, and I'm so happy to be part of their family. I love all of these people very much.

Which brings me to one more thing that happened while I was working on this book: I got married. There's nobody I'd rather be locked down with or have a pandemic-delayed marriage to than my wife, Abbie. She put up with me without complaint through months of my writing this book under self-imposed house arrest, somehow never getting mad when the dirty dishes stacked up or my side of the room got too messy. She checked my work, listened to my gripes, and helped me believe in myself. She is the strongest, most caring, supportive, and thoughtful person I know, and I love her very much.

SOURCES

The following sources were used in addition to the author's firsthand reporting. Note that a web address is provided only when a standard internet search might be insufficient.

CHAPTER 1

"The Esports Economy Will Generate At Least $465 Million in 2017," *Newzoo*, February 16, 2015.

"Twitch Revenue and Usage Statistics (2020)," Business of Apps, accessed through Internet Archive, https://web.archive.org/web /20200605153158/https://www.businessofapps.com/data/twitch -statistics/.

Jurre Pannekeet, "Newzoo's Esports Business Predictions for 2021: Esports Will Propel Gaming into a Bigger Industry than Traditional Professional Sports," *Newzoo*, August 29, 2018.

Phil Kollar, "The Past, Present and Future of *League of Legends* Studio Riot Games," *Polygon*, September 13, 2016.

Christopher Palmeri, "*Fortnite* Now Has 200 Million Players, Up 60% From the Last Count," *Bloomberg*, November 26, 2018.

Colleen Taylor, "Sources: Apple Paid $7 Million for Color Labs," *TechCrunch*, November 19, 2012.

Steven Davidoff Solomon, "$1 Billion for Dollar Shave Club: Why Every Company Should Worry," *New York Times*, July 27, 2016.

Jason Del Rey, "Dollar Shave Club just sold for $1 billion to Unilever," *Vox*, July 19, 2016.

CHAPTER 2

"The New Home Sewing Co. of Orange, Massachusetts," Museum of Our Industrial Heritage, accessed through Internet Archive, https:// web.archive.org/web/20151218124736/https://industrialhistory

.org/histories/the-new-home-sewing-machine-co-of-orange
-massachusetts/.

"About Orange," Orange, Massachusetts: The Friendly Town, https://
www.townoforange.org/about-orange.

Alejandra Reyes-Velarde and Javier Panzar, "Jacksonville shooting victim
Elijah Clayton was a skilled football player on the field and online,"
Los Angeles Times, August 27, 2018.

Jose Pagliery, Curt Devine, and Drew Griffin, "Jacksonville shooter had
history of mental illness and police visits to family home," CNN,
August 28, 2018.

CHAPTER 3

"Groupon Expands to New Markets in Florida," Business Wire, October
12, 2010, https://web.archive.org/web/20200807103828/https://
www.businesswire.com/news/home/20101012006607/en/Groupon
-Expands-Markets-Florida.

Douglas MacMillan and Joseph Galante, "Groupon Prankster Mason Not
Joking in Spurning Google," *Bloomberg*, December 6, 2010.

Andrew Dietderich, "EPrize gets $32 million in financing," *Crain's
Detroit Business*, February 1, 2006.

Ingrid Lunden, "How Atlanta's Calendly turned a scheduling nightmare
into a $3B startup," *TechCrunch*, January 26, 2021.

Samantha Sharf, "WeWork Offloads Managed By Q For A Fraction Of
What It Paid," *Forbes*, March 3, 2020.

Gillian Tan, Kristen V. Brown, and Crystal Tse, "Ginkgo Agrees to
$17.5 Billion Merger With Harry Sloan SPAC," *Bloomberg*, May 11,
2021.

Matthew DeBord, "GM paid a lot less for Cruise Automation than
everyone thought," *Business Insider*, July 21, 2016.

Tim Levin, "Microsoft is the latest investor to join GM's Cruise in a
round that values the self-driving firm at $30 billion," *Business
Insider*, January 19, 2021.

"Next steps for our experimental fiber network," Google Blog, March 26,
2010.

Miguel Helft, "Cities Rush to Woo Google Broadband Before Friday
Deadline," *New York Times*, March 26, 2010.

"Greenville, South Carolina Creates the World's First and Largest
People-Powered Google Chain With Over 2,000 Eco-Friendly LED

Glow Sticks," Greenville Feels Lucky, accessed through Internet Archive, https://web.archive.org/web/20140201214231/http:/www .wearefeelinglucky.com/.

"The 5 Strangest City Pitches for Google's New Fiber-Optic Service," PCMag, March 7, 2010.

John D. Sutter, "Topeka 'renames' itself 'Google, Kansas,'" CNN.com, March 2, 2010.

David Serchuk, "The 'Google Fiber' effect on economic development? It's real," American City Business Journals, February 25, 2016.

Jeremy Hobson, "How Google Fiber Changed Kansas City,"WBUR.org, November 10, 2017.

CHAPTER 4

Housing Information Portal: Census Tract 5410, Wayne, MI, Data Driven Detroit, https://hip.datadrivendetroit.org/profiles /14000US26163541000-census-tract-5410-wayne-mi/.

Sydney Fine, "Michigan and Housing Discrimination, 1949–1968," *Michigan Historical Review*, Vol. 23, No. 2 (Fall 1997), accessed through JSTOR.

"1967 Detroit Riots," History.com, September 27, 2017.

Sandy McClure and Andrea Ford, "Drugs and fear at housing project," *Detroit Free Press*, March 12, 1982, https://www.crimeindetroit .com/documents/031282%20Drugs%20and%20Fear%20at%20 Housing%20Project.pdf.

Andrea Ford, "Kids jump rope to songs of heroin growing up in Jeffries Homes," *Detroit Free Press*, March 17, 1982, https://crimeindetroit .com/documents/031782%20Kids%20Jump%20Rope%20to%20 Songs%20of%20Heroin.pdf.

Thomas Sugrue, "Origins of the Urban Crisis: Race and Inequality in Postwar Detroit," (Princeton University Press, 2014), 23, 95–98.

CHAPTER 5

Michael Vitez, "From West Philly to Gagaland," *Philadelphia Inquirer*, February 24, 2013.

CHAPTER 6

Amanda Lenhart, "Chapter 3: Video Games Are Key Elements in Friendships for Many Boys," Pew Research Center, August 6, 2015.

Jess Condit, "Swedish media house buys world's largest eSports company," Engadget, July 1, 2015.

Paul Steinbach, "PlayOn! Sports CEO David Rudolph Discusses NFHS Network," Athletic Business, July 2013.

Jason Krell, "High School esports growth means better outcomes for more students," Medium, May 22, 2019.

James Kozachuk, Cyrus K. Foroughi, Guo Freeman, "Exploring Electronic Sports: An Interdisciplinary Approach," Proceedings of the Human Factors and Ergonomics Society Annual Meeting, accessed through ResearchGate.net.

CHAPTER 7

Julia Alexander, "*Fortnite* hits 125 million players in less than a year, says Epic Games," Polygon, June 12, 2018.

"Number of *League of Legends* monthly active users (MAU) from 2011 to 2016," Statista.

CHAPTER 8

Nitasha Tiku, "Black tech founders say venture capital needs to move past 'diversity theater,'" *Washington Post*, June 10, 2020.

Mfonobong Nsehe, "The Black Billionaires 2020," *Forbes*, March 7, 2018.

Jesse Singal, "Gaming's summer of rage," *Boston Globe*, September 20, 2014.

Beth Teitell and Callum Borchers, "GamerGate anger at woman all too real for gamemaker," *Boston Globe*, October 30, 2014.

Jim Edwards, "FBI's 'Gamergate' file says prosecutors didn't charge men who sent death threats to female video game fans—even when suspects confessed," *Business Insider*, February 16, 2017.

CHAPTER 9

"Ford High School," *U.S. News & World Report*.

CHAPTER 10

Mark David, "South Mapleton Drive Houses a Bevy of the Rich and Famous," *Variety*, August 28, 2014.

Kieran Darcy and Jacob Wolf, "How Blizzard convinced sports billionaires to buy into the *Overwatch* League," ESPN.com, July 26, 2018.

Annie Pei, "Activision Blizzard holds first-ever *Overwatch* League Grand Finals," CNBC, July 30, 2018.

Nicole Carpenter, "*Overwatch* League drew in 10.8 million viewers for the grand final, according to Blizzard," Dot Esports, August 8, 2018.

Valerie Honeycutt Spears, "No *Fortnite* in Kentucky high school e-sports competitions, KHSAA says," *Lexington Herald Leader*, January 27, 2020.

Chris Ferguson, et al., "News Media, Public Education and Public Policy Committee," *The Amplifier Magazine*, June 12, 2017.

J. Breuer, J. Vogelgesang, T. Quandt, and R. Festl, "Violent video games and physical aggression: Evidence for a selection effect among adolescents," *Psychology Of Popular Media Culture*, February 16, 2015.

Philip Bump, "If video games spur gun violence, it's only in the United States," *Washington Post*, March 8, 2018.

Patrick M. Markey and Christopher J. Ferguson, *Moral Combat: Why the War on Violent Video Games Is Wrong*, BenBella Books, 2017.

Greg Toppo, "Do violent video games make kids violent? Trump thinks they could," *USA Today*, February 20, 2018.

Christopher J. Ferguson, "Does movie or videogame violence predict societal violence? It depends on what you look at and when," *Journal of Communication*, Vol. 65 (2015), accessed through Issuu.

CHAPTER 12

"Internet Gaming Disorder," American Psychiatric Association, https://www.psychiatry.org/File%20Library/Psychiatrists/Practice/DSM/APA_DSM-5-Internet-Gaming-Disorder.pdf.

Alice Park, "'Gaming Disorder' Is Now an Official Medical Condition, According to the WHO," *Time*, May 29, 2019.

World Health Organization, "6C51 Gaming disorder," *International Classification of Diseases 11th Revision*, https://icd.who.int/dev11/l-m/en#/http%3a%2f%2fid.who.int%2ficd%2fentity%2f1448597234.

Peter Gray, "Sense and Nonsense About Video Game Addiction," *Psychology Today*, March 11, 2018.

Mark Knudson, "Opinion: CHSAA sanctioning eSports is the worst idea ever," *Coloradoan*, June 16, 2018.

Anesa Hosein, "Girls' video gaming behaviour and undergraduate degree selection: A secondary data analysis approach," *Computers in Human Behavior*, Vol. 91, February 2019, accessed through ScienceDirect.

"Only spring sport Hawaii state champ set to be crowned in esports," KITV.com, May 20, 2020.

Dean Takahashi, "Epic Games seeking to sell stake for $750 million at $17 billion valuation," *VentureBeat*, June 15, 2020.

Noah Smith, "The giants of the video game industry have thrived in the pandemic. Can the success continue?" *Washington Post*, May 12, 2020.

Peter Temin, *The Vanishing Middle Class: Prejudice and Power in a Dual Economy* (The MIT Press, 2018), 41, 101–109, 118, 153, 156–157.

Ta-Nehisi Coates, "The Myth of an Affirmative-Action President," *The Atlantic*, August 29, 2012.

ABOUT THE AUTHOR

KEVIN J. RYAN is an award-winning journalist who has spent the past decade covering business, sports, education, and technology. He reports on entrepreneurship and tech startups at *Inc.* magazine, where he hosted the *Inc. Uncensored* podcast, and has previously written for *ESPN The Magazine*, CNBC, and the *Long Island Press*. He lives in Queens, New York, with his wife, Abbie, and their dog, Flutie.